A Bash In The Tunnel

A Bash In The Tunnel

James Joyce by the Irish

edited by

John Ryan

CLIFTON BOOKS

New England House, New England Street, Brighton BN1 4HN

Registered Office:
Clifton House, 83-117 Euston Road, London N.W.1

ISBN 0 901255 19 X

Printed in Great Britain
GRAPHIC ART SERVICES (BRIGHTON) LTD.

For Anna Livia

Acknowledgements

The editor's thanks are due to the following for permission to use material published in this book: Faber and Faber Ltd. for extracts from *OUR EXAGMINATION ROUND HIS FACTIFICATIONS FOR INCAMINATION OF 'WORK IN PROGRESS'* by Samuel Beckett and others (1929), also for the use of an extract from *MY BROTHER'S KEEPER* (1958) by Stanislaus Joyce; Jonathan Cape for the extract taken from *OLIVER ST. JOHN GOGARTY* by Ulick O'Connor (1964); Farrar Strauss and Young for an extract from *SILENT YEARS* by J. F. Byrne (1953).

The editor is greatly indebted to Kevin O'Byrne and Tom Haran for their kindness and patience in the final preparation of the manuscript.

James Joyce by Sean O'Sullivan R.H.A.

This sketch is reproduced by the kind
permission of Mr. White, Curator, National
Gallery of Ireland.

Under the dented hat
with high black band;

that long face, sloping
like a gable down
to the jutting jaw;
sallow skin, scant
moustache, swallowed

by dark, sudden—
ly glinting glasses

those slender fingers
cramped around a
walking stick or
white wine glass;
it could be my

father or yours;
any worn, life

tempered man if
the caption lacked
the detail – bright as
heresiarch or fallen
angel – of his name.

John Montague

Contents

INTRODUCTION. 9

A BASH IN THE TUNNEL by Brian Nolan . . . 15

DANTE . . . BRUNO . . . VICO . . . JOYCE
by Samuel Beckett 21

THE MYSTICISM THAT PLEASED HIM: A NOTE ON
THE PRIMARY SOURCE OF JOYCE'S *ULYSSES* by
W. B. Stanford 35

DEAR MR JOYCE by Edna O'Brien 43

WHO KILLED JAMES JOYCE? by Patrick Kavanagh . 49

A RECOLLECTION OF JAMES JOYCE by Joseph Hone . 53

TIRED LINES, OR TALES MY MOTHER TOLD ME
by Aidan Higgins 55

JOYEUX QUICUM ULYSSE . . . SWISSAIRIS
DUBELLAY GADELICE by Niall Montgomery . . . 61

JOYCE AND GOGARTY by Ulick O'Connor . . . 73

THE BUD by Stanislaus Joyce 101

JOYCE WITHOUT FEARS: A PERSONAL JOURNEY
by John Jordan 135

FATHER CONMEE AND HIS ASSOCIATES
by Eoin O'Mahony 147

DRUMS AND GUNS, AND GUNS AND DRUMS.
HURRAH! HURRAH! by Patrick Boyle 157

A SHORT VIEW OF THE PROGRESS OF
JOYCEANITY by Denis Johnston 163

CHILDE HORRID'S PILGRIMACE by Andrew Cass . . 169

JAMES JOYCE – THE INTERNATIONALIST
by Arthur Power 181

Contents

DOWNES'S CAKESHOP AND WILLIAMS'S JAM by
Bernard Share 189

DOCTORS AND HOSPITALS by Dr J. B. Lyons . . . 193

STEPHEN HERO AND *A PORTRAIT OF THE ARTIST
AS A YOUNG MAN:* THE INTERVENTION OF
STYLE IN A WORK OF THE CREATIVE IMAGINA-
TION by Francis Harvey 203

THE UNRAISED HAT by Monk Gibbon 209

THE CATHOLIC ELEMENT IN *WORK IN PROGRESS*
by Thomas McGreevy 213

DISEASES OF THE OX by John Francis Byrne . . . 221

THE ARTIST ON THE GIANT'S GRAVE
by Benedict Kiely 235

WHAT THE IRISH PAPERS SAID The obituary memoirs
appearing in the Irish papers of January 1941 . . . 243

NOTES ON CONTRIBUTORS 251

INDEX 255

Introduction

In 1951, whilst I was editor of the Irish literary periodical *Envoy*, I decided that it would be a fitting thing to commemorate the tenth anniversary of the death of James Joyce by bringing out a special number dedicated to him which would reflect the attitudes and opinions of his fellow countrymen towards their illustrious compatriot.

To this end I began by inviting Brian Nolan to act as honorary editor for this particular issue. His own genius closely matched, without in anyway resembling or attempting to counterfeit, Joyce's. But if the mantle of Joyce (or should we say the waistcoat?) were ever to be passed on, nobody would be half so deserving of it as the man who, under his other guises of Flan O'Brien and Myles Na gCopaleen, proved himself incontestably to be the most creative writer and mordant wit that Ireland had given us since Shem the Penman himself.

The exigencies of space and finance in our small journal allowed only for the inclusion of eight of the writers who are represented in this present volume while our very small circulation (less than a thousand copies) meant that the edition was almost immediately out of print. These essays have never been reprinted until now. The present title *A Bash in the Tunnel* comes from Nolan's foreword to that number.

Since then there has been a continuous demand for republication. It was agreed, therefore, not only to provide for this need but at the same time considerably to expand the scope of the original work by adding material of a similar subject matter that had appeared earlier by Irish writers and friends and also such work as had been produced in the following years. In addition, much has been newly commissioned from Irish writers of today, who, if not Joyce's contemporaries in the strictest sense, grew up when his living presence was felt. Alas,

Introduction

Brian Nolan, who died in 1966, was unable to assist me in this compilation and I must pray that he would have approved.

A formidable corpus of Joycean scholarship and pseudo-scholarship has emerged since the writer's death, much of it of excruciating abstruseness. This book hopes to be none of these things: it is a book by *Irish writers* about an *Irish writer*. To this extent I believe it to be unique.

Joyce was quintessentially an Irishman to the extent that Wilde, Shaw or Yeats could never be. This quality was the great source of his genius, the inexhaustible mine from which he would hew *Ulysses* and *Finnegans Wake*.

To understand Joyce at all, this fact has to be faced. In seeing Joyce through the eyes of the Irish (not always smiling) we shall see the man more clearly and, I believe, understand the writer more fully.

JOHN RYAN

A Bash in the Tunnel

Brian Nolan

James Joyce was an artist. He has said so himself. His was a case of Ars gratia Artis. He declared that he would pursue his artistic mission even if the penalty was as long as eternity itself. This appears to be an affirmation of belief in Hell, therefore of belief in Heaven and in God.

A better title for this article might be: 'Was Joyce Mad?' By Hamlet, Prince of Denmark. Yet there is a reason for the present title.

Some thinkers – all Irish, all Catholic, some unlay – have confessed to discerning a resemblance between Joyce and Satan. True, resemblances there are. Both had other names, the one Stephen Dedalus, the other Lucifer; the latter name, meaning 'Maker of Light', was to attract later the ironical gloss 'Prince of Darkness'! Both started off very well under unfaultable teachers, both were very proud, both had a fall. But they differed on one big, critical issue. Satan never denied the existence of the Almighty; indeed he acknowledged it by challenging merely His primacy. Joyce said there was no God, proving this by uttering various blasphemies and obscenities and not being instantly struck dead.

A man once said to me that he hated blasphemy, but on purely rational grounds. If there is no God, he said, the thing is stupid and unnecessary. If there is, it's dangerous.

Anatole France says this better. He relates how, one morning, a notorious agnostic called on a friend who was a devout Catholic. The devout Catholic was drunk and began to pour forth appalling blasphemies. Pale and shocked, the agnostic rushed from the house. Later, a third party challenged him on this incident.

'You have been saying for years that there is no God. Why then should you be so frightened at somebody else insulting this God who doesn't exist?'

'I still say there is no God. But that fellow thinks there is. Suppose a thunderbolt was sent down to strike him dead. How did I know I wouldn't get killed as well? Wasn't I standing beside him?'

Another blasphemy, perhaps – doubting the Almighty's aim. Yet it is still true that all true blasphemers must be believers.

What is the position of the artist in Ireland?

Shortly before commencing to assemble material for this essay, I went into the Bailey in Dublin to drink a bottle of stout and do some solitary thinking. Before any considerable thought had formed itself, a man – then a complete stranger – came, accompanied by his drink, and stood beside me: addressing me by name, he said he was surprised to see a man like myself drinking in a pub.

My pub radar screen showed up the word 'toucher'. I was instantly much on my guard.

'And where do you think I should drink?' I asked. 'Pay fancy prices in a hotel?'

'Ah, no,' he said. 'I didn't mean that. But any time I feel like a good bash myself, I have it in the cars. What will you have?'

I said I would have a large one, knowing that his mysterious reply would entail lengthy elucidation.

' I needn't tell you that that crowd is a crowd of bastards,' was his prefatory exegesis.

Then he told me all. At one time his father had a pub and grocery business, situated near a large Dublin railway terminus. Every year the railway company invited tenders for the provisioning of its dining cars, and every year the father got the contract. (The narrator said he thought this was due to the territorial proximity of the house, with diminished handling and cartage charges.)

The dining cars (hereinafter known as 'the cars') were customarily parked in remote sidings. It was the father's job to load them from time to time with costly victuals – eggs, rashers, cold turkey and whiskey. These cars, bulging in their lonely sidings with such fabulous fare, had special locks. The father had the key, and nobody else in the world had authority to open the doors until the car was part of a train. But my informant had made it his business, he told me, to have a key too.

'At that time,' he told me, 'I had a bash once a week in the cars.'

One must here record two peculiarities of Irish railway practice. The first is a chronic inability to 'make up' trains in advance, i.e. to estimate expected passenger traffic accurately. Week after week a long-distance train is scheduled to be five passenger coaches and a car. Perpetually, an extra 150 passengers arrive on the departure platform unexpectedly. This means that the car must be detached, a passenger coach substituted, and the train despatched foodless and drinkless on its way.

The second peculiarity – not exclusively Irish – is the inability of personnel in charge of shunting engines to leave coaches, parked in far sidings, alone. At all costs they must be shifted.

That was the situation as my friend in the Bailey described it. The loaded dining cars never went anywhere, in the long-distance sense. He approved of that. But they were subject to endless enshuntment. That, he said, was a bloody scandal and a waste of the taxpayers' money.

When the urge for a 'bash' came upon him, his routine was simple. Using his secret key, he secretly got into a parked and laden car very early in the morning, penetrated to the pantry, grabbed a jug of water, a glass and a bottle of whiskey and, with this assortment of material and utensil, locked himself in the lavatory.

Reflect on that locking. So far as the whole world was concerned, the car was utterly empty. It was locked with special, unprecedented locks. Yet this man locked himself securely within those locks.

Came the dawn – and the shunters. They espied, as doth the greyhound the hare, the lonely dining car, mute, immobile, deserted. So they coupled it up and dragged it to another siding at Liffey Junction. It was there for five hours but ('that crowd of bastards,' i.e. other shunters) it was discovered and towed over to the yards behind Westland Row Station. Many hours later it was shunted on to the tail of the Wexford Express but later angrily detached owing to the unexpected arrival of extra passengers.

'And are you sitting in the lavatory drinking whiskey all the time?' I asked.

'Certainly I am,' he answered, 'what the hell do you think lavatories in trains is for? And with the knees of me trousers wet with me own whiskey from the jerks of them shunter bastards!'

His resentment was enormous. Be it noted that the whiskey was not in fact his own whiskey, that he was that oddity, an unauthorized person.

'How long does a bash in the cars last?' I asked him.

'Ah, that depends on a lot of things,' he said. 'As you know, I never carry a watch.' (Exhibits cuffless, hairy wrist in proof.) 'Did I ever tell you about the time I had a bash in the tunnel?'

He had not – for the good reason that I had never met him before.

'I seen meself,' he said, 'once upon a time on a three-day bash. The bastards took me out of Liffey Junction down to Hazelhatch. Another crowd shifted me into Harcourt Street yards. I was having a good bash at this time, but I always try to see, for the good of me health, that a bash doesn't last more than a day and night. I know it's night outside when it's dark. If it's bright it's day. Do you follow me?'

'I think I do.'

'Well, I was about on the third bottle when this other shunter crowd come along – it was dark, about eight in the evening – and nothing would do them only bring me into the Liffey Tunnel under the Phoenix Park and park me there. As you know I never use a watch. If it's bright, it's day. If it's dark, it's night. Here was meself parked in the tunnel opening bottle after bottle in the dark, thinking the night was a very long one, stuck there in the tunnel. I was three-quarters way into the jigs when they pulled me out of the tunnel into Kingsbridge. I was in bed for a week. Did you ever in your life hear of a greater crowd of bastards?'

'Never.'

'That was the first and last time I ever had a bash in the tunnel.'

Funny? But surely there you have the Irish artist? Sitting fully dressed, innerly locked in the toilet of a locked coach where he has no right to be, resentfully drinking somebody else's whiskey, being whisked hither and thither by anonymous shunters, keeping fastidiously the while on the outer face of his door the simple word ENGAGED!

I think the image fits Joyce; but particularly in his manifestation of a most Irish characteristic – the transgressor's resentment with the nongressor.

A friend of mine found himself next door at dinner to a well-known savant who appears in *Ulysses*. (He shall be nameless, for he still lives.) My friend, making dutiful conversation, made mention of Joyce. The savant said that Ireland was under a deep obligation to the author of Joyce's *Irish Names of Places*. My friend lengthily explained that his reference had been to a different Joyce. The savant did not quite understand, but ultimately confessed that he had heard certain rumours about the other man. It seemed that he had written some dirty books, published in Paris.

'But you are a character in one of them,' my friend incautiously re-marked.

The next two hours, to the neglect of wine and cigars, were occupied with a heated statement by the savant that he was by no means a character in fiction, he was a man, furthermore he was alive and he had published books of his own.

'How can I be a character in fiction,' he demanded, 'if I am here talking to you?'

That incident may be funny, too, but its curiosity is this: Joyce spent a lifetime establishing himself as a character in fiction. Joyce created, in narcissus fascination, the ageless Stephen. Beginning with importing real characters into his books, he achieves the magnificent inversion of making them legendary and fictional. It is quite preposterous. Thousands of people believe that there once lived a man named Sherlock Holmes.

Joyce went further than Satan in rebellion.

Two characters who confess themselves based on Aquinas: Joyce and Maritain.

In *Finnegans Wake*, Joyce appears to favour the Vico theory of inevitable human and recurring evolution – theocracy: aristocracy: democracy: chaos.

'A.E.' referred to the chaos of Joyce's mind.

That was wrong, for Joyce's mind was indeed very orderly. In composition he used coloured pencils to keep himself right. All his works, not excluding *Finnegans Wake*, have a rigid classic pattern. His personal moral and family behaviours were impeccable. He seems to have deserved equally with George Moore the sneer about the latter – he never kissed, but told.

What was really abnormal about Joyce? At Clongowes he had his dose of Jesuit casuistry. Why did he substitute his home-made chaosistry?

It seems to me that Joyce emerges, through curtains of salacity and blasphemy, as a truly fear-shaken Irish Catholic, rebelling not so much against the Church but against its near-schism Irish eccentricities, its pretence that there is only one Commandment, the vulgarity of its edifices, the shallowness and stupidity of many of its ministers. His revolt, noble in itself, carried him away. He could not see the tree for the woods. But I think he meant well. We all do, anyway.

What is *Finnegans Wake?* A treatise on the incommunicable night-mind? Or merely an example of silence, exile and punning?

Some think that Joyce was at heart an Irish dawn-bursting romantic, an admirer of de Valera, and one who dearly wished to be recalled to Dublin as an ageing man to be crowned with a D. Litt. from the national and priest-haunted university. This is at least possible, if only because it explains the preposterous 'aesthetic' affectations of his youth, which included the necessity for being rude to his dying mother. The theme here is that a heart of gold was beating under the artificial waistcoat. Amen.

Humour, the handmaid of sorrow and fear, creeps out endlessly in all Joyce's works. He uses the thing in the same way as Shakespeare does but less formally, to attenuate the fear of those who have belief and who genuinely think that they will be in hell or in heaven shortly, and possibly very shortly. With laughs he palliates the sense of doom that is the heritage of the Irish Catholic. True humour needs this background urgency: Rabelais is funny, but his stuff cloys. His stuff lacks tragedy.

Perhaps the true fascination of Joyce lies in his secretiveness, his ambiguity (his polyguity, perhaps?), his leg-pulling, his dishonesties, his technical skill, his attraction for Americans. His works are a garden in which some of us may play. All that we can claim to know is merely a small bit of that garden.

But at the end, Joyce will still be in his tunnel, unabashed.

Dante... Bruno... Vico... Joyce

Samuel Beckett[1]

The danger in the neatness of identifications. The conception of Philosophy and Philology as a pair of nigger minstrels out of the Teatro dei Piccoli is soothing, like the contemplation of a carefully folded ham sandwich. Giambattista Vico himself could not resist the attractiveness of such coincidences of gesture. He insisted on complete identification between the philosophical abstraction and the empirical illustration, thereby annulling the absolutism of each conception – hoisting the real unjustifiably clear of its dimensional limits, temporalizing that which is extratemporal. And now here am I, with my handful of abstractions, among which notably: a mountain, the coincidence of contraries, the inevitability of cyclic evolution, a system of Poetics, and the prospect of self-extension in the world of Mr Joyce's *Work in Progress*. There is the temptation to treat every concept like a 'bass dropt neck fust in till a bung crate', and make a really tidy job of it. Unfortunately such an exactitude of application would imply distortion in one of two directions. Must we wring the neck of a certain system in order to stuff it into a contemporary pigeon-hole, or modify the dimensions of that pigeon-hole for the satisfaction of the analogymongers? Literary criticism is not book-keeping.

Giambattista Vico was a practical roundheaded Neapolitan. It pleases Croce to consider him as a mystic, essentially speculative, '*disdegnoso dell empirisimo*'. It is a surprising interpretation, seeing that more than three-fifths of his *Scienza Nuova* is concerned with empirical investigation. Croce opposes him to the reformative materialistic school of Ugo Grozio, and absolves him from the utilitarian pre-

[1]From *Our Exagmination Round His Factification for Incamination of Work in Progress* (Faber & Faber 1929)

occupations of Hobbes, Spinoza, Locke, Bayle and Machiavelli. All this cannot be swallowed without protest. Vico defines Providence as: '*una mente spesso diversa ed alle volte tutta contraria e sempre superiore ad essi fini particolari che essi uomini si avevano proposti; dei quali fini ristretti fatti mezzi per servire a fini piu ampi, gli ha sempre adoperati per conservare l'umana generazione in questa terra*'. What could be more definitely utilitarianism? His treatment of the origin and functions of poetry, language and myth, as will appear later, is as far removed from the mystical as it is possible to imagine. For our immediate purpose, however, it matters little whether we consider him as a mystic or as a scientific investigator; but there are no two ways about considering him as an *innovator*. His division of the development of human society into three ages: Theocratic, Heroic, Human (civilized), with a corresponding classification of language: Hieroglyphic (sacred), Metaphorical (poetic), Philosophical (capable of abstraction and generalization), was by no means new, although it must have appeared so to his contemporaries. He derived this convenient classification from the Egyptians, via Herodotus. At the same time it is impossible to deny the originality with which he applied and developed its implications. His exposition of the ineluctable circular progression of Society was completely new, although the germ of it was contained in Giordano Bruno's treatment of identified contraries. But it is in Book 2, described by himself as '*tutto il corpo . . . la chiave maestra . . . dell' opera*', that appears the unqualified originality of his mind; here he evolved a theory of the origins of poetry and language, the significance of myth, and the nature of barbaric civilization that must have appeared nothing less than an impertinent outrage against tradition. These two aspects of Vico have their reverberations, their reapplications – without, however, receiving the faintest explicit illustration – in *Work in Progress*.

It is first necessary to condense the thesis of Vico, the scientific historian. In the beginning was the thunder: the thunder sets free Religion, in its most objective and unphilosophical form – idolatrous animism: Religion produces Society, and the first social men are the cave-dwellers, taking refuge from a passionate Nature: this primitive family life receives its first impulse towards development from the arrival of terrified vagabonds: admitted they are the first slaves: growing stronger, they exact agrarian concessions, and a despotism has evolved into a primitive feudalism: the cave becomes a city, and the feudal system a democracy: then an anarchy: this is corrected by a return to monarchy: the last stage is a tendency towards interdestruction: the nations are dispersed, and the Phoenix of Society arises out of their ashes. To this six-termed social progression corresponds a six-termed progression of human motives: necessity, utility, convenience, pleasure, luxury, abuse of luxury; and their incarnate manifestations: Polyphemus, Achilles, Caesar and Alexander, Tiberius, Caligula and Nero.

At this point Vico applies Bruno – though he takes very good care not to say so – and proceeds from rather arbitrary data to philosophical abstraction. There is no difference, says Bruno, between the smallest possible chord and the smallest possible arc, no difference between the infinite circle and the straight line. The maxima and minima of particular contraries are one and indifferent. Minimal heat equals minimal cold. Consequently transmutations are circular. The principle (minimum) of one contrary takes its movement from the principle (maximum) of another. Therefore not only do the minima coincide with the minima, the maxima with the maxima, but the minima with the maxima in the succession of transmutations. Maximal speed is a state of rest. The maximum of corruption and the minimum of generation are identical: in principle, corruption is generation. And all things are ultimately identified with God, the universal monad, Monad of monads. From these considerations Vico evolved a Science and Philosophy of History. It may be an amusing exercise to take an historical figure, such as Scipio, and label him No. 3; it is of no ultimate importance. What is of ultimate importance is the recognition that the passage from Scipio to Caesar is as inevitable as the passage from Caesar to Tiberius, since the flowers of corruption in Scipio and Caesar are the seeds of vitality in Caesar and Tiberius. Thus we have the spectacle of a human progression that depends for its movement on individuals, and which at the same time is independent of individuals in virtue of what appears to be a preordained cyclicism. It follows that History is neither to be considered as a formless structure, due exclusively to the achievements of individual agents, nor as possessing reality apart from and independent of them, accomplished behind their backs in spite of them, the work of some superior force, variously known as Fate, Chance, Fortune, God. Both these views, the materialistic and the transcendental, Vico rejects in favour of the rational. Individuality is the concretion of universality, and every individual action is at the same time superindividual. The individual and the universal cannot be considered as distinct from each other. History, then, is not the result of Fate or Chance – in both cases the individual would be separated from his product – but the result of a Necessity that is not Fate, of a Liberty that is not Chance (compare Dante's 'yoke of liberty'). This force he called Divine Providence, with his tongue, one feels, very much in his cheek. And it is to this Providence that we must trace the three institutions common to every society: Church, Marriage, Burial. This is not Bossuet's Providence, transcendental and miraculous, but immanent and the stuff itself of human life, working by natural means. Humanity is its work in itself. God acts on her, but by no means of her. Humanity is divine, but no man is divine.

This social and historical classification is clearly adapted by Mr Joyce as a structural convenience – or inconvenience. His position is in no way a philosophical one. It is the detached attitude of Stephen Dedalus in *Portrait of the Artist* . . . who describes Epictetus to the Master of Studies as 'an old gentleman who said that the soul is very like a bucketful of water.' The lamp is more important than the lamp-lighter. By structural I do not only mean a bold outward division, a bare skeleton for the housing of material. I mean the endless substantial variations on these three beats, and interior intertwining of these three themes into a decoration of arabesques – decoration and more than decoration. Part I is a mass of past shadow, corresponding therefore to Vico's first human institution, Religion, or to his Theocratic age, or simply to an abstraction – Birth. Part 2 is the lovegame of the children, corresponding to the second institution, Marriage, or to the Heroic age, or to an abstraction – Maturity. Part 3 is passed in sleep, corresponding to the third institution, Burial, or to the human age, or to an abstraction – Corruption. Part 4 is the day beginning again, and corresponds to Vico's Providence, or to the transition from the Human to the Theocratic, or to an abstraction – Generation. Mr Joyce does not take birth for granted, as Vico seems to have done. So much for the dry bones. The consciousness that there is a great deal of the unborn infant in the lifeless octogenarian, and a great deal of both in the man at the apogee of his life's curve, removes all the stiff interexclusiveness that is often the danger in neat construction. Corruption is not excluded from Part I nor maturity from Part 3. The four 'lovedroyd curdinals' are presented on the same plane – 'his element curdinal numen and his enement curdinal marrying and his epulent curdinal weisswasch and his eminent curdinal Kay o' Kay'! There are numerous references to Vico's four human institutions – Providence counting as one! 'A good clap, a fore wedding, a bad wake, tell hell's well'; 'their weatherings and their marryings and their buryings and their natural selections'; 'the lightning look, the birding cry, awe from the grave, everflowing on our times'; 'by four hands of forethought the first babe of reconcilement is laid in its last cradle of hume sweet hume'.

Apart from this emphasis on the tangible conveniences common to humanity, we find frequent expressions of Vico's insistence on the inevitable character of every progression – or retrogression: 'The Vico road goes round and round to meet where terms begin. Still onappealed to by the cycles and onappalled by the recoursers, we feel all serence, never you fret, as regards our dutyful cask . . . before there was a man at all in Ireland there was a lord at Lucan. We only wish everyone was as sure of anything in this watery world as we are of everything in the newlywet fellow that's bound to follow! 'The efferfreshpainted lily in beautific repose upon the silence of the dead from Pharooh the next first down to ramescheckles the last bust thing.' 'In fact, under the close eyes of the inspectors the traits featuring the chiaroscuro coalesce, their contrarieties eliminated, in one stable somebody similarly as by the providential warring of heartshaker with housebreaker and of dramdrinker against freethinker our social something bowls along bumpily, experiencing a jolting series of prearranged disappointments, down the long lane of (it's as semper as oxhousehumper) generations, more generations and still more generations' – this last a case of Mr Joyce's rare subjectivism. In a word, here is all humanity circling with fatal monotony about the Providential fulcrum – the 'convoy wheeling encircling abound the gigantig's lifetree'. Enough has been said, or at least enough has been suggested, to show how Vico is substantially present in the *Work in Progress*. Passing to the Vico of the Poetics we hope to establish an even more striking, if less direct, relationship.

Vico rejected the three popular interpretations of the poetic spirit, which considered poetry as an ingenious popular expression of philosophical conceptions, or an amusing social diversion, or an exact science within the reach of everyone in possession of the recipe. Poetry, he says, was born of curiosity, daughter of ignorance. The first men had to create matter by the force of their imaginations, and 'poet' means 'creator'. Poetry was the first operation of the human mind, and without it thought could not exist. Barbarians, incapable of analysis and abstraction, must use their fantasy to explain what their reason cannot comprehend. Before articulation comes song; before abstract terms, metaphors. The figurative character of the oldest poetry must be regarded, not as sophisticated confectionery, but as evidence of a poverty-stricken vocabulary and of a disability to achieve abstraction. Poetry is essentially the antithesis of Metaphysics: Metaphysics purge the mind of the senses and cultivate the disembodiment of the spiritual; Poetry is all passion and feeling and animates the inanimate; Metaphysics are most perfect when most concerned with universals; Poetry, when most concerned with particulars. Poets are the sense, philosophers the intelligence, of humanity. Considering the Scholastics' axiom: *'niente e nell'intelleto che prima non sia nel senso'*, it follows that poetry is a prime condition of philosophy and civilization. The primitive animistic movement was a manifestation of the *'forma poetica dello spitiro'*.

His treatment of the origin of language proceeds along similar lines. Here again he rejects the materialistic and transcendental views: the one declaring that language was nothing but a polite and conventional symbolism; the other, in desperation, describing it as a gift from the Gods. As before, Vico is the rationalist, aware of the natural and inevitable growth of language. In its first dumb form, language was gesture. If a man wanted to say 'sea', he pointed to the sea. With the spread of animism this gesture was replaced by the word 'Neptune'. He directs our attention to the fact that every need of life, natural, moral and economic, has its verbal expression in one or other of the 30,000 Greek divinities. This is Homer's 'language of the Gods'. Its evolution through poetry to a highly civilized vehicle, rich in abstract and technical terms, was as little fortuitous as the evolution of society itself. Words have their progressions as well as social phrases. 'Forest-cabin-village-city-academy' is one rough progression. Another: 'mountain-plain-riverbank'. And every word expands with psychological inevitability. Take the Latin word 'Lex'.

1   Lex = Crop of acorns
2   Ilex = Tree that produces acorns
3   Legere = To gather
4   Aquilex = He that gathers the waters
5   Lex = Gathering together of people, public assembly
6   Lex = Law
7   Legere = To gather together letters into a word, to read

The root of any word whatsoever can be traced back to some pre-lingual symbol. This early inability to abstract the general from the particular produced the type-names. It is the child's mind over again. The child extends the names of the first familiar objects to other strange objects in which he is conscious of some analogy. The first men, unable to conceive the abstract idea of 'poet' or 'hero', named every hero after the first hero, every poet after the first poet. Recognizing this custom of designating a number of individuals by the names of their prototypes, we can explain various classical and mythological mysteries. Hermes is the prototype of the Egyptian inventor: so, for Romulus, the great law-giver, and Hercules, the Greek hero: so for Homer. Thus Vico asserts the spontaneity of language and denies the dualism of poetry and language. Similarly, poetry is the foundation of poetry and language. When language consisted of gesture, the spoken and the written were identical. Hieroglyphics, or sacred language, as he calls it, were not the invention of philosophers for the mysterious expression of profound thought, but the common necessity of primitive peoples. Convenience only begins to assert itself at a far more advanced stage of civilization, in the form of alphabetism. Here Vico, implicitly at least, distinguishes between writing and direct expression. In such direct expression, form and content are inseparable. Examples are the medals of the Middle Ages, which bore no inscription and were a mute testimony to the feebleness of conventional alphabetic writing: and the flags of our own day. As with Poetry and Language, so with Myth. Myth, according to Vico, is neither an allegorical expression of general philosophical axioms (Conti, Bacon), nor a derivative from particular peoples, as for instance the Hebrews or Egyptians, nor yet the work of isolated poets, but an historical statement of fact, of actual contemporary phenomena, actual in the sense that they were created out of necessity by primitive minds, and firmly believed. Allegory implies a threefold intellectual operation: the construction of a message of general significance, the preparation of a fabulous form, and an exercise of considerable technical difficulty in uniting the two, an operation totally beyond the reach of the primitive mind. Moreover, if we consider the myth as being essentially allegorical, we are not obliged to accept the form in which it is cast as a statement of fact. But we know that the actual creators of these myths gave full credence to their face-value. Jove was no symbol: he was terribly real. It was precisely their superficial metaphorical character that made them intelligible to people incapable of receiving anything more abstract than the plain record of objectivity.

Such is a painful exposition of Vico's dynamic treatment of Language, Poetry and Myth. He may still appear as a mystic to some: if so, a mystic that rejects the transcendental in every shape and form as a factor in human development, and whose Providence is not divine enough to do without the cooperation of Humanity.

On turning to the *Work in Progress* we find that the mirror is not so convex. Here is direct expression – pages and pages of it. And if you don't understand it, Ladies and Gentlemen, it is because you are too decadent to receive it. You are not satisfied unless form is so strictly divorced from content that you can comprehend the one almost without bothering to read the other. This rapid skimming and absorption of the scant cream of sense is made possible by what I may call a continuous process of copious intellectual salivation. The form that is an arbitrary and independent phenomenon can fulfil no higher function that that of stimulus for a tertiary or quartary conditioned reflex of dribbling comprehension. When Miss Rebecca West clears her decks for a sorrowful deprecation of the Narcissistic element in Mr Joyce by the purchase of 3 hats, one feels that she might very well wear her bib at all her intellectual banquets, or alternatively, assert a more noteworthy control over her salivary glands than is possible for Monsieur Pavlo's unfortunate dogs. The title of this book[1] is a good example of a form carrying a strict inner determination. It should be proof against the usual volley of cerebral sniggers: and it may suggest to some a dozen incredulous Joshuas prowling around the Queen's Hall, springing their tuning-forks lightly against finger-nails that have not yet been refined out of existence. Mr Joyce has a word to say to you on the subject: 'Yet to concentrate solely on the literal sense or even the psychological content of any document to the sore neglect of the enveloping facts themselves circumstantiating it is just as harmful; etc.' And another: 'Who in his heart doubts either that the facts of feminine clothiering are there all the time or that the feminine fiction, stranger than the facts, is there also at the same time, only a little to the rere? Or that one may be separated from the other? Or that both may be contemplated simultaneously? Or that each may be taken up in turn and considered apart from the other?'

Here form *is* content, content *is* form. You complain that this stuff is not written in English. It is not written at all. It is not to be read – or rather it is only to be read. It is to be looked at and listened to. His writing is not *about* something; *it is that something itself* (a fact that has

---

[1] *Our Exagmination Round His Factification for Incamination of Work in Progress*

been grasped by an eminent English novelist and historian whose work is in complete opposition to Mr Joyce's). When the sense is sleep, the words go to sleep. (See the end of *Anna Livia*.) When the sense is dancing, the words dance. Take the passage at the end of Shaun's pastoral: 'To stir up love's young fizz I tilt with this bridle's cup champagne, dimming douce from her peepair of hideseeks tight squeezed on my snowybreasted and while my pearlies in their sparkling wisdom are nippling her bubbles I swear (and let you swear) by the bumper round of my poor old snaggletooth's solidbowel I ne'er will prove I'm untrue to (theatre!) you liking so long as my hole looks. Down.' The language is drunk. The very words are tilted and effervescent. How can we qualify this general aesthetic vigilance without which we cannot hope to snare the sense which is for ever rising to the surface of the form and becoming the form itself? St Augustine puts us on the track of a word with his *'intendere'*; Dante has: *'Donne ch'avete intelletto d'amore'*, and *'Voi che, intendendo, il terzo ciel movete'*; but his *'intendere'* suggests a strictly intellectual operation. When an Italian says today *'Ho inteso,'* he means something between *'Ho udito'* and *'Ho capito'*, a sensuous untidy art of intellection. Perhaps 'apprehension' is the most satisfactory English word. Stephen says to Lynch: 'Temporal or spatial the aesthetic image is first luminously apprehended as self-bounded and self-contained upon the immeasurable background of space or time is not it . . . You apprehend its wholeness.'

There is one point to make clear: the beauty of *Work in Progress* is not presented in space alone, since its adequate apprehension depends as much on its visibility as on its audibility. There is a temporal as well as a spatial unity to be apprehended. Substitute 'and' for 'or' in the quotation, and it becomes obvious why it is as inadequate to speak of 'reading' *Work in Progress* as it would be extravagant to speak of 'apprehending' the work of the late Mr Nat Gould. Mr Joyce has desophisticated language. And it is worth while remarking that no language is so sophisticated as English. It is abstracted to death. Take the word 'doubt': it gives us hardly any sensuous suggestion of hesitancy, of the necessity for choice, of static irresolution. Whereas the German 'Zweifel' does, and, in lesser degree, the Italian 'dubitare'. Mr Joyce recognizes how inadequate 'doubt' is to express a state of extreme uncertainty, and replaces it by 'in twosome twiminds'. Nor is he by any means the first to recognize the importance of treating words as something more than mere polite symbols. Shakespeare uses fat, greasy words to express corruption: 'Duller shouldst thou be than the fat weed that rots itself in death on Lethe wharf.' We hear the ooze squelching all through Dickens' description of the Thames in *Great Expectations*. This writing that you find so obscure is a quintessential extraction of language and painting and gesture, with all the inevitable economy of hieroglyphics. Here words are not the polite contortions of twentieth-century printer's ink. They are alive. They elbow their way on to the page, and glow and blaze and fade and disappear. 'Brawn is my name and broad is my nature and I've breit on my brow and all's right with every feature, and I'll brune this bird or Brown Bess's bung's gone bandy.' This is Brawn blowing with a light gust through the trees or Brawn passing with the sunset. Because the wind in the trees means as little to you as the evening prospect from the Piazzale Michelangiolo – though you accept them both because your non-acceptance would be of no significance – this little adventure of Brawn means nothing to you; and you do not accept it, even though here also your non-acceptance is of no significance. H. C. Earwigger, too, is not content to be mentioned like a shilling-shocker villain, and then dropped until the exigencies of the narrative require that he be again referred to. He continues to suggest himself for a couple of pages, by means of repeated permutations on his 'normative letters', as if to say: 'This is all about me, H. C. Earwigger: don't forget this is all about me!'

This inner elemental vitality and corruption of expression imparts a furious restlessness to the form, which is admirably suited to the purgatorial aspect of the work. There is an endless verbal germination, maturation, putrefaction, the cyclic dynamism of the intermediate. This reduction of various expressive media to their primitive economic directness, and the fusion of these primal essences into an assimilated medium for the exteriorization of thought, is pure Vico, and Vico applied to the problem of style. But Vico is reflected more explicitly than by a distillation of disparate poetic ingredients into a synthetical syrup. We notice that there is little or no attempt at subjectivism or abstraction, no attempt at metaphysical generalization. We are presented with a statement of the particular. It is the old myth: the girl on the dirt track, the two washerwomen on the banks of the river. And there is considerable animism: the mountain 'abhearing', the river puffing her old doudheen. (See the beautiful passage beginning: 'First she let her hair fall and down it flussed.') We have type-names: Isolde – any beautiful girl: Earwigger – Guinness's brewery, the Wellington

monument, the Phoenix Park, anything that occupies an extremely comfortable position between the two stools. Anna Livia herself, mother of
Dublin, but no more the only mother than Zoroaster was the only
oriental stargazer. 'Teems of times and happy returns. The same anew.
Ordovico or viricordo. Anna was, Livia is, Plurabelle's to be. North-
men's thing made Southfolk's place, but howmultyplurators made
eachone in person.' Vico and Bruno are here, and more substantially
than would appear from this swift survey of the question. For the
benefit of those who enjoy a parenthetical sneer, we would draw
attention to the fact that when Mr Joyce's early pamphlet *The Day of
Rabblement* appeared, the local philosophers were thrown into a state
of some bewilderment by a reference in the first line to 'The Nolan'.
They finally succeeded in identifying this mysterious individual with
one of the obscurer ancient Irish kings. In the present work he appeared
frequently as 'Browne and Nolan' the name of a very remarkable
Dublin bookseller and stationer.

To justify our title, we must move north, '*Sovra'l bel fiume d'Arno
alla gran villa*'. . . . Between '*colui per lo cui verso – il meonio cantor
non a piu solo*' and the 'still today insufficiently malestimated note-
snatcher, Shem the Penman', there exists considerable circumstantial
similarity. They both saw how worn out and threadbare was the
conventional language of cunning literary artificers, both rejected any
approximation to a universal language. If English is not yet so definitely
a polite necessity as Latin was in the Middle Ages, at least one is justified in declaring that its position in relation to other European languages
is to a great extent that of mediaeval Latin to the Italian dialects.
Dante did not adopt the vulgar out of any kind of local jingoism nor
out of any determination to assert the superiority of Tuscan to all its
rivals as a form of spoken Italian. On reading his *De Vulgari Eloquentia*
we are struck by his complete freedom from civic intolerance. He
attacks the world's Portadownians: '*Nam quicumque tam obscenae
rationis est, ut lucum suae nationis delitosissimm credat esse sub sole,
huic etiam prae cunctis propriam volgare licetur, idest maternam locutionem.
Nos autem, cui mundus est patria* . . . etc.' When he comes to examine the
dialects he finds Tuscan: '*turpissimum . . . fere omnes Tusci in suo
turpiloquio obtusi . . . non restat in dubio quin aliud sit vulgare quod
quaerimus quam quod attingit populus Tuscanorum.*' His conclusion is
that the corruption common to all the dialects makes it impossible to
select one rather than another as an adequate literary form, and that

he who would write in the vulgar must assemble the purest elements from each dialect and construct a synthetic language that would at least possess more than a circumscribed local interest: which is precisely what he did. He did not write in Florentine any more than in Neapolitan. He wrote a vulgar that *could* have been spoken by an ideal Italian who had assimilated what was best in all the dialects of his country, but which in fact was certainly not spoken nor ever had been. Which disposes of the capital objection that might be made against this attractive parallel between Dante and Mr Joyce in the question of language, i.e. that at least Dante wrote what was being spoken in the streets of his own town, whereas no creature in heaven or earth ever spoke the language of *Work in Progress*. It is reasonable to admit that an international phenomenon might be capable of speaking it, just as in 1300 none but an inter-regional phenomenon could have spoken the language of the Divine Comedy. We are inclined to forget that Dante's literary public was Latin, that the form of his Poem was to be judged by Latin eyes and ears, by a Latin Esthetic intolerant of innovation, and which could hardly fail to be irritated by the substitution of '*Nel mezzo del cammin di nostra vita*' with its 'barbarous' directness for the suave elegance of: '*Ultima regna canam, fluido contermina mundo,*' just as English eyes and ears prefer: 'Smoking his favourite pipe in the sacred presence of ladies' to: 'Rauking his flavourite turfco in the smukking precincts of lydias.' Boccaccio did not jeer at the '*piedi sozzi*' of the peacock that Signora Alighieri dreamed about.

I find two well made caps in the *Convivio*, one to fit the collective noddle of the monodialectical arcadians whose fury is precipitated by a failure to discover 'innocefree' in the Concise Oxford Dictionary and who qualify as the 'ravings of a Bedlamite' the formal structure raised by Mr Joyce after years of patient and inspired labour: '*Questi sono da chiamare pecore e non uomini; chè se una pecora si gittasse da una ripa di mille passi, tutte l'altre le andrebbono dietro; e se una pecora per alcuna cagione al passare d'una strada salta, tutte le altre saltano, eziando nulla veggendo da saltare. E io ne vidi già molte in un pozzo saltare, per una che dentro vi salto, forse credendo di saltare un muro*'. And the other for Mr Joyce, biologist in words: '*Questo* (formal innovation) *sarà luce nuova, sole nuovo, il quale sorgerà ore l'usato tramonterà e darà luce a coloro che sono in tenebre e in oscurità per lo usato sole che a loro non luce.*' And, lest he should pull it down over his eyes and laugh, behind the peak; I translate '*in tenebre e in oscurita*' by 'bored to extinction'. (Dante makes a curious mistake speaking of the origin of language, when he rejects the authority of Genesis that Eve was the first to speak, when she addressed the Serpent. His incredulity is amusing: *'inconvenienter putatur tam egregium humani generis actum, vel prius quam a viro, foemina profluisse'*. But before Eve was born the animals were given names by Adam, the man who 'first said goo to a goose'. Moreover it is explicitly stated that the choice of names was left entirely to Adam, so that there is not the slightest biblical authority for the conception of language as a direct gift of God, any more than there is any intellectual authority for conceiving that we are indebted for the 'Concert' to the individual who used to buy paint for Giorgione.)

We know very little about the immediate reception accorded to Dante's mighty vindication of the 'vulgar', but we can form our own opinions when, two centuries later, we find Castiglione splitting more than a few hairs concerning the respective advantages of Latin and Italian, and Poliziano writing the dullest of dull Latin Elegies to justify his existence as the author of *Orfeo* and the *Stanze*. We may also compare, if we think it worth while, the storm of ecclesiastical abuse raised by Mr Joyce's work, and the treatment that *The Divine Comedy* must certainly have received from the same source. His Contemporary Holiness might have swallowed the crucifixion of *'lo sommo Giove'*, and all it stood for, but he could scarcely have looked with favour on the spectacle of three of his immediate predecessors plunged head-foremost in the fiery stone of Malebolge, nor yet the identification of the Papacy in the mystical procession of Terrestial Paradise with a *'puttana sciolta'*. The *De Monarchia* was burnt publicly under Pope Giovanni XXII at the instigation of Cardinal Beltrando and the bones of its author would have suffered the same fate but for the interference of an influential man of letters, Pino della Tosa. Another point of comparison is the preoccupation with the significance of numbers. The death of Beatrice inspired nothing less than a highly complicated poem dealing with the importance of the number three in her life. Dante never ceased to be obsessed by this number. Thus the Poem is divided into three Cantiche, each composed of 33 Canti, and written in terza rima. Why, Mr Joyce seems to say, should there be four legs to a table, and four to a horse, and four seasons and four Gospels and four Provinces in Ireland? Why twelve Tables of the Law, and twelve Apostles and twelve months and twelve Napoleonic marshals and twelve men in Florence called Ottolenghi? Why should the Armistice be celebrated at the eleventh hour of the eleventh day of the eleventh month? He cannot tell you because he is not God Almighty, but in a thousand years he will tell you, and in the meantime must be content to know why horses have not five legs, nor three. He is conscious that things with a common numerical characteristic tend towards a very significant interrelationship. This preoccupation is freely translated in his present work: see the 'Question and Answer' chapter, and the Four speaking through the child's brain. They are the four winds as much as the four Provinces, and the four Episcopal Sees as much as either.

A last word about the Purgatories. Dante's is conical and consequently implies culmination. Mr Joyce's is spherical and excludes culmination. In the one there is an ascent from real vegetation – Ante-Purgatory – to ideal vegetation – Terrestrial Paradise: in the other there is no ascent and no ideal vegetation. In the one, absolute progression and a guaranteed consummation: in the other, flux – progression or retrogression, and an apparent consummation. In the one movement is unidirectional, and a step forward represents a net advance: in the other movement is non-directional or multi-directional, and a step forward is, by definition, a step back. Dante's Terrestrial Paradise is the carriage entrance to a Paradise that is not terrestrial: Mr Joyce's Terrestrial Paradise is the tradesmen's entrance on to the sea-shore. Sin is an impediment to movement up the cone, and a condition of movement round the sphere. In what sense, then, is Mr Joyce's work purgatorial? In the absolute absence of the Absolute. Hell is the static lifelessness of unrelieved immaculation. Purgatory a flood of movement and vitality released by the conjunction of these two elements. There is a continuous purgatorial process at work, in the sense that the vicious circle of humanity is being achieved, and this achievement depends on the recurrent predomination of one of two broad qualities. No resistance, no eruption, and it is only in Hell and Paradise that there are no eruptions, that there can be none, need be none. On this earth that is Purgatory, Vice and Virtue – which you may take to mean any pair of large contrary human factors – must in turn be purged down to spirits of rebelliousness. Then the dominant crust of the Vicious or Virtuous sets, resistance is provided, the explosion duly takes place and the machine proceeds. And no more than this; neither prize nor penalty; simply a series of stimulants to enable the kitten to catch its tail. And the partially purgatorial agent? The partially purged.

The Mysticism That Pleased Him

A Note on the Primary Source of Joyce's *Ulysses*

W. B. Stanford

In a conversation at Zürich in 1917, Joyce remarked: ' ... I was twelve years old when I studied the Trojan War but the story of Ulysses alone remained in my recollection. It was the mysticism that pleased me ... '[1] This presents two problems: what did Joyce mean by 'mysticism' in this context, and from what source did he, knowing no Greek, first derive it?

Joyce can hardly have meant mysticism in its primary religious sense. The better-known ancient and modern accounts of the Troy tale never suggest that either Ulysses or any other Homeric hero had a desire to attain to the Beatific Vision through contemplation and spiritual asceticism. In the *Iliad* and *Odyssey*, it is true, Pallas Athene constantly guides and cherishes Ulysses; but there is nothing mystical in Ulysses's attitude towards her or in any other aspect of his eminently pragmatic piety. Abnormally, three vernacular writers, Dante, Pascoli and Kazantzakis, do present some non-classical adventures of Ulysses with marked mysticism; but their work was, for various reasons, linguistic and chronological, inaccessible to Joyce at the age of twelve. We must look elsewhere for both the nature and the source of the mysticism that pleased him.

If one takes 'mysticism' in its secondary and more literary sense, as 'spiritually allegorical, of occult meaning', the first problem is solved at once. Though Homer himself probably intended no allegories in his epics, his interpreters very soon began to discover them for him. As early as 525 BC Theagenes of Rhegium used allegorical interpretations to defend Homer from attacks by contemporary theologians and moralists,

---

[1] Herbert Gorman, *James Joyce*, 1941, p. 222.

explaining that the names of the gods were best understood as representing elements of nature or else mental and moral qualities. Apollo, for example, should be understood as a symbol of fire, Poseidon of water, Hermes of intelligence and Leto of forgetfulness.

The lively imaginations of later Greek critics developed this kind of allegorical exegesis energetically. In the Alexandrian epoch scholastic subtleties went to ludicrous extremes in discerning occult meanings for straightforward descriptions. For instance, Penelope's web that kept the Suitors at bay was interpreted as a system of dialectic, the warp being the premises, the woof the conclusion, and her torch the light of reason. The Neo-Platonists, most notably Porphyry and 'Heraclides Ponticus', added a genuinely mystical quality to these allegorizations. The wanderings of Ulysses became one of their favourite symbols for the vicissitudes of the soul among the phenomena of the physical world. And, significantly for *Ulysses*, sometimes Daedalus, the inventor of flight, was set beside him as a parallel emblem of the soul's aspiration. Early Fathers of the Church took over this allegorical attitude to Ulysses, and added their own ingenuities. Origen did not think it improper to compare Ulysses tied to the mast as he passed the Sirens with Our Lord nailed to the Cross.[1]

The 'mysticism' remained active, even dominant at times, in the Ulysses tradition till the seventeenth century in Western Europe. But then, under the influence of scientific rationalism, religious purism and literary humanism, it almost vanished in the Augustan and neoclassical treatments of the myth. Calderon's *Love the Greatest Enchantment* and *The Sorceries of Sin,* are the last great allegorical presentations of Ulysses in Western literature before Joyce's *Ulysses*. The prevailing ethos in almost all characterizations of Ulysses from Fénelon's *Télémaque* onwards is humanistic, not mystical. This, of course, was no innovation. Homer, Sophocles, Euripides, Virgil, Ovid, Lydgate,

---

[1] S. Foster Damon in *James Joyce: Two Decades Of Criticism,* ed. Seon Givens, 1948, p. 204, refers to Neo-Platonic symbolisms in *Ulysses*. They are specially prevalent in the Proteus episode. For Ulysses and Daedalus as symbols of the soul's wanderings, see P. Courcelle in *Revue des Etudes Anciennes,* 1944, pp. 65–93; they are also mentioned together by Vico in his *New Science,* par. 634. Vico's allegorical approach to Homer, though the reverse of mystical, is a notable exception to the then current literary fashion, which is more typically displayed in his friend Metastasio's *Achilles in Scyros* with its pasteboard conventional Ulysses. Christian interpretations of Ulysses Bound to the Mast, and of the Moly, have been discussed in *Griechische Mythen in christlicher Deutung* by Hugo Rahner (Zürich, 1945), pp. 229–492.

du Bellay, Ascham, Shakespeare, and many other writers in the Ulysses tradition, had been primarily interested in the moral and humane aspects of Joyce's 'favourite hero' (as he described him in his school essay).[1] But here the significant fact is that the mystical interpretation of Ulysses had never been so much neglected in Western European literature as in the two centuries preceding Joyce's youthful rediscovery of it.[2]

Pope, in the preface to all his powerful translations of Homer, had blamed Chapman in these terms: 'He appears to have had a strong affectation of extracting new meanings out of his author: insomuch as to promise, in his rhyming preface, a poem of the mysteries he had revealed in Homer; and perhaps he endeavoured to strain the obvious sense to this end'.[3] The Augustans, serene in their deistical and scientific optimism, did not care for mysteries. Their Romantic successors, seeing Homer through Augustan glasses and finding him too marmoreal, looked elsewhere – to Ossian, Werther or Prometheus – for their heroes. There is no mysticism in the Ulysses of Landor, Tennyson, de Tabley, Phillips or Robert Bridges – Joyce's immediate English predecessors in the Ulysses tradition – nor, so far as I can find, in any Western European portrait of Ulysses from Goethe's projected *Ulysses auf Phaa* in the 1780s to Gerhard Hauptmann's *Der Bogen des Odysseus* in 1914.

Where, then, did Joyce find the mysticism that pleased him? The answer is to be found in the syllabus for the Intermediate Examination in 1894. The course set for English literature in the Preparatory Grade included the first seven chapters of Lamb's *Adventures of Ulysses*, in

---

[1] For Joyce's essay on Ulysses as 'My Favourite Hero' in his third year at Belvedere, see Gorman, *James Joyce*, p. 45.

[2] The fact that some scholars, like Max Müller, were discovering solar myths and the like while Joyce was a boy is hardly significant here. Their learned speculations could hardly have impinged on the mind of a twelve-year-old, Greekless schoolboy. But doubtless Joyce read about them later and welcomed them, as he welcomed Berard's theory of the Semitic origins of the *Odyssey*.

[3] Pope was, presumably, referring to the lines in Chapman's 'To the Reader' (121ff) which describe how earlier translators had "fail'd to search his deep and treasurous heart" because they had not "the fit key of Nature", "with Poesy to open Poesy",

> Which, in my poem of the mysteries
> Reveal'd in Homer, I will clearly prove.

But, in the absence of any such subsequent poem, may we not take it, allowing for Chapman's sinuosities of style and thought, that he merely meant his translation?

Andrew Lang's or John Cooke's edition. Joyce, then twelve years old, took the Second Paper in English on the afternoon of Wednesday the thirteenth (the date he dreaded later) of June, 1894. He had to answer five general questions, all far from 'mystical', on the wanderings of Ulysses. His total mark in English was 455 out of 1,200, not good in comparison with his 700 out of 1,200 in Latin. Perhaps he lost marks on the uninspiring subjects for composition. If he had been in the Junior Grade he could have written on 'Ulysses' and might have surprised a certain W. Magennis, M.A., who was among the Junior Grade examiners in English. As it was, they were not impressed, writing in their report:

> The compositions, with some exceptions, lacked arrangement. Those on 'Ulysses' for the most part consisted of extracts from Lamb, more or less accurately reproduced, but badly connected: the writers too frequently restricted themselves to a narrative of the hero's wanderings after the capture of Troy, and gave undue prominence to the incident in the cave of Polyphemus . . . Many excellent essays were written on the subject of 'Animal Pets' . . .

Apparently there was no mysticism there either. Next year, however, when Joyce was in the Junior Grade, he had an opportunity of writing on 'Slow rises Worth by Poverty depressed', a subject almost as significant for his later career as 'Ulysses'. W. Magennis examined and reported then too. Later he came to know James Joyce as something more than a number on an examination script.[1]

But how did Lamb's *Adventures of Ulysses* convey this sense of mystical meaning to the young Joyce? Lamb's presentation is by no

---

[1] For the facts in this paragraph see the *Programme of Examinations . . . for* 1894 (pub. 1893), the *Examination Papers . . . for* 1894 and (the results of) *Examinations Held in* 1894, published by the Intermediate Examination Board, Dublin. (I am grateful to the officials of the National Library, Dublin, and the Department of Education, secondary branch, for help here.) In this and subsequent reports there is some noteworthy biographical material still to be used. Professor Stanislaus Joyce had kindly corroborated my conjecture that his brother's interest in Ulysses was first aroused by Lamb's book, before I discovered it on the Intermediate course. V. Larbaud in *Criterion,* i, 1922, p. 99, states that Joyce had been attracted by 'a translation' of the Odyssey (Lamb's work is not quite this) at school, and had frequently read it over again for 'love of Ulysses'. Joyce used the edition of Lamb's work by John Cooke (a graduate of T.C.D.) published by Browne & Nolan, Dublin (no date: probably 1893). I owe thanks to Father R. Coyle, S. J., of Belvedere, Mr P. A. Gibney (Joyce's schoolmate) and Messrs Browne & Nolan for help in establishing this fact. I hope to discuss Cooke's edition elsewhere. It includes Lamb's own preface.

means explicitly mystical. Indeed the first sentence of his short preface states that his book was intended as a supplement to Fénelon's very mundane and humanistic *Télémaque*. But, as Lamb admits later in his preface, the main influence on his style and attitude was 'one obsolete version'. He means Chapman's translation which now, thanks to Lamb's revival of its imaginative riches and Keats's sonnet 'On first looking into Chapman's Homer', is no longer an obsolete or forgotten work. But Pope's scornful remark on its 'mysteries' probably had sealed its disfavour in the eighteenth century.

Chapman's mind was more akin to Sir Thomas Browne's or to Porphyry's than to Ovid's or Shakespeare's (whose Ulysses, in *Troilus and Cressida*, is magnificently practical). Chapman constantly sought delphic oracles and Alexandrian allegorisms in 'Homer, Prince of Poets'. His prose 'Preface to the Reader' in his *Iliads* begins with a discourse on esoteric truth, for 'Poesy is the flower of the Sun, and disdains to open to the eye of a candle'. In the Epistle Dedicatory to his *Odysseys* he avers (with characteristic tortuousness):

> Nor is this all-comprising Poesy fantastic or mere fictive; but the most material and doctrinal illations of truth . . . Wherein, if the body (being the letter of history) seems fictive; and beyond possibility to bring into act, the sense then and allegory, which is the soul, is to be sought . . .

Later, in the same Epistle, he breaks into verse and speaks of Homer's 'heaven-strong mysteries', and tells how (after Homer's death had dispelled the 'bloody mist' of misunderstanding, poverty and spite):

> then truth's light
> Glimmer'd about his poem; the pinch'd soul
> (Amidst the mysteries it did enrol)
> Brake powerfully abroad.

One could quote many other expressions of this apocalyptic approach to Homer from Chapman's prefaces and translations and many examples of 'allegory, which is the soul'.[1]

---

[1] Chapman is quoted from Richard Hooper's editions of the *Iliads* (edition 1865) and *Odyssey* (1857), pp. lxxxvi and xlix, li–lii. In the former, p. xlvi, he quotes Samuel Sheppard's poem 'On Mr Chapman's Incomparable Translation of Homer's Works' (published 1651), which claims that Chapman surpassed
all that on them take
Great Homer's misticke meaning plain to make,
Yeeld him more dark with farr-fetcht allegories,
Sometimes mistaking clean his learned stories.

Chapman addressed his interpretations to sophisticated Elizabethan and Jacobean courtiers. Lamb wrote his *Adventures of Ulysses* mainly for young readers. Consequently, he wisely avoided any elaborate allegorisms. He preferred, as he says in his preface, to adapt Homer's tale for the sake of 'a rapidity to the narration', and 'to give it more the air of romance'. But he emphasizes the note of wonder and magic whenever he can.[1] The 'agents' in his tale, he tells his readers, 'besides men and women, are giants, enchanters, sirens: things which denote external force or internal temptations, the twofold danger which a wise fortitude must expect to encounter in its course through this world'. In displaying this thaumaturgy, Lamb had to fight the prevailing taste. His publisher, Godwin, objected to some of the more horrific details in the grimmer episodes. Lamb defended them in a spirited letter:

> The giant's vomit [in Homer's account of the Cyclops incident] was perfectly nauseous, and I am glad you pointed it out. I have removed the objection. To the other passages I can find no other objection but what you may bring to numberless passages, besides, such as of Scylla snatching up the six men, etc., that is to say, they are lively images of 'shocking' things. If you want a book, which is not occasionally to shock, you should not have thought of a tale which was so full of anthropophagi and wonders. I cannot alter these things without enervating the Book, and I will not alter them, if the penalty should be that you and all the London booksellers should refuse it. But speaking as author to author, I must say that I think the 'terrible' in these two passages seems to me so much to preponderate over the nauseous as to make them rather fine than disgusting.

'A tale so full of anthropophagi and wonders': the Sir Thomas Brownian phrase emblemizes the essential quality of both Lamb's and Chapman's versions in contrast to the anthropocentric humanism of Fénelon or Pope. To emphasize it Lamb even deserted both Chapman and Homer by skipping the Telemacheia, and beginning at once with Ulysses' supernatural adventures. (It should be remembered that the Preparatory Grade Course which Joyce had to study – though doubtless

---

[1] Lamb introduces at least one quite unclassical interpretation when he equates the twelve children of Aeolus with the twelve winds. (There is nothing of this in Chapman.) On this and many other innovations, see E. H. Gardner's edition (1921) to which I owe the quotation from Lamb's letter to Godwin (*Letters*, ed. E. V. Lucas, vi, 386).

he read to the end of the book for himself – was restricted to the chapters describing these adventures in fairyland, Ulysses' return home and his revenge on the Suitors being reserved for the maturer Junior Grade minds.) Constantly, in his story, Lamb adds touches of wonder not to be found in Chapman or Homer. Thus, Circe 'could command the moon from her sphere, or unroot the solid oak from its place to make it dance for their diversion, and by the help of her illusions (like Bella Cohen later) she could vary the taste of pleasures, and contrive delights, recreations and jolly pastimes, to *fetch the day about from sun to sun, and rock the tedious year as in a delightful dream.* The Siren's song is such as 'has made the gods stoop, and *heaven drowsy with the harmony*', and 'the celestial harmony' of their voices 'no tongue can describe'; 'the Moly is a small unsightly root, its virtues but little known, and in low estimation; the dull shepherd treads on it every day with his clouted shoes; but it bears a small white flower which is medicinal against charms, blights, mildews and damps'.[1] These concepts and many others like them, though not plainly allegorical, would suggest mystical meanings to a young imaginative mind better than any didactic gloss. Wonder, as the ancient Greeks knew well, is the mother of speculative philosophy.

Much of Joyce's later reading would strengthen this sense of mysticism in the Ulysses myth; Dante, above all, in *Inferno*, xxvi:

> For every true-born mysticist
> A Dante is unprejudiced . . . ,

with, perhaps, Calderon's two plays already mentioned (they were accessible to Joyce at the National Library in Denis Florence Mac Carthy's opalescent and most unjustly neglected translations), Pascoli's *Ultimo Viaggio* and the various Neo-Platonic and allegorical commentators. But Joyce never forgot his debt to Charles Lamb. Twice, in

---

[1] Can this description have suggested the potato-moly motif to Joyce? Lamb's references to the small, unsightly root and the treading of the dull shepherd are quite unhomeric. Further, can it be that the name Bloom contains an intentional reference to the blossom of the moly which is emphasized by Homer and his successors including Lamb and Calderon? Most significant for this is a scene in Hauptmann's play *The Bow of Odysseus* (which Joyce read when he was beginning to compose *Ulysses* in 1914), where the word 'Blume' recurs twice in connection with Ulysses and Antinoos calls him 'der Blumlein'–Moly-Mann. 'Poldy Bloom' has a suggestive assonance here. And in a sense 'Molly' Bloom was his moly against the delusions and illusions of life too.

letters[1] to his Aunt Josephine, in 1922, when she was mystified by his final essay on the Ulysses theme, he told her that the best introduction to it was Lamb's *Adventures of Ulysses*. It still is.

---

[1] I am grateful to Mr Niall Sheridan for having told me of these letters and for lending me photostats of them. They are dated 10.11.22 (from Nice) and 21.12.22 (from Paris).

Dear Mr Joyce

Edna O'Brien

Was he garrulous? Did he wear a topcoat? Did he hanker after an estate? Did he play chess or cribbage? Once at evening time was he observed to step out, get into a carriage and immediately and for some mystifying reason get out again and disappear into the house? In short was he a neurotic? Such questions we always ask about the deceased great, trying in our forlorn way to identify with them, to find some point of contact, some malady, some caprice that brings us and them nearer. Such questions are not satisfactorily answered in works of fiction (writers being consummate magpies) nor in the testimonies of friends because friends are prone to lie in the interests of love, hate, imperviousness or venom. Ex-lovers are equally unreliable, being for ever besotted or irredeemably wounded. But letters tell. Letters are like the lines on a face, testimonial. In this case they are the access to the man that encased the mind that was the genius of James Joyce, Aquarian, Dubliner.

He started to study medicine three times. No two occupations are closer than that of doctor and novelist. Both are trying to arrive at a truth of some kind and hence a remedy to living. Had he qualified he would have been bound to have gone on and been a gynaecologist, he with his obsession with womb and ovary and Holles Street hospital. In his youth he was suspicious, contemptuous, unaccommodating. He saw his countrymen as being made up of yahoos, adulterous priests and sly deceitful women. He classed it as the 'venereal condition of the Irish'. Like the wild geese he had a mind to go elsewhere; it was not to follow an alien king but to commence a revolution in word. He wanted to be continentalized. He liked the vineyards. He had a dream of Paris. He likened it to a lantern in the wood of the world for lovers. He had a craze for languages. In literature his heroes were Cardinal Newman and

Henrik Ibsen. To Ibsen he wrote: 'Your work on earth draws to a close and you are near the silence. It is growing dark for you.' He was nineteen at that time. Young men do not usually know such things, unless there is already on them the shadow of their future. There was on him. He descended into blindness. The eyes are the nearest to the brain. He was beset by glaucoma, cataract, iris complaint, dissolution of the retina. His nerves were like the twitterings of wrens. His brain pandemoniacal. The sirens were always on. He was having to take aspirin, iodine, scopolamine. It had its funny side, this daily harassment of his. His eye doctor had a bet with him that if the front wall of the lens of his eye was removed a cataract would decide to form itself on the back wall. He admitted that with such cryptic wit a man like that could have written *Ulysses*. He was prone to betting. He wagered a pound of dried apricots with his friend Ezra Pound that his play *Exiles* would not be produced although at the time there was a management in an agreeable tizz about it. A pound of apricots, a pound of chops, plum pudding mass and canticles. Religious motifs may have dogged him and Latin words and Hades and Potsdam and melancolores and Atrahora and the Portuguese for Devil but he remained a plain-spoken man. In a tart and almost vulnerable rejoinder he was driven to point out to his aunt that receiving a copy of *Ulysses* was not like receiving a pound of chops and he urged her to give cognizance to that fact and get it back from whatever hooligan had swizzled her out of it, under the name of borrowing. His mind was for ever commuting. In the next letter, or the letter following, he plied her with questions. Had such and such a house ivy on its sea-front wall, how many steps were there down to the sea, could a man climb over a certain railing into Eccles Street? To him words were not literature but numerals, digits, things that when he strung them together in his wild, prodigious way took on another light, another lustre and were the litany of his lapsed Catholic soul. He liked hymnbooks and tittle-tattle and all tongues to be welded in together. The English he strove for was pidgin, nigger, cockney, Irish, Bowery and biblical. To avoid being cloying, to run no risk of being literary, he always prefaced or postscripted his incandescent phrases with a joke. When asking Italo Svevo to collect a briefcase, he first described it with fiendish accuracy, its oilskin cloth, the approximate weight, the approximate measurement and the protrusion which struck him as having likeness to a nun's belly. Then he said: 'In this briefcase I placed the written symbols of the languid lights which occasionally flashed across my soul.'

Only by giving a pedestrian complexion to the whole thing could he communicate his real feeling, rather like having to make a declaration of love to a banana skin.

Love. Love as we practise it makes dotards of us all. Blackmailers. Infants. It is a solace to know that he sublimely fell into those traps. No detachment, no grand phrases but raging boiling lust and suspiciousness and doubt. His love object, and the only one as far as we know, was from Galway, the city of his tribal name. Are such things total chance. She had reddish-brown hair and he wanted that she had fuller breasts and fat thighs. To achieve that he urged that she drink cocoa. Back in Dublin without her, where he was on the ludicrous mission of helping to have cinemas opened, he was wrecked with thoughts of their youth, their courtship, her absence. Was his son really his son? Was not the blood-stain the first time rather slight? Could he be smacked by her? Or better still flogged? Could he be her child? Could she be his mother? The brown stains on her girlish drawers sent him off on another rhapsody. Desire and shame, shame and desire. His own words for all his own feelings were that they were mad and dirty.

The madness was there all right, the madness that through the long hours of day and night, when he attained divinity through language, murdered his eyes, his nerves and later his stomach. He went far into far latitudes but he always came back. He came back with such weird reliability. He had to. He had to cope with poverty, piracy, lawsuits. Money was always on their agenda, or rather the absence of it. Borrowing and lending. Checking the prices of food, of furniture, hotel rooms and, much, much later, the cost of mental institutions. He had dreams of grandeur. There were some very fine furs he wanted to buy for Nora. There was a necklace that he had made for her in Dublin, while at the same time he was sending his brother a telegram to say that he was arriving home on the morrow, penniless. He suggested the kind of linoleum they get for the kitchen, the kind of curtains and an armchair where he could loll. He asked his brother for Jesus' sake not to attack him with bills.

He attended to his own talent, not in the interest of bombast or self-aggrandisement, but rather like a faithful watchman. He had the fixity of the great and therefore no need of vanity. He estimated that three shillings would be a reasonable price for *Ulysses*. A tiresome book he admitted. At that same time he was dogged by a fear that the printing house would be burnt down or that some untoward catastrophe would

happen to it. He assisted Miss Beach in wrapping the copies, he autographed the de luxe editions, he wrote to influential people, he hawked
packages to the post office. He knew that the illustrious would change
their minds many a time before settling down to a final opinion and he
knew that many another would know as much about it as the Parliamentary side of his arse. If there was a good review he rejoiced, simply because
it might lead to another sale, maybe. If there was a bad review he asked
sagely what method of suicide he ought to embark on. He was a distant
man. Ambiguous. He wrote reams and reams and yet there was no
knowing for certain what he felt about the people he wrote to. A slitherer,
Jesuitically trained, and with a scorching wit. Getting shamrock so that
it was then a cloudscreen, a sham screen, and from that to something
else, derived from Syrian or Burmese or Heaven or Hell. Metamorphosis
it is called. Then back to the bathbuns. If he had a sign on his person it
would be Beware of the Miserere. He liked regional dishes. He liked a
white wine that was named St Patrice. He knew that Oxford was where
the best shirts were made. He asked an affluent friend for a spare tie
and upon getting it was filled with a deferential effusion. Blind as only
the visioned can be. His mind a conglomeration of colour, trinities,
rainbows, double rainbows, Joyce knows what. Iridescent and onomato-
peic and sensifacient, all together. He must have often longed to have
his brain dry-cleaned or exposed to the gales of the Atlantic Ocean.
When he learned that the wild flowers of Carthage survived the devas-
tations of centuries he likened that indomitableness to being the lilts of
children. He had two children, Lucia and Giorgio.

It was where his family pinged and impinged that his profound heart
was bared. He believed that a mysterious malady had caught hold of
them when they were small, in Switzerland. Lucia wanted to be a dancer
and then an artist. Giorgio wanted to be a singer. Neither of them
realized their ambitions. At first he feared that their existence might
sever him and Nora. As they grew older their needs became paramount.
When they were absent from home he wrote daily and maundered into
many languages, because he had seen to it that they were multilingual.
For his son he copied out songs, sent sheet music, wished maybe that
he be another John McCormack whom he both admired and ridiculed
in that sparring way of his. Never the genius but always the father,
livening them up with some story, some little memory that danced
through his mind. Always in the cause of levity, always.

Fathers and daughters. That terrible clench. He named her Lucia after the patron saint of eyes. She had to have an operation to have one of hers straightened. First she wanted to be a dancer, then an artist, a graphic artist. She was given to premonitions. She had the wisdom of the serpent and the gentleness of the dove, as he said. Again as he said, she was gay, sweet and ironic, but given to bursts of anger and eventually she had to be put in a straitjacket. He strove to right her. He must have minded terribly not being God, he who had nearly attained a divinity through language. He praised her rubrics, her lettering, her designs. Long before he had loved the graphic fantasies of the old Irish monks. She was not Cézanne, as he noted, but he wanted her life to have point. It was more than fatherly concern, he saw into her. He tried to save her from institutions but she passed the line of demarcation, made too far a walk out into the mental Azores and had to be committed. One asylum was called St Nazaire. So like Nazareth. So like Joyce.

Towards the end of his life there came a thaw, a burstingness. He was famous then. There were picnics arranged in his honour. When he went to his favourite Paris restaurant the orchestra played 'It's a Long Way To Tipperary'. He was bowed to at the opera. But it was not fame that caused him to mellow so, surely it was growth. He called on people, sent greetings, blessings, telegrams, entertained those he met with his clear tenor tones. He sent Mr Yeats an autographed copy of *Work in Progress* and said that if Mrs Yeats cared to unsew the first pages of *Ulysses* he would happily sign it for them. He sent *Pomes Penyeach* to the library at Galway University. They had a special reading desk made and he was delighted that his book, with Lucia's letterings, was on display for all the ex-hooligans to see. The spleen was going out of his mind. He was the father of a family, a scattered family. He remembered Christmas, birthdays, old friends, he lifted a glass to old times. He had come to a height. He had achieved monumence both in his work and in his being. In neutral Switzerland where he and Nora went to be near Lucia he got pains that could only be relieved by morphine. The doctors and surgeon had a concilium and took him to the Red Cross hospital where they operated. There was a hole in his stomach resulting from an ulcer that had been his constant but undiagnosed companion for years. Two days later he died. It was January. He was bordering on sixty. It is hard not to want to believe in immortality, considering the death of dear Mr Joyce.

Who Killed James Joyce?

Patrick Kavanagh

I find it difficult to form any particular opinion about Joyce. I have one advantage over certain others: I was never an original admirer of Joyce and so have not had the normal reaction, that readjusting of one's values which is common in regard to one's enthusiasms. It often happens in the case of a person with whom we were in love. We react violently to right the balance. I read *Ulysses* for the first time about seven years ago. Since then, it has been my second favourite bedside book.

What I think a mistake is reading deep symbolism into *Ulysses*, drawing comparisons. *Ulysses* is a very funny book, and it is also a very wearying book. It is almost entirely a transcription of life. Joyce added nothing – except possibly Stephen, and he gave us Stephen completely in the *Portrait*.

There is nothing wrong with Joyce, who, as Chesterton said about someone else, is sane enough; it is his commentators who are mad.

Almost the most outstanding quality in Joyce is his Catholicism or rather his anti-Protestantism. Joyce, through Stephen, in the *Portrait* must have done more damage to Protestantism than any modern apologist.

His reason made him a bad Catholic, but whatever the defects of Catholicism, he saw that Protestantism was a compendium of all those defects.

There was nothing in Joyce's life of noble self-sacrifice – except the fact that he went off with a penniless girl. Perhaps it was the artist in him which gave this kink to his character!

Yet I am constantly reminded of the number of writers who achieved the depths of hell's despair simply because they happened to get a woman without the spondulicks. I could name a score of dramatic tragedies from literature and from life which could have been solved by money. O'Casey's *Juno and the Paycock* couldn't exist if the will hadn't been botched or they had won the Sweep. Everywhere I find this problem which most people attribute to some tremendous integrity. This may be so, for the ways of God are strange and He sometimes makes a man turn away from the door of Midas's counting house. It has happened to myself. I am nearly incapable of not falling out with anyone who isn't as poor as myself. If Joyce had had a thousand a year would he have written *Ulysses* as he did?

Prosperity takes a lot of the bitterness out of life. It is more than possible that Joyce could not have remembered with the same awful hate that boon companion in the canary waistcoat, Buck Mulligan. And there is also Mr Deasy whose wonderful thumb-nail portrait we might have lost.

It seems to me that God, through the agency of society, manages to breed a race of artists by the process of starvation and all kinds of indignity due to poverty. Is it not on the cards that an artist can be bred artificially in this way? Or must he have the kink in him originally?

He has got to hate society, that is nearly certain.

Remember Dante exiled; Goethe crying: 'Beware of what you pray for in youth for you will get it in middle age.' Ah, yes, the story of men who, generally, against their wills, were miserable.

Sometimes you get the artificial breed who betakes himself to a mews where, on a stretcher bed, he subsists on a diet of brown bread and champagne. But these are the phonies who love society and who are loved by it. So it appears that my theory of artificial artistic insemination does not work out.

Art is life squeezed through a repression.

Milton, Homer, blind.

Byron and Shelley, two wealthy men, did manage to achieve misery and sudden death.

Joyce and Eliot have a good deal in common: they are both materialists which may be one reason why they have become a fashion. Society knows where it stands with mere matter. (I am not too sure of my argument here: society has also a deep affection for the immaterial.)

What I am trying to say is that Joyce has little, or none, of that ethereal commodity known as inspiration. He is the very clever cynical man who has found a formula.

In the end this introvert formula which feeds on itself exhausts its material. A true creator is always trying to be a little more than matter.

Finnegans Wake is the delirium of a man with no more to say. He has melted down even the matrix.

– You, Cochrane, what city sent for him?

– Tarentum, sir.

There is, in this writing here, a strange intangible quality which helps to destroy my argument. There is something which enlarges the imagination, excites the reader creatively.

But the *Portrait of the Artist* is Joyce's testament.

And yet, as I read through some of the more violent parts of *Ulysses,* I feel that Joyce is an unmannerly child enjoying destruction. Hate and pride.

It is a form of idealism. We feel that when the cities are flattened and civilization destroyed, something better will arise. It is a delusion.

Who killed James Joyce?
I, said the commentator,
I killed James Joyce
For my graduation.

What weapon was used
To slay mighty Ulysses?
The weapon that was used
Was a Harvard thesis.

How did you bury Joyce?
In a broadcast Symposium.
That's how we buried Joyce,
To a tuneful encomium.

Who carried the coffin out?
Six Dublin codgers
Led into Langham Place
By W. R. Rodgers.

Who said the burial prayers? –
Please do not hurt me –
Joyce was no Protestant,
Surely not Bertie?

Who killed Finnegan?
I, said a Yale-man,
I was the man who made
The corpse for the wake man.

And did you get high marks,
The Ph. D.?
I got the B. Litt.
And my master's degree.

Did you get money
For your Joycean knowledge?
I got a scholarship
To Trinity College.

I made the pilgrimage,
In the Bloomsday swelter,
From the Martello Tower
To the cabby's shelter.

A Recollection of James Joyce

Joseph Hone

It was in 1909 – the summer, I think – that I read Joyce's *Dubliners* in manuscript. The stories were written out in cheap notebooks in a copperplate hand that would have won, for a schoolboy, a prize in calligraphy. They were handed to me by George Roberts, the managing director of Maunsel & Co., a publishing firm of which I was then a member. Roberts was a very good judge of a book, besides being a fine printer; but one, at least, of the stories gave him pause: such is my recollection. This was 'Ivy Day in the Committee Room', in which Dublin's grave councillors are depicted in discussing, among other matters, the private life of King Edward VII. As I look back, it occurs to me that the firm's hesitation, so far as this particular story was concerned, may have been due to a desire not to prejudice itself with Lady Aberdeen, the then Lord Lieutenant's wife, by whom it had been commissioned to publish tracts relative to her anti-tuberculosis campaign. But of this I am not certain.

I took the manuscript home, the issue still undecided, and I am ashamed to think of the length of time I had it in my possession. A month or two at least. It visited with me the house of a friend near Bray, Victor Le Fanu, a nephew of the novelist, Joseph Sheridan Le Fanu, the agent for Lord Meath's estates, and in my mind's eye I can still see it lying open on the table of his book-room, for I had invited his opinion upon it. Le Fanu, formerly a famous rugby international, was a good classical scholar, and in the midst of his country pursuits he found time to read a great deal. Kipling, Meredith and Stevenson were his favourite novelists, and I did not expect that he would take very kindly to *Dubliners*. Nor did he; the life described was off his beat. But he read the stories carefully, and, recognizing their remarkable quality, took more interest in them than in the usual Maunsel publications.

Apparently, Joyce learned that I had been given it to read, and on my way home, while stopping at Marseilles, I had a letter of complaint from him, dated Trieste, and forwarded to me from Dublin. In my reply I may have asked him whether he would assent to the exclusion of 'Ivy Day' from the collection; but, at all events, whatever it was that I said, it furnished him with a pretext for submitting the story in the next year, after King Edward's death, to his successor, George V. Subsequently, he published an account of his grievance against Maunsel and of his appeal to Caesar (which, of course, was abortive) in a communication to Arthur Griffith's *Sinn Fein;* but I was out of Ireland then, and only heard of this long afterwards, when someone told me, or I read somewhere, that he had quoted 'a Mr Hone writing from Marseilles' in his covering letter to the King. I have never consulted his version of the episode, and I must confess that I feel a disinclination to do so now, though my memory might be thereby refreshed.

On reference to the bibliography of Joyce in the London edition of *Ulysses* I find that the letter to *Sinn Fein* appeared in August 1911. It was a year or two after this that I had my one and only encounter with the author. I was then living in London and had ceased to be a partner of Maunsel & Co., but I used to call at an agency which the firm had opened in the Bloomsbury district. On my way there, one morning, I met a young man, leading a small boy by the hand, who introduced himself as the author of *Dubliners*. I can still point to the spot where we stood and talked; but I remember nothing of what passed between us except his saying that he had 'crossed Europe' to see me. From this it may be concluded that he was still in communication with Maunsels about *Dubliners*. I fancy, however, that it was at the instance of Ezra Pound, who had heard of him from Yeats, that he had come to London. And it was through Pound's good offices that he, at last, found a publisher for *Dubliners*.

Tired Lines, or Tales My Mother Told Me

Aidan Higgins

These are random notes from one who was born into an Irish Catholic family near Dublin and spent four evasive years in James Joyce's old boarding school. Lucan features. ('Before there was a man in all Ireland there was a lord at Lucan'.)

I was born in County Kildare five years after the publication of *Ulysses*, in the fifth year of the nineteen allotted to the composition of its nocturnal sequel. Dublin, Cosgrave's city, Alfie Byrne's city, Dev's city, Joyce's city, Gitter and Gewitter, the grey city, lay twelve miles in one direction and the Jesuit college where he had briefly boarded as a young boy was about five miles in the opposite direction, beyond the defunct village of Clane and the misnamed farmhouse known as the Jolly Farmers. No sounds of merriment issued from it in my period at the same school, where Joyce was *not* remembered. Other famous OBs who had made their mark in the world were remembered and had an honoured name: the patriot Kettle, lost in Somme or Flanders mud, and others who had distinguished themselves at Bar or Bench or Business; but Joyce had made another kind of mark, and his old Alma Mater would prefer to forget him. A Jesuit and Greek scholar put it well: 'Jice? (to rhyme with lice). We're not proud of him'.

James Joyce was forty-five when I was born, I was twelve when he died. He was dead ten years when I went to his school and his passing had left no impression on me. Indeed I confused his name with another wordslinger who was then making a name for himself – the traitor 'Lord Haw-Haw'. Another Joyce.

Being read to by my mother, in the country then, when she was alive, reading by paraffin lamps a generation before television, and (a little later) seeing maybe a film a year up to the age of fifteen and sixteen, gave me a lifelong addiction to print. Marlay Abbey was a mile away, the name occurs in some lines of Yeats; towards the end of her life Lady Gregory visited it. Two centuries earlier Vanessa van Homrigh had lived there, written imploring, indiscreet, demanding, pathetic, futile letters to the Dean, who came sometimes on horseback – irascible, testy man mounted on docile Houyhnhnm – but more often not. She consoled herself by planting trees to commemorate his coming, tried to forget his going. Swift (perhaps secretly married to Stella) in a rage broke with her and she succumbed to an old-fashioned ailment: a broken heart. Sir Charles Napier, soldier and historian, lived opposite at Oakley Park. I often cycled between those glass-topped walls as a boy, along a narrow, walled road on which Fr. Prout, then a teacher at Clongowes (move on a century), had taken a group of his boys – none too sober – from a friend's house in the village where he had been arguing politics, the favourite Irish pastime, and loaded them on to turf carts and taken them back to the school; for this irregularity he was sent elsewhere. F. S. Mahony.

A century later the turf carts were moving as slowly between city and bog, bog and city; I put them in a novel, to stop them moving in my head, long after they had ceased moving on the roads.

Joyce, young and chronically impecunious, had walked the twelve miles to the village, looking for a loan from a rich man, and walked back as poor as he had set out. The trip wasn't altogether wasted, for the name of the village appears in *Finnegans Wake*.

The author Richard Rumbold had lived at Madame Popoff's beyond Castletown, attended Cambridge, published *My Father's Son* and been refused communion by Fr. Ronald Knox. He died later (or took his own life) under odd circumstances in Italy. Cyril Connolly, who had relatives at Castletown, reviewed his posthumous *Message in Code*. From an auction at the Abbey my mother brought away *Green Hills of Africa*. She knew Gogarty, who sent her inscribed copies of his books. I read *As I Was Walking Down Sackville Street;* my mother told me of the libel action; I didn't care overmuch for the gossipy style of the thing, nor, despite the promise of its title, for *Tumbling in the Hay*. My mother met Noel Coward in the Shelbourne Hotel, where Kate O'Brien could be seen writing in the lounge. Shelley had released fire balloons from a bedroom window. So, where I grew up, there were authors (or their ghosts) around.

My mother considered Yeats both mystical and silly, perhaps

because of his known interest in the occult. Joyce, to her way of thinking, was 'low'. It is a prejudice shared today by the critic V. S. Pritchett.
Nothing inspiring could be expected from such a lower middle class
person; his morals were suspect. The low bard might also be a cad
(*pace* Pritchett). It is a curious view.

I read *Dubliners* in a County Council lending library copy as mauled
and dog-eared and annotated (words and phrases dangerous to faith and
morals scraped out by a careful hand) as a manual, and was as depressed
by it as its author had perhaps intended. The *Portrait* was quite another
story; it made my hair fly back. The all-too-familiar lachrymose
dithyrambic beat of the old stuff that had preceded it, from something
as impoverished and mean-spirited as *Watergate* up to the later con-
coctions of O'Connor, had not prepared one for this, and it made it
impossible for Irish writers to write that way again. How critical of his
country and his fellow countrymen and (not least) himself, Joyce, was,
after what had preceded him; oppression had bred a talent for self-
adulation – all Paddies were patsies at heart. One had anticipated a
scoundrel, and encountered a most moral man. The exhibitionary
needs of a fictional plot – what poet Montague has aptly called 'the
fireside chattiness of most Irish story-telling' – did not seem to concern
him at all (which was a relief); he wrote out his own life.

The whole of Whitman's work is deliberate. (R. L. Stevenson).

In those days (I am referring to the period 1935–55 when a very
strict censorship of books had made Irish bookshops reservoirs of
mediocrity, when indeed there was not a bookshop in Dublin or Cork
or Galway – all university cities – worthy of the name; with the County
Council lending libraries manned by amateur theologians who would not
endanger their immortal souls by stocking banned and in some cases,
unbanned or neverbanned goods; and this, in a nice inversion of
values, also applied to some of the 'better' Dublin bookshops; on top of
the official censorship there was an unofficial censorship) *Ulysses* was
hard to come by: it was not banned but neither was it for sale in any of
the bookshops – a very 'Irish' paradox, surely, under 'the close eye of
the inspectors'.

Those who had actually read it, or parts of it, possibly for its known
salacious content (reputedly very high), were sorely puzzled by it, as
puzzled as the British sailors in Nice, thirty years later, with the
Traveller's Library *Watt* (the light that failed). There was the
Davi-Dasi and there was Genet and there was *Story of O* and there was

Watt with its textural lacunae and its ferocious punctuation (Beckett's exasperation with a tradition that appeared to him a good deal less than futile was already beginning to show its hand), about as far removed from pornography as a handbook on ballistics. How were the poor salts to know where the smut was?

Some thought *Ulysses* shocking, as indeed it was (Joyce had brought back the Deep Forest and the Grunting Boar, and both were uncomfortable to encounter); others considered it 'unhealthy'; while the majority pronounced it unreadable and vile. And in Ireland to mention it to anyone in Holy Orders was like bringing up a heresy in the worst of all possible taste: the notion that man in his innermost being was low. Only his dreams were high, even lofty.

Ulysses, being forbidden fruit, had to be imported illegally from the same neighbouring kingdom that had already burnt entire editions at *their* Customs. On me it had a shattering effect. If the *Portrait,* so perfect in its form, so elegantly carried through, had bent the back of the Old Tradition, then the Blue Book of Eccles (as Joyce whimsically referred to it in *Finnegans Wake)* broke it into its component parts, right down the centre of its ten-century-old venerable and vulnerable vertebra. It was an extraordinary achievement for one man.

In *Ulysses,* in a sense, lay the combined talents of sixteen gifted writers; it was said by critics, when it came out in 1922, that it was fifty years ahead of its time; now, almost fifty years later, that still applies. An American author friend of mine put it like this: 'Those who were writing while he was writing in Paris will only be remembered because they knew him. That man was a genius in a high grade hat. Tell him I said so'.

Ulysses ended the old complacent and acceptable way of writing, very Irish and often dull. Not in the matter perhaps, lifted from life; but in the manner certainly. Nobody had written like this before and probably no one would again. So that to say today, as critics are prone to do, that So-and-so 'writes like Joyce' is patent nonsense. They have said it of my own poor efforts, so I know it to be nonsense. I do not write like Joyce. In my beginnings as a writer I spent seven years reading Joyce, and maybe another four forcing myself *not* to imitate him. Three or four novels, written by ambitious Irish hands and said to be 'like Joyce' by critics trying, one can only suppose, to be mischievous, have appeared in my time, in Dublin. They are all published in England, and appear in the spring and fall, big bad novels bloated as toadstools.

Whereas it would be truer to say that So-and-so wrote as though

James Joyce had never existed, which is not to deny such work, hard come by as all such work is, certain virtues of its own, but virtues of a very limited sectarian order taken from an old and, I hope, now defunct tradition. Enough on that subject.

Joyce, in *Ulysses*, brought something to Irish literature which had never been there before; it was something the people had – his people, the Irish – waiting for a Joyce to discover it, represent it to them; perhaps only by living and working out of the country all his life, with it always in his mind, could it be done, as he had done it; and perhaps for that very reason they found it particularly objectionable, even abhorrent. He had lived too long away from them, and knew them better than they knew themselves. His fellow countrymen looked upon Joyce then, and still do, rather as the sixteenth-century Poles must have looked upon the astronomer Copernicus. A genuine case of diabolic possession. For the Irish, if they believed in anything, believed in the Devil.

For me, the great discoveries in my own literature have been *Portrait* (which I read around the period that I read Gosse's *Father and Son*, George Moore's *Confessions of a Young Man*, which Moore had the cheek to compare with Joyce's *Portrait;* Rousseau's *Confessions*, Samuel Butler's *Way of All Flesh)* and *Ulysses*. Then Samuel Beckett's *Murphy* and Brian Nolan's *At Swim-Two-Birds*. Both these latter eccentric works had, in different ways, something of the grubbiness that Joyce had sought.

Nolan, a writer who hid behind not one but a couple of *nom-de-plumes*, was a legendary character in his own lifetime, a legendary drinker, the legendary author of a book, *At Swim-Two-Birds*, and had kept the legend alive in an unlikely place – a daily column in the *Irish Times*. In the heyday of the column it had a readership of, I suppose, less than 50,000, but even so he had a readership 90 per cent or even higher than the best sales an Irish 'best-seller' could hope for; for the Irish do not read, and least of all buy books – Shaw, that mercenary man, remarked on it.

Beckett's early novel shared the same publishing fate as *At Swim-Two-Birds;* both came out around 1939, and a year later it was difficult to find a copy of either. Both were 'underground classics', as the phrase goes, until they were re-issued after the war. Both, today, are source books, the starts of long chains of associations. *Murphy* was set in London and Dublin, a peculiarly endearing work, treated by its author in a high-handed way that no other Irish writer, then or now, could even approximate to; echoes of it are apparent in Iris Murdoch's early *Under the Net*. It was a preparation for the more exigent manner of the later French novels published by *Les Editions de Minuit*. Beckett wrote in French, Nolan wrote in Irish; where do the Gaelic revivalists put his play, *An Beal Bocht?*

Malone Dies and *Molloy* are written with a clarity and bile that recall Swift. But already apparent in the latter is the 'balls-aching boredom' with fictional themes that was to blight his later fiction like a disease in trees. I confess that I cannot follow him into *The Unnameable*, much less beyond it into *How It Is*. These astringent philosophical works are beyond the patience of most. Beckett is a comic writer, and a great one, until the end of *Molloy*, but if he is a comic writer after that, then so is Augustine of Hippo. *Monotonie um der Drehpunkt*. Beckett's novels are not read in Ireland. He was one of the twelve who contributed to *Our Exagmination*. His fate – an appropriate one for a first disciple – is to be crucified upside down.

Who follows Beckett, himself following so closely on Joyce? *Cadenza? Inish? Death of a Chieftain?* Each of these, in their different ways, to a greater or lesser degree, have something of that lordly asperity that characterizes the better work done by Irish authors. And perhaps other exceptions could be made. But for the rest – linear, traditional, benign and dull; complacent and narrow playwrights, generally rural based, and excruciating novelists, generally from Dublin – the way lies back; back into the past.

Come in, *Esther Waters!* Come back, *Knocknagow!* Inbred habits are hardest to break; the 'fireside chattiness' lives on. Come in, Jim Jice!

He could hear, of course, all kinds of words changing colour like those crabs about Ringsend in the morning, burrowing quickly into all colours of different sorts of the same sand where they had a home somewhere beneath or seemed to. Then he looked up and saw the eyes that said or didn't say the words the voice he heard said . . .

The words are coming back, and inside the wrappings of the words there would be thoughts lying there.

> *Frisch weht der Wind*
> *Der Heimat zu,*
> *Mein Irisch Kind,*
> *Wo weilest du?*

The Vico Road goes round and round to meet where terms begin. A good clap, a fore wedding, a bad wake; hume sweet hume.

Joyeux Quicum Ulysse . . .
Swissairis Dubellay Gadelice

Niall Montgomery

The Joyce-Joyeux correspondence is not stressed by the subtle overseas doctors in whom, under martial aid, are vested the exegetic rights in the Swiss master's work. Yet it was Joyce who with *Ulysses* gave the belly back its Homeric laugh, Joyce who with *Finnegans Wake* planted a verbatim bomb in the slip-happy land of Paranomasia. Neither operation was painless, but the well-read indigenes of the mental reservations now obey the Punal Laws, the stitches are out of the literary body, and a smile won't pinch the wounded skin.

Andrew Cass shows that the mature writer – almost a stage European – who wrote *Ulysses* is not to be confounded with Stephen Dedalus, but embarrassing autobiographical hints in *Finnegans Wake* suggest that Joyce took his factitious exile at least as seriously as du Bellay. 'Plus mon petit *Life* que le mont Palatin . . . ?'

The pun, used almost involuntarily, is common in Dublin chat, and figures in *Ulysses* as a sort of 'tic Joyeux'. 'Poached eyes on ghost' is perhaps not all that casual, but what is good there, anywhere, is more the fun than the pun.

Academic machinery – one thinks of the engines rigged up by Bergson and M. Eastman – cannot handle fun: that is one reason why the college despatches on Joyce have not been too gay. The critical plant laid down in the Renaissance and turned over to steam during the Great Peace includes elaborate jigs which derogations of the human brain and its noble operator will knock out of gear. There *Finnegans Wake* and *Ulysses* have been tossed around – sometimes the critics themselves ended up in the jigs. It is time to dismantle that German factory and outlaw the ritual mensuration of the crepuscholars.

Dublin is the wittiest city in christendom, said a learned antichrist, according to its inhabitants. To Aldous Huxley, Sousa of all 'christian minstrelsy', fun must certainly be a betrayal of the simian in the temple, and the pun, insanitary artifact, a suggestion of the survival of the other crowd. Charlie, says Mr Joyce, you're my darwing. That is the sort of guffaw his commentators have 'explained' with misplaced diffidence.

Joyce's work comes at the full glory of Protestant civilization, in the centre of which man is discovered – thinking! The considering cap is old hat to Catholics, too ignorant to know that it confers divinity upon the wearer. They are baffled when Rousseau, first gentleman in Europe born without original sin, elects for special praise and mention a sodality held by them in most misprision – the human race. With the Irish – election agents of the faithful – universal contempt is an occupational disease. And Joyce was not just a Catholic; he was an Irish Catholic.

The leper, a deceased Dublin journalist remarked, does not change his spats. Oriental readers may not know that Irish Catholic is no mere racial label: it is generic, a condition that deed poll or simple affidavit cannot cure, and Joyce, like Stalin, is the product of a Catholic school.

Thus there are in *Finnegans Wake* things which a man of intellect will find irritating and insulting. That is how they were intended. Here the – literally – unforgettable dialogue of the old Maynooth Catechism is more helpful than the learning of Campbell and Robinson.

Q. What do you mean by mysteries of religion?
A. Mysteries of religion are revealed truths which we cannot comprehend.
Q. Why does God require of us to believe mysteries of religion?
A. God requires of us to believe mysteries of religion that we may pay him the homage of our understanding.

It is not a high fee, but – by a coincidence? – it is that demanded by the creator of the Western Word – *pas singe, messieurs*. Mr Cass has indicated Mr de Valera's 'alter ego' role in *Finnegans Wake*: there he is most often 'Dev', the name given to another ruler in the Chançun de Willame.

O hi, bel sire, dist Viuïen le ber.

I ço conuis ben que ueirs e uifs est Dev,

Qui uint en terre pur son pople saluer, . . .

Oddly, the monosyllable is, in Joyce's book, the only echo of that fine piece of eleventh-thirteenth-century verse (?)

The mind, distinguished wheelbarrow in which prejudices collected at the cradle are trundled for dumping outside the grave, is unsafe at 20,000 feet. Joyce leaves those heights to broomstruck heretics: the 'Jeune audacieux' of the *Portrait* is Dedalus, not Icarus. W. B. Yeats, hammering his thoughts into unity, is a figure of the good designer working toward simplicity. The unsimple thought, pearl of philosophy, appals by reason of inedibility until its sartorial uses are seen.

Critics happy to find tameness and obscurity in Joyce's philosophical masters are as shrewd as those who explain Yeats's work in terms of his psychical safari. 'Je n'hésite pas,' says Picasso, 'lorsqu'on me montre par exemple un carton de dessins anciens, à y prendre tout ce que veux.' Joyce took all he wanted from the philosophers, raped their cruel Circe, language, put her to work digging etymological roots, and died laughing.

If there is a philosophers' ward in our last home, perpetually red faces are there worn by Giambattista Vico and Giordano Bruno, as they watch a roll of *bronnanoleum* lapping endlessly on a *vicocylometer* to another part of Dante's infirmary: inside is J. A. Joyce, shaking with mnemonia. Yet the Vico structure in *Finnegans Wake* is at least as important as the golden section and root-five rectangle grid in the design of the Parthenon.

The scholastic mind's supreme act is to know that it cannot know. Words, immemorial indices of thought, shrivel in such a tropic. The first Pope was, traditionally, briefed with a pun, and, in fact, the papal power of interpretation cut the Church off from profane philosphy, that argument about definitions unsettled till Messrs Ogden and Richards glossed 'the Meaning of Meaning' and showed the essentially British nature of thought by inventing a saxonphone. By contrast, the Roman Church, its liturgy long frozen in the algebra of byzantine Latin, has many tongues in its cheek.

Philosophy is the cult of the insoluble, the Monte Carlo of the spirit. Some of the players have systems, but the bank is never broken. Joyce's metaphysic accepts the insolubility – when he stole Vico's system it was to bankrupt literature, in the service of art. An artist has no message, no mission, and Joyce isn't even a heretic; the *Osservatore Romano* has praised his work. His theological difficulties were really social; he felt it was not the thing to be a Dublin Catholic.

This innocence left him free, almost in infancy, to investigate the conditions and fix the limits of his art. It is astonishing that the 'last' cyclofoliate page of his big comedy is envisaged in a key plan and out-line specification devised thirty years earlier.

Herbert Gorman, who holds readers in debt for the information that John Stanislaus Joyce 'always wore a monocle in one eye', publishes in his 'definitive' biography notes, dated February and March 1903, each not initialled merely but signed 'James A. Joyce'. The tone is repulsive – the voice is the voice of Stephen but the hand is the same that later in the century writes 'The voice is the voice of Jokeup, I fear'.

An interpretation, in two sentences, of Aristotle on art notes, better than a Zervos conversation, the future character of painting – Picasso, a year older, was still making pictures like the Blue Period 'La Vie'. A definition of sculpture interests for its exclusion of the *genre* Calder; a short aesthetical catechism is precise and funny, but the main clauses of the Joyce factory act are in the paragraph on tragedy and comedy.

> . . . an improper art aims at exciting in the way of comedy the feeling of desire but the feeling which is proper to comic art is the feeling of joy. Desire, as I have said, is the feeling which urges us to go to something but joy is the feeling which the possession of some good excites in us. Desire, the feeling which an improper art seeks to excite in the way of comedy, differs, it will be seen, from joy. For desire urges us from rest so long as we possess something. Desire, therefore, can only be excited in us by a comedy (a work of comic art) which is not sufficient in itself inasmuch as it urges us to seek some-thing beyond itself; but a comedy (a work of comic art) which does not urge us to seek anything beyond itself excites in us the feeling of joy. All art which excites in us the feeling of joy is so far comic and according as this feeling of joy is excited by whatever is substantial or accidental in human fortunes the art is to be judged more or less excel-lent; and even tragic art may be said to participate in the nature of comic art so far as the possession of a work of tragic art (a tragedy) excitesin us the feeling of joy. From this it may be seen that tragedy is the imperfect manner and comedy the perfect manner in art . . .

The critics ignore this schoolboy stuff. Professor Levin of Harvard, best of the psychoanalysts who have written on Joyce, sees it this way:

> If we could eliminate the causes of misunderstanding, by some process of critical chemistry, we should find that his genius was far happier – far less tragic and more humorous – than the brooding morbidity of his books would indicate . . .

The definition of reading as some process of critical chemistry is fancy.

. . . The motley of a Rabelais, under happier circumstances, would have sat more comfortably upon him . . .

This side of the grave only the *happier circumstances* of Hollywood or Moscow affect a writer's writing. French clergymen don't wear motley.

. . . The *saeva indignatio* was a reaction to his age; the *vis comica* was his natural bent . . .

Operate with both and Equity calls the whole shop out?

. . . With his mind so divided against itself, so full of unshared emotions, he inevitably hit upon the formula of Renan – irony and pity. These are both admirable qualities, but we may observe that the writers who cultivate them have seldom succeeded in combining them; they lavish the irony on the world and save the pity for themselves. The result is the wavering tone of the *Portrait of the Artist* and even *Ulysses;* sympathy has critical reservations and criticism has sentimental weaknesses.

Dr Levin reads too rapidly; with such standards he will see only faulty characterization in *Gulliver's Travels,* improbabilities in *Don Quixote.* Both *Ulysses* and the *Portrait* deserve a second reading, bearing in mind the objective absence from both of the adult Joyce. Both books are comic sections of the monstrous Stephen: the 'longueurs' in both are products of the head – the Joyce heart is a motor, never a control.

In *Finnegans Wake,* in spite of the old grudges and the deep scars, Joyce attains – at a stupendous price – a robustious serenity. In security, his writing grows more impersonal; both artist and public are less in evidence.

Dr Levin's insistence on the grudges and scars of the lout who pulled a fast one on the Sackville Street rustics by becoming a European literary man is embarrassing. Beware of them whom God has marked, runs a cruel saying of the Dublin slums; it describes the blackmail operated in literary criticism by psycho-analysis. The suggestion that Joyce's art is distorted by recollection of 'Robber and Mumsell, the pulpic dictators' is theatrical. At the Wake, with great respect to Dr Levin, Joyce's detachment has the autonomy of frenzy; the 'divine comic' is beside himself with laughter.

Joyce, who was at Clongowes before he was educated, at Belvedere, never lost the schoolboy's delight in the explosion of digestive gases. Just such a salute from the great Fenian cyclist marks, in the Wake, a revolution of the joyce wheel.

Loud heap miseries upon us yet entwine our arts with laughters low, prays the Trieste maestro, while in New England grave Dr Levin, on behalf of the Automobile Association, comments

> pedestrian readers will not forgive a novelist or a dramatist for such conceits, though they accept them from a humorist or a poet . . .

There is a difficulty. Digestive and other instruments, seldom absent from the works of the American masters, are there handled respectfully for psychological or pornographical ends only. Joyce lacks the piety of a true cloacal student; even *Ulysses* is more a public labyrinth than a Celtic toilet. Digestion in Faulkner is no joke; it's not part of the Eliot catharsis. But a masterpiece is not funny and Mr Eliot – himself – has not merely praised *Finnegans Wake* but has praised his own praise, in a passage where it is compared with one of the most laughless items in the history of song, Mr Perse's *Anabase*.

> I believe that this is a piece of writing of the same importance as the later work of James Joyce, as valuable as *Anna Livia Plurabelle*. And this is a high estimate indeed.

Joyce, perhaps, returns the compliment with:

> No, assuredly they are not justified, those gloom-pourers who grouse that letters have never been quite their old selves again since that weird weekday in bleak Janiveer (yet how palmy date in a waste's oasis!) when to the shock of both, Biddy Doran looked ad literature.

Even Campbell and Robinson, authors of the wonderful *Eschatolentele-quai to Fino Gonzague,* say emphatically *Finnegans Wake* is not a book of sweetness and light, and this is odd since they, unlike the present writer, have read it. Joyce, in a Leonardo mood, says it contains 'some most dreadful stuff in a murderous mirror-hand'. The mirror it turns on language is the same that in *Ulysses* and the earlier books is held up to life.

The door slammed behind her.
Mr Casey freeing his arms from his holders, suddenly bowed his head on his hands with a sob of pain.
– Poor Parnell! he cried loudly. My dead king!

With four ridiculous words the writer ends the agony he has been making for any male Irish reader, sleepily smiling while pouring the icy water. That is the perfect manner in art, with s. indignatio and *v.c.* – illegally? – in combined operation.

Devastatingly, the colonial critics reject this view. Joyce does offend in taste, says Dr William Carlos Williams. Joyce is sentimental in his handling of his material. He does deform his drawing and allow defective characterizations to creep in. And Dr Levin complains that the Italian writer gives a 'suspiciously convincing impersonation of Dickens . . .' What ticket did Dickens carry – comic writer or tragic writer?

The scarred, grudge-stuffed manqué has immortalized Edwardian foundation garments; his obsession with garters is a great madness.

Richard: And you gave him your garter. Is it allowed to mention that?
Beatrice (with some reserve): If you think it worthy of mention.

He did. The astonishing figure runs right through the books till it reaches, in *Finnegans Wake*, appropriate climax in an inventory of the writer's properties.

. . . schoolgirl's, young ladies', milkmaids', washerwomen's, shopkeepers' wives', merry widows', ex nuns', vice abbess's, pro virgins', super whores', silent sisters', Charleys' aunts', grandmothers', mothers'-in-laws', fostermothers', godmothers' garters . . .

And was there ever another Clongownian who got such value out of the word 'drawers'?

In *Exiles*, even the stage directions are funny.
Robert Hand, in evening dress, is seated at the piano . . . He rises and, pulling out a pump from behind the piano, walks here and there in the room ejecting from it into the air sprays of perfume.

Swift is not harder on the male nation than that.

'Dowling was no German, and that's a sure five' wins no lama's laugh, but Cranly deserves a grin when he says to the dreary Stephen, Credo ut vos sanguinarius mendax estis quia facies vostra monstrat ut vos in damno malo humore estis. It is Joyce's amused consciousness of Dedalus, perpetually in damno malo humore, that makes the early books. Cranly's language recalls the archaic French of the young Hussonet in that more terrifying Portrait of the Artist, *L'Education Sentimentale*.

> And what star is that, Poldy? says she.
> By God, she had Bloom cornered. 'That one, is it?' says Chris Callinan. 'Sure that's only what you might call a pinprick.' By God, he wasn't far wide of the mark. Lenehan stopped and leaned on the river-wall, panting with soft laughter.
> – I'm weak, he gasped.

Common persons of the writer's generation stopped and leaned with Lenehan, whose 'hands moulded ample curves of air'. An infant elected for his companions' pedantic enjoyment.

> – 'Eh, mister! Your fly is open, mister!' pointing out that only a master's mirror could catch that second 'mister'. Scholarly children could chant the passage which ends

> – I wouldn't do anything at all in that line, Davy Byrne said. It ruined many a man the same horses

and marvel at the precision of the dropped comma. With teardimmed eyes, beyond the threshold of risibility, they

> beheld Him even Him, ben Bloom Elijah, amid clouds of angels ascend to the glory of the brightness at an angle of forty five degrees over Donohoe's in Little Green Street like a shot off a shovel

and wondered at the only capitalized street in that meticulous script. When the caretaker hung his thumbs in the loops of his gold watch chain and spoke in a discreet tone, they waited for the great syntactic delirium of

> Not a bloody bit like the man, says he.
> That's not Mulcahy, says he, whoever done it.
> – That's all done with a purpose, Martin Cunningham explained to Hynes.

- I know, Hynes said, I know that.
- To cheer a fellow up Martin Cunningham said.
It's pure good-heartedness; damn the thing else.
It's all done with a purpose, and it is done to cheer a fellow up, but the fellow is J. A. Joyce. The mourners are entitled to their laugh – that's what a wake is for – but Joyce was no music-hall entertainer, in spite of the view that *Finnegans Wake* was written with one eye on Broadway.

The etymological slaughter in *Finnegans Wake* is an inevitable development of the language of *Ulysses*, in the sense that the internal combustion engine is an inevitable development of the horse. (Joyce as the Henry Ford of literature is not fanciful; he took Vico's line on Homer seriously – at least two of his friends had the work in progress thrown at them with an instruction to finish the bloody thing.) Even in *The Sirens* he is playing more with the sentence than the word. Mulligan's 'new art colour for our Irish poets: snot-green,' for instance, were it in Finnegan, would come out as 'expecterovert'.

Tzara's no precursor, even on the strength of a 1920 offering like 'qui t'a di "écume hâchée de prodigieuses tristesses-horloge" t'offre un mot qu'on ne trouve pas dans le Larousse et veut atteindre ta hauteur'. That's fashionable stuff; Joyce rode no hobbyhorse in the café revolutions of the twenties, and wasn't seen in Kiltic toilette with the keeners in the new century, as 'He was down with the whooping laugh'.

The political view, characteristic of the century, of destruction as the best guarantee of peace is reflected in art, where the only discipline is pneumatic drill. Schönberg's dodecaphony shatters tonality: Picasso's ikonoplasm breaks symbols down to the horror of their appearance: the Joyce 'verbomb' rocked the Indo-European speech structure. Like the politicians, they only did it for the laugh.

The word was Joyce's oyster: like Picasso he knew there was no fun for him in the modish obsession with the soul. He was no hierophant, but the epiphant – who never forgets; the psychophants don't forgive his neglect of their lady. 'He shows no more concern for his hero,' says Dr Levin, 'than a geneticist for a fruit-fly.' A novel needs a hero. 'No psychoanalyst,' he adds, 'could account for the encyclopedic sweep of Earwicker's fantasies or the acoustical properties of his dreamwork'. An encyclopedic sweep would be just the man to handle that circus oddity, the psychoanalyst, in his search for the serious novel of spiritual growth and sexual decay that Joyce had the impertinence not to write.

Chez moi, says Picasso, in his last speech here, un tableau est une somme de destructions. The potamous image suits *Finnegans Wake,* which is just such a Somme. Picasso, says Miss Stein, can express things seen not as one knows them but as they are when one sees them without remembering having looked at them. 'The strangest feature of this dream vision,' continues Dr Levin, 'is that it lacks visual imagery'. Joyce scored no Anglo-Afrodisiacal ballet, designed no décor, never heard of automatic writing. Language is the plane where he sees as one sees without remembering having looked, but the wreckage of potted speech shows his idea of words in palimpsestuous relation. In action, the artist has no memory, even when he's creating an oral instrument for remembering, a harmnemonica.

Language, crystallized into symbols, from word, through phrase, sentence and paragraph into the larger formulae of correspondence, conversation and literature, was ready for his magnifying gloss. Things like the Drumgondola tram, remembrandts, risicide, laotsey taotsey, hereospont, dianablowing, biografiend, andrewpaulmurphyc, albiogenselman, acoustrolobes, a gorgon of selfridgeousness, skyterriers – *djoytsch* for Domini canes – useless to Hollywood, are a sight for sore eyes in braille.

A talk on space-time is interrupted when up through a crack in the platform come Marx, Origen, a dogma, Darwin, Lamarck, a dog and a smell of burning.

(you must not be allowed to forget that this is all contained, I mean the system, in the dogmarks of origen on spurios).

Who else, with so few blasts, could rouse from the famous nations of the dead so many ninny ghosts? This is not a new language, but a stylish economical way of using the old material, of making hystery the nightmare from which no one who reads *Finnegans Wakes* without a laugh.

The nineteenth-century bible haunts the *echodex shaunaiticus.* Each time he hits the note, he plays it hard, and notes the fragmented tones on the score – the origin of spices, the ouragan of spaces. Americans use breakdown as a synonym of analysis: these noisy demolitions are echo syntheses. Had Joyce found the philosopher's tone?

(Despite other references to racial and genetic theories, the book has nowhere the tribute to August Weissmann that readers would be happy to recognize in the inexpensive symbol VIIISMAN. Ungenerous?)

In records made in jazz's middle period, an adventurous trumpeter at times is heard giving his music something like that treatment. He gets a note, holds, then hammers it, blows it inside out, sets it on fire, ends up with something else, maybe not so good. Joyce plays a theme from Shakespeare, Chicago style, thus:

For a burning would is come to dance inane.
Glamours hath moidered's lieb and herefore Coldours must leap no more. Lack breath must leap no more.

A pleasant glimpse of the unhappy Scotch tycoon pneumatically debarred from o'erleaping himself! Ben Jonson was kinder *du côté de chez* the Swan, not funnier. Joyce's own unplanned laughter is said to have ended early readings from work in progress. The writing which he says is 'as easy ach beth cac duff' is careless in parts.

In that book of ghosts and echoes, for instance – some of them thematic, others treated like figures in the exposition and development of a sonata – his development of at least one figure is slightly sloppy.

My name is Norval: on the Grampian hills
My father feeds his flocks . . .

appears at page 569.35 as My name is novel and on the Granby in hills: at 570.1 it has become Mine name's Apnorval and o'er the Grand-beyond mountains . . .

Interesting, certainly, but surely
My name is Nerval: on th' Elysian Champs
My lordship feeds his lobster . . .

would have been a graceful tribute to another wasted talent?

Again, when, in specifically nightmayoral overtures, 'Rex Ingram Pageantmaster' appears, and the reader – recalling the purgatorial correspondences stressed by Beckett and McGreevy, Vico's pia et pura, Joyce's Anna, thinks of Nello d'Inghiramo dei Pannocchieschi, podestà of Volterra, he finds that further allusion to the podestà's wife, La Pia, mentioned in the fifth canto of the Purgatorio, simply isn't in the text!

The essays of Joyce's friends and collaborators, Samuel Beckett and Thomas McGreevy, antedating the publication of the book by ten years, have been surpassed in volume and curiosity by subsequent criticism but not in clarity of vision or lucidity of exposition, qualities which clash with the offensive illiteracies of their fellow contributors to the Exagmination:

it invalidates its own major pretence to being an inclusive whole . . .
(William Carlos Williams)

. . . supra hunc petrum edifico eglesiam mean . . . (Eugene Jolas).
The word 'usqueadbaugham' is Gaelic for whiskey (Elliot Paul).

Finnegans Wake, a fair-sized book with an economical sense-space
factor, took seventeen years to write, and is distributed at thirty
shillings. Yet it places the critics in the same dilemma as the dirt-track
and all-in wrestling fans – is it value? Is the thing sincere? Even the
gladiator's death doesn't convince the mature sportsman; negotiated
euthanasia is not cricket. The voice of Baudelaire in Mr Eliot's best
cellar, echoing through the wake – . . . my shemblable! My freer! . . . –
scares the estimators.

Professor Harry Levin, of Harvard, author of the excellent *James
Joyce – a critical introduction* has a similar problem in measuring the
earlier books; are they up to standard?

If Joyce's treatment of Stephen is true to himself, we have no right
to interpose any other criteria.

Consumer research has rarely spoken with so cultivated a voice, but
failure to know the examiner's mind is more serious for an American
than for a European artist. The 'deep scars' Dublin made on Joyce seem
mild compared with imperial America's processional exposition of his
and W. B. Yeats's friend, Ezra Pound, chained, in a cage.

April 1951.

Joyce and Gogarty

Ulick O'Connor[1]

When Oliver Gogarty went to America in 1939 on a lecture tour he was to find that part of his fame for Americans lay in the fact that he figured as Buck Mulligan in James Joyce's novel *Ulysses*.

There is no doubt that the original of Buck Mulligan was Gogarty. Gogarty admitted the fact in public on many occasions. He lived in the Martello Tower with Joyce, as Mulligan does with Stephen Dedalus in the novel. Oliver Gogarty saved three men from drowning in the Liffey. Mulligan saves seven. The name Malachi Mulligan has the same metrical arrangement as Oliver Gogarty.

'Two dactyls tripping and sunny like the buck himself,' says Mulligan, referring to his Christian and surnames. Twenty years before Joyce wrote this, George Moore had discussed dactyls in the name Oliver Gogarty. He had given Gogarty's name to a character in his novel *The Lake*, a renegade priest called Oliver Gogarty. When Mrs Gogarty, Oliver's mother, complained, Moore chirruped back, 'Madam, supply me with two such joyous dactyls and I will gladly change the name'. Joyce would have heard about Moore's remark from Gogarty and it almost certainly gave him the inspiration for Malachi Mulligan's name in *Ulysses*.

Padraic Colum tells me that Buck Mulligan's dialogue is a pretty accurate description of Gogartian conversation in the period during which Joyce knew Gogarty.

The talk of the 'Buck' in the opening of *Ulysses*, the interjection from him in the library and the hospital are as right as could be – not only the words but the pace of the words.

---

[1] From *Oliver St. John Gogarty*, by Ulick O'Connor. (Jonathan Cape 1964)

Passages from *Ulysses* suggest the conversational techniques which Moore, Colum and A.E. noted in Gogarty. Colum remembers his conversation as an astonishing verbal display with 'its sudden shifts and inexplicable transitions, its copious quotations of poetry, along with frequent plain statements of practical issues', while Moore has commented on Gogarty's power of perceiving distant analogies as he talked and relating them to the subject on hand. These qualities are suggested in Mulligan's conversation as he talks with Stephen on the parapet of the Martello Tower in the opening chapter of *Ulysses*.

(Mulligan) came over to the gunrest and, thrusting a hand into Stephen's upper pocket, said 'Lend us a loan of your noserag to wipe my razor.' Stephen suffered him to pull out and hold up on show by its corner a dirty crumpled handkerchief. Buck Mulligan wiped the razorblade neatly. Then, gazing over the handkerchief, he said: 'The bard's noserag. A new art colour for our Irish poets: snot-green. You can almost taste it, can't you?

He mounted to the parapet again and gazed out over Dublin Bay, his fair oakpale hair stirring slightly.

'God,' he said quietly. 'Isn't the sea what Algy calls it: a grey sweet Mother? The snot-green sea. The scrotum-tightening sea. Epi oinopa ponton. Ah, Dedalus, the Greeks. I must teach you. You must read them in the original Thalatta! Thalatta! She is our great sweet mother. Come and look'.

Stephen stood up and went to the parapet. Leaning on it he looked down on the water and on the mailboat clearing the harbour mouth of Kingstown.

'Our mighty mother,' Buck Mulligan said. He turned abruptly his great searching eyes from the sea to Stephen's face.

The 'Algy' referred to is the poet Algernon Swinburne. Quotations from Swinburne abound in Gogartian epistles. In a letter written in June 1904, he actually quotes the Swinburne phrase which Joyce puts on Mulligan's lips: 'our grey sweet mother'.

When *Ulysses* appeared in 1922 and Gogarty saw himself depicted as Mulligan, he was furious. It seemed to him in the nature of a betrayal that Joyce should have written about him as he did.

'That bloody Joyce whom I kept in my youth has written a book you can read on all the lavatory walls on Dublin,' he snarled to a friend who questioned him about the book shortly after it appeared. When Norah Hoult, wishing to place Gogarty as a character in one of her novels, gave him smoke-blue eyes because, as she said, Joyce was always right about such things, Gogarty replied indignantly that this was not so. Augustus John, who was a close friend of Gogarty's, could never draw him out on the subject of Joyce. Likewise, when John went to sketch Joyce in Paris, he could get no response from his sitter when he brought up Gogarty's name. Another artist, Sean O'Sullivan, did elicit a comment from Joyce while he was engaged in painting him; he happened to mention that Gogarty was a successful surgeon in Dublin. 'God help anyone who gets into the hands of that fellow', is how Joyce received the information.

As late as 1938, when Philip Toynbee was visiting Gogarty in Ely Place, Dublin, he mentioned Joyce's name, and the only reply he got from his host was 'James Joyce is not a gentleman'. When he went to America in 1939, Gogarty created a sensation in literary circles by attacking aspects of Joyce's work which he looked on as confused and lacking in artistic merit. Those critics who praised the obscurities in Joyce's work he regarded with contempt. On a brochure sent to me from New York in 1954, Gogarty had noted down his reactions to this type of criticism. The brochure dealt with a forthcoming 'study' of *Ulysses* and was heavily studded with neo-Freudian jargon.

'Bloom lived in No. 3 Clare Street, Dublin,' Gogarty wrote. 'Yet the Jews have made him a symbol of the blossoming earth. Can Joyce adulation go further than this?'

Why should Gogarty have taken umbrage at the portrait of himself that appeared in *Ulysses?* At first glance it may seem paradoxical that he should have complained at a depiction of himself which showed him as a handsome Greco-Celt, with the wit and brilliance of a Regency gallant. But when *Ulysses* appeared in 1922, Gogarty had become a considerable public figure in his own country: he was by then one of the leading surgeons in Dublin and was about to become a senator of the new Irish state. If he had become associated with the wild, carefree, Rabelaisian character of the Buck, it could have done him harm in public life. Remember that Joyce had obtained much of the material out of which he had created Mulligan from Gogarty's own lips and from letters which he had received from him when they were on terms of intimate friendship. To use such material later on, careless of whether it might injure the person concerned or not, was an act which could be construed as treacherous, and Gogarty regarded it as such. There are, as well, secret little gibes in *Ulysses* which must have galled Gogarty when he read them. There is, for instance, a sneering reference to Gogarty's father, a brilliant and fashionable doctor, held in high repute before his death at the age of fifty-three. Mr Richard Ellman, incidentally, repeats Joyce's slander in his biography of Joyce, relying on no other authority than the reference in *Ulysses*.

The irony of the matter is that while Gogarty with some reason regarded Mulligan's portrait as a betrayal, Joyce nurtured a paranoid belief that he would be betrayed by Gogarty at some stage. In the novel, Buck Mulligan is shown as abandoning Stephen when trouble starts in Westland Row. Mulligan is the Judas on that night. Joyce undoubtedly had a fixation on this subject. He saw betrayal in situations where none existed. He wrote to Stanislaus in 1906 expressing his confidence that Gogarty would betray his friend Arthur Griffith and the Sinn Fein movement: 'No doubt whatsoever exists in my mind about this. It is my final view of his character, a native Irish growth'. How wrong Joyce was in his prognostication can be seen from the fact that Gogarty remained Griffith's intimate friend until Griffith died in 1922, after being elected President of the Dail Eireann.

In fact, Gogarty's acts towards Joyce were those of a generous and faithful friend. He rejoiced in Joyce's creative gifts and for this reason he gave him money and lent him clothes so that the artist might practise his craft undisturbed. One of the reasons he had conceived the idea of living in the Martello Tower in Sandycove was that Joyce had told him he wanted a year to write his novel, and the Tower seemed to Gogarty the best place in which to house his friend for the task. Gogarty states this in a letter to an Oxford friend written in 1904. In these circumstances, to find an implication of betrayal against him in *Ulysses* must have been a bitter pill to Gogarty.

The relationship between Joyce and Gogarty was a complex one. They shared many common interests, and a certain compatibility of temperament attracted each to the other. But it would have required a more equable temperament than either possessed to reconcile the divergencies in their backgrounds and outlook on life.

They met for the first time in the summer of 1901. Gogarty was then twenty-two years of age; Joyce, nineteen. Gogarty, who had met Joyce casually on another occasion, went up boldly to him in a tram and asked him if he wrote poetry. Joyce replied, tersely, 'Yes'. This didn't deter Gogarty from asking Joyce to tea on the following Thursday. Joyce arrived, as he had promised, at Fairfield, which was quite near the centre of the city. He found, to his astonishment, that he and Gogarty had much in common. He had known Gogarty's reputation in the city as a cyclist, swimmer and fashionable man-about-town, but he hadn't suspected that he was a poet as well. Gogarty's extraordinary memory for Greek and Latin verse fascinated Joyce.

Himself a shy visitor at the feast of the world's learning, he was charmed to find a friend who could quote Virgil, Homer and Catullus as easily as another might Shelley or Wordsworth. In return, he would sing for Gogarty airs from the psalm-books of the lutanists or some old forgotten song of the Elizabethans that he had salvaged from an obscure music sheet. His favourite airs were Dowland's 'Weep no more, Sad Fountains' and a piece which began:

Farewell and adieu to you, sweet Spanish Ladies,
Farewell and adieu to you, ladies of Spain,
For we have received orders to sail for old England,
And we hope that one day we may meet again.

Gogarty induced Joyce to adopt his method of writing verses on a sheet of vellum, one verse to a single sheet. After a while Joyce began to come out regularly to Fairfield to show his new work to Gogarty and discuss it with him. They used to go together to the garden behind the house and sit on a pair of old green seats that stood under a great semi-circle of yews, the same bower of beauty to which Gogarty took the Trinity Dons. Mulberry bushes grew on the lawn, protected from the north wind by the trees, and behind lay the kitchen garden and a large orchard. 'On the east a stone wall, topped with foxgloves red and white, self-sown from the herbarium beneath, let the level sun flood in over the bay, and stipple the dark yew hedge with points of moving gold. The beds were marked with boxwood margins and contained foxglove, mullein, digitalis, lily of the valley, bryony and thyme.' Here the pair composed, fragile verses, whose mood indicates how their imaginations were influenced by the prospect of nature about them:

My love is in a light attire
Among the appletrees,
Where the gay winds do most desire
To run in companies.

And where the sky's pale blue cup
Over the laughing land,
My love goes lightly, holding up
Her dress with dainty hand.

(James Joyce)

My Love is dark, but she is fair,
As dark as damask roses are,
As dark as woodland lake water
That mirrors every star.

But as the moon who shines by night,
She wins the darker air
To blend its beauty with her light,
Till dark is doubly fair.

(Oliver Gogarty)

Another factor which bound them together was that both young men were in loquacious revolt against what they regarded as the smug, conventional outlook of the Dublin middle classes. Padraic Colum remembers that the two seemed to be engaged in some enterprise – an apostolate of irreverence. 'The rationalism of Catholicism and the stupidity of British imperialism were satirized by them in verse are anecdote.' Gogarty's Rabelaisian ballads, which Joyce circulated enthusiastically round the city, are one example of their joyous rejection of the attitudes of bourgeois belief. Also they flouted convention by their open visits to the Nighttown area in Dublin.

Another way in which their iconoclasm exhibited itself was in the perpetration of practical jokes. On one occasion Joyce decided to run Gogarty for the Vice-Chancellor's poetry prize in the Royal University. Gogarty had not known, until Joyce told him, that, as a former student, he was eligible for the Gold Medal. He had already won two of his three Vice-Chancellor medals for poetry in Trinity. Gogarty hurriedly composed a poem on the set theme, which was, in 1903, the Death of Shelley, and allowed Joyce to write in the last line for him: 'Shines on three soldier of song Leonida'. He duly won the Gold Medal. Joyce and he proceeded to the main door of the Conferring Hall of the Royal to obtain a dispensation which would enable Gogarty to absent himself from the presentation of the medal. To have been present at the ceremony would have meant hiring a special gown. The porter answered them.

'Is this the Royal University?' Gogarty said.

'You know bloody well it is,' the porter replied.

'It was a flower show last time I was here', said Gogarty, which was literally true, as the hall had been used for a flower exhibition. Since the Royal University was only an examining body, its premises were often used for other purposes. Permission was refused for him to absent himself. So he and Joyce bought a gown out of a rag man's sack, and amid cheers he went up for his medal, looking as if he had been through a cyclone. That night, from a sanctuary in the Kips[1], Joyce dispatched a pawn ticket to Sir James Meredith, the Vice-Chancellor of the University, for the value of the medal, which was £25.

Just how much Joyce and Gogarty were in revolt against the popular mind can be gathered from the fact that neither of them was sympathetic to the Celtic aspects of the Literary Revival which was taking place around them. Gogarty feared the 'Celtic chloroform', which he maintained 'would freeze out the Sapphic current of his soul', and declared his opposition to what he termed 'the epidemic of the disinterred', a reference to the fashion of writing about the Celtic heroes, which was popular at the time. Joyce considered that the Celt had contributed nothing 'but a whine to Europe'. This was their outlook in a period which was throwing up 'Celtic' poets of the calibre of Yeats, A.E., James Stephens, Synge and Colum. But with the exception of Colum, all these writers were of Protestant, Anglo-Irish stock. Gogarty and Joyce, on the other hand, came from an older stock of Irishmen whose connections with the cultural inheritance of Europe had been minimized since the bulk of the Catholic aristocracy and upper class had left Ireland for Europe after the siege of Limerick in 1693. Young intellectuals of Joyce and Gogarty's class tended to turn outwards towards Europe for a renewal of the inspiration their ancestors had shared when they were part of the Western tradition. Tom Kettle, a contemporary of Joyce and Gogarty, spoke the mind of his generation when he wrote: 'If Ireland is to become truly Irish she must first become European.' If they turned to ancestral image at all, it was the Scandinavian strain in the Irish stock that attracted them rather than the Celtic one. Tom Kettle, whose name was of Norse origin, used to talk of his ancestors 'who came out of the sea'. Joyce's works are laced with references to the Viking adventurers who built Dublin in the ninth century.

---

[1] The Dublin Brothel area

Here Dane-Vikings . . . ran to beach, their blood beaked prows
riding low on a molten pewter surf.   (*Ulysses*, page 67)

It pleased Gogarty to note in Dublin street-children survivals of
Scandinavian traits: 'snub-nosed and hawser-haired like their roving
ancestors'. In his poem 'Fog-Horns' he recalls the era when the blond-
beards settled the east coast of Ireland and founded his native city:

> The fog horns sound
> With a note so prolonged
> That the whole air is thronged,
> And the sound is to me,
> In spite of its crying,
> The most satisfying,
> The bravest of all the brave
>   sounds of the sea.
>
> From the fjords of the North
> The fogs belly forth
> Like sails of the long ships
> That trouble the earth.
> They stand with lose sail.
> In the fords of the Gael:
> From Dark Pool to White Ford
>   the surf-light is pale.
>
> The chronicles say
> That the Danes in their day
> Took a very great prey
> Of women from Howth.
> They seem to imply
> That the women were shy,
> That the women were loath
> To be taken from Howth.
> From bushy and thrushy
>   sequestering Howth.

No mist of the Druid
Could halt or undo it
When long ships besetted
The warm sands wave-netted.
In vain might men pray
To be spared the invader
To that kind eye of gray,
To the Saint who regretted
Sea-purple Ben Edar.
They sailed to the town
That is sprung from the sea
Where the Liffey comes down
Down to roll on the Lea.

Where the long ships had grounded.
You hear them again
As they called to the Dane,
And the glens were astounded.
War horns sounded,
And strong men abounded
When Dublin was founded . . .

Only a few months after their first meeting, Joyce and Gogarty had already become a familiar pair in the city streets. For a year or so they were seldom out of each other's company. There are people still in Dublin who can recall seeing them striding along arm in arm, a handsome pair of mockers whispering irreverences in each other's ears. Whenever a remark of Gogarty's particularly pleased Joyce, he would stop deliberately, throw back his head, and guffaw loudly.

There were certain similarities in their appearance. Both had long Celtic faces and pale complexions. They had blue eyes of such a singular kind that people meeting them for the first time were immediately struck by their quality. Joyce's eyes were steel blue: Gogarty's were darker in shade. Their hair was brown, though, as has been pointed out, Gogarty's was often streaked with gold from the bleaching of the sun. Joyce could not afford to dress with much taste, but Gogarty was known round the city for his elegant bearing and primrose waistcoats. One student remembers Gogarty's superb aplomb as he emerged from Trinity, and greeted two plumed whores with a sweeping, regal bow.

Joyce, before Gogarty met him, had already become a character in the city. He was aloof in bearing and demeanour; but he had a caustic tongue and a sense of showmanship that enabled him to keep apart from the herd and at the same time to impress his personality upon the public mind. He always managed somehow to create an air about himself and have his exploits talked about around the town. Too poor to dress elegantly, he nevertheless, from his meagre sartorial resources, managed to assemble a number of items which gave him a distinctive appearance. He was usually seen in grey flannels, yachting cap and tennis shoes, with a blackthorn stick under his arm. This led Gogarty to say to him one day: 'Where's she moored, Commander?' This was typical of Gogarty. He liked to elaborate on Joyce's character and present him to the public in as interesting a fashion as possible. Colum recalls that it was solely as a character and partly a Gogartian creation that Joyce was known to Dubliners at that time. Gogarty had different names for Joyce. At one time he used to refer to him as 'Kinch'. This was in imitation of the cutting sound of a knife. 'Kinch says' was an opening gambit for a Gogartian monologue. At another time his name for Joyce was 'Dante'. He had achieved his ambition by getting Joyce to shave – and he had done so by showing Dante's profile and suggesting that without the down on his chin, Joyce would bear a resemblance to the Florentine. After Joyce came back from Paris he had taken to lilting a new ballad called 'Cadet Roussel': this gave Gogarty an idea foi a new Joycean title. 'Have you seen Cadet Roussel?' became his greeting for a while.

In December 1903 Joyce went off to Paris with the intention of studying medicine. In January Gogarty went to England to spend two terms at Oxford University. One happy result of their separation was that they communicated with each other by letter, and as Joyce hung on to his Gogartiana like a leech, there is in existence today at Cornell University a formidable body of correspondence which passed from Gogarty to Joyce during the period they were apart from each other. With a few exceptions Joyce's letters to Gogarty were destroyed in the fire at Gogarty's country home in 1923, when his house was burnt down by the anti-Treaty forces.

Gogarty's purpose in going to Oxford was to have a shot at winning the Newdigate Prize for English verse. Dowden felt that his favourite pupil, having won the Vice-Chancellor's prize three times running in Trinity, stood a chance of bringing off the double by winning the Oxford award as well. The matter was arranged through Macran, who saw to it that Gogarty should meet F. W. Lee, a Fellow of Worcester College, for tea while he was in Dublin. Lee was so impressed that he arranged that Gogarty should go up for two terms to Worcester and work under W. H. Hadow, the philosopher, who was also a friend of Macran's.

Gogarty arrived in Oxford on 25th January 1904, including in his baggage, T. S. C. Dagg remembers, a barrel of Guinness stout – an example of the Dubliner's contempt for that beverage if brewed on any but Liffey water.

At Bletchley Station he noticed a star falling. Was it to be a good or bad omen for his Newdigate?

He made a friend at Worcester College of George Bell, who has recalled the impression that Gogarty made on him at that time:

Oliver was filled with poetry and a fascinating and inspiring companion. He was fond of the Gardens at Worcester, and he and I in the summer of 1904 often met on the Lawns there. We used to walk by the river past the locks and admire the laburnums.

George Kennedy Alexander Bell was destined to be Bishop of Chichester from 1929 to 1958. He was a prominent figure in English public life, one of the leaders of the Ecumenical movement in the twenties, a patron of the drama and an enlightened humanist.

The rumour of the entertaining Irishman spread in Oxford, and Gogarty was in constant demand. When the punting parties began they proved ideal for Mahaffy's[1] pupil. Propped up with cushions, he would lie back and talk, his mind stimulated by the pleasant natural surroundings while his companions attended to the movement of the boat. When they tied up for lunch his talk flowed on, continued through the meal, until they departed, when Gogarty would settle himself comfortably, in the cushions again, words bubbling from his lips, in what seemed to his English friends an inexhaustible fountain of wit, erudition and improvisation.

As at Trinity his flair for the picaresque made him the subject of student tales. He drank the sconce at Worcester. This entailed drinking five pints of beer from a silver cup in one go, without letting the cup down from his lips. The performance nearly froze Gogarty's tonsils off, but he went through with it.

'I was weaned on pints,' he explained.

He joined the Oxford Gaelic Society which was an offshoot of the new enthusiasm for the language in Ireland. The Oxford students took

---

1 John Pentland Mahaffy, professor of Greek, later Provost of Trinity College, Dublin. Tutor of Oscar Wilde and a celebrated conversationalist and wit.

weekly classes in Irish. One of them was Dermot Trench, son of Arch-bishop Trench. Another was an aristocratic and wealthy Spaniard of Irish descent, Senor O'Neill. O'Neill possessed a magnificent motor-car and chauffeur. He was rather pretentious about his rare chariot, and not inclined to allow his fellow students to share a seat with him in it. One day while he was out of town Gogarty succeeded in convincing O'Neill's chauffeur that he had permission to use the car. He then drove round Oxford dressed in a fur coat (also O'Neill's) visiting the different tradesmen to whom he owed money, and they were numerous. The tradesmen were summoned to the window of the car as it stopped at each shop, and peremptorily asked why they had been plying the occu-pant with bills. Mesmerized by his magnificence, they muttered apologies, some of them offering to send up additional goods immediate-ly, offers of which Gogarty at once availed himself. When someone with him in the car reminded him that a wine-dealer from whom he had just ordered a cask of wine was already owed £4, Gogarty replied loftily: 'Well now I owe him eight.' They then drove to Blenheim, Gogarty directing the chauffeur from the back seat with taps of his stick on the shoulder. Later he and his guests enjoyed wine and foodstuffs which had been sent post-haste to Gogarty's rooms by shop-owners terrified of losing the patronage of so magnificent a customer.

O'Neill was furious when he found out the trick that had been played on him. Apparently his sense of humour was more Iberian than Irish. I am indebted for this anecdote to Mr William Dinan who was up at Oxford at the same time as Gogarty.

Gogarty worked hard at his Newdigate poem. But when the results were posted up he found he was only proxime accessit. His friend Bell had won the prize. With typical modesty Gogarty maintained that Bell had written a better poem. Dowden when Gogarty showed him Bell's poem agreed that this was so, and Gogarty wrote at once to Bell telling him of Dowden's opinion. One reason for Gogarty's lack of success may have been that the form prescribed was heroic couplets, which he regarded as the metre 'of Alexander Pope and all the bores of the eighteenth century, Goldsmith excepted'.

In the meantime he and Joyce had been corresponding constantly. These letters are studded with archaic turns of speech which Gogarty, Joyce, Elwood and Co. often used among themselves as if in recognition of the fact that they belonged to a more gracious and elated age than the one they were living in. Phrases such as Gogarty's:

Inform me how thou liltest; at present I wind the pastoral pipe.
By the Christ's crust I am sorry I cannot make haste to help you.
Let me know if thou wouldst fain travel.
I am travelling. Verily verily I say unto thee in answer to thy urging,
I am living in College. Neither in town or on the town.

or Joyce's:

You will not have me faithfully, Adieu then inconsequent.

Gogarty in his letters often breaks into biblical parody:

This epistle pleaseth me. Thou art yet in London, but a little while
and thou shalt see me. Thy remarks concerning chastity pained me,
but not so much as chastity. Most marvellous foul sin in chiding sin,
when thou thyself hast been a libertine.

In another epistle of this kind, Joyce is felicitated on having been the
recipient of the 'stigmata' after an over-ardent but incautious pursuit of
Venus among the drabs of dockland.

In a letter written from Dublin to Joyce in France, Gogarty parodies
the Kiltartan dialect of English words and Irish idiom, which Lady
Gregory used in her plays and which had become a popular mode of
expression with the Celtic Twilight writers.

Dear Joyce,
It is myself that write to answer the letter you kindly sent me and I
writing for it in Ireland. For a long time I have been wanting to
speak to you and tell you what I was thinking about you. Yourself it
is that must have had the strange thoughts about me for not writing
to you, and you so long gone from the old place where you were born
and reared. There are fine poets in our country who have been making songs in the tounge (sic) in which the sons of Usna were betrayed.

By the time that Gogarty was established at Worcester, Joyce had
given up medicine and gone back to Dublin to be near his mother, who
was dying. Gogarty wrote to him describing the delights of the Towery
city and asking Joyce to come over and spend some weeks with him,
the travelling expenses to be undertaken by Gogarty. The letter addressed 'from the Bard Gogarty to the wandering Aengus', a pet name
Gogarty had for Joyce, borrowed from a figure in a Yeats poem, and
one which Joyce later makes Mulligan confer on Stephen Dedalus in

Ulysses. From the opening sentences it will be seen that Gogarty had undertaken the task of subsidizing from his meagre resources Joyce's living expenses:

> The only explanation of my tardiness in forwarding funds to you is my difficulty in obtaining them. The 10/– I hope reached you. Fairview is not an office for changing postal orders into cash. However, I guessed you would be directed to the General Post Office from Fairview P.O. Chamber Music immediately springs into my mind from the appearance of the above abbreviation. Go and see the holy women – disguised if you like as the gardiner *(sic)* – then send me a detailed account of the position of my lady of love. I fear she has no money and is unwilling to ask for it. Poor Jennie is a good soul. This cunning Druid, O Wandering Aengus, obtained but a 2nd place in the Newdigate, further cause for impecuniosity. My Alexandrines I think are traditional – hence these tears – damn tradition and the impenetrability of professors' souls, but perhaps to damn tradition is to reject Rome and England, and we must have the one as we must have lingerie on ladies and we require the other as the ladies. However, good luck – O Aengus of the Birds. Sing sweetly so that the stones may move and build a causeway *(sic)* to Oxford. Yesterday I was under the poplars green on the blue waters. I wish you would seriously think of coming over here for a week. I have two new suits, one for you; and everything you need – the credence of shopkeepers without which faith we cannot be healed. Good luck old man.

Another letter is more specific in its demand that Joyce should pay a visit to Oxford.

Be Jaysus Joyce

> You must come over here for a day or two next fortnight, I want your advice. The single from Dublin to Oxford is twenty-seven shillings: I shall send you travelling expenses. (I couldn't trust you with more.) Let me know if you will come thus. I want to get dhrunk, dhrunk *(sic)*.

One begging letter of Joyce's drew a poetic reply from Gogarty; in parody of 'A.E.', Gogarty had lent so much money to Joyce that he had none left for himself to take him out of Oxford.

I thought, beloved, to have bought for you
A gift of quietness for ten and six,
Cooling your brow, and your landlady too
With ready spondulicks.

Homeward I go not yet because of those
Who will not let me leave, lest they repine,
For from the Bank the stream of quiet flows
Through hands that are not mine.

But O my Knight: I send to you the stars
That light my very creditable gains
And out of Oxenford though on my arse
My scorn of all its pains.

Gogarty was always anxious to secure Joyce against his creditors by getting him to capitalize on his really exquisite tenor voice. From Oxford he wrote urging Joyce to make practical use of his musical gift and promising to get him engagements.

When I return to Thule, I shall get you many engagements I hope, to sing at entertainments. Revenge yourself by singing for the garrison. Educated people in Ireland are the garrison – the soul is the garrison of the body. I am revenging myself on the Professors of Poetry here by Socratian corruption of youth. Have you read Aphrodite, by Pierre Louys?

Gogarty even went to the extent of copying out unpublished Elizabethan songs from the Bodleian in Oxford so that Joyce might have fresh material for his concert repertoire.

There are a lot of unpublished Elizabethan Lyrics in the Bodleian some of which I am transcribing. One or two of the drinking songs are excellent, I shall send them to you when time allows.

One of the letters addressed to 'James Augustus Joyce, Scorner of Mediocrity and Scourge of the Rabblement' introduces those two gallant aspirants to the healing profession who later figure in *Ulysses*, 'Medical Dick and Medical Davy'. Gogarty's ballad about their activities is, unfortunately, unprintable. In another letter he reports a conversation which readers of *A Portrait of the Artist* will recognize as substantially the same as the one that takes place between the blasphemous student, Temple, and Stephen Dedalus on the steps of the National Library.

I discovered a disciple of yours, a two year medical at the Play. He divides his rustic hair in the middle and doesn't shave his meagre beard. He with a fearful joy informed me that he was an Atheist.

Joyce's Pupil (volunteering): I am an Atheist, you know, I am an Atheist.

Gogarty: Yes. What does that mean?

J's Pupil: You know, I don't believe in God.

Gogarty: No. And what is God?

J's Pupil: Oh! Everyone knows about God – God is – any fool could tell you what God is. I don't believe in religion. (Clearly here he becomes interested.)

Gogarty: Indeed. What is religion?

J's Pupil: I don't go to Church or to Mass.

Gogarty's last term at Oxford came to an end in June 1904. According to William Dinan, a fellow student with Gogarty at Oxford, Gogarty's popularity suffered a slight set-back in his last few weeks there.

At a lunch I gave in Worcester a scholar called Seton got drunk, became a nuisance and bored Gogarty. Gogarty got up and made a rather irreverent remark which gave offence, as Seton was a Church student; though Gogarty didn't know that he was, when he made the remark. It got round Oxford, and a set rather gave Gogarty the cold shoulder. You see he was a typical Trinity man. In Trinity they don't give a damn about the conventions; its life is part of the life of a large city. But in Oxford where society is closer, introvert, you have to keep the conventions. You could break the Law with impunity provided you didn't contravene a convention at the same time.

On 13th June Gogarty wrote to the Bursar, Mr W. Gerrant, to notify him that he had completed his term, and to convey his thanks to the Bursar for giving him 'such beautiful rooms'. Oxford did much for Gogarty. His mind flowered there like the chestnut trees he used to see between the towers of Worcester. At Trinity it had been mostly with the Fellows that he discussed poetry and philosophy. But at Oxford he found he could confess his enthusiasm for Beauty unabashed, in conversation with students like G. K. A. Bell, Christopher Stone, Compton Mackenzie and other friends there. It was not considered a pose to spread oneself on a phrase of poetry or to show enthusiasm for painting or architecture.

A lover of Arnold's poetry before he went to Oxford, many of its surroundings had magical associations for him. He spent a lot of his time walking the countryside, or riding to more distant places on an Indian motor-cycle he bought from a dealer named William Morris, the future Lord Nuffield.

He continued to pour out his thoughts to George Bell in letters written during the two or three years following the time he went down from Oxford. In his first letter written to Bell in June, after Gogarty had returned to Dublin, we can discern the influence of the ardour of his Oxford period. Compare this passage, for instance, with the hard cynical humour of his letters to Joyce quoted a few pages previously.

He describes a visit to Howth Hill in company with a girl. Howth is the long peninsula which stretches over Dublin Bay.

This was the most happy day I ever wish to spend. First of all I rose at 3.30 and saw dawn then – a letter from you. Then a talk with a Platonic friend (John Eglinton), sphering and unsphering the spirit of Plato, and, after lunch, a visit to the beautiful Hill of Howth, 'all but island,' the northern arm of our beautiful bay that takes the morning to its breast – the southern arm is the 'Golden Spears' of which I praised to you ere this. The air was Lesbian. I climbed the fields and gradually reached a woody land that looks towards Lambay island and the dim northern hills. Below the mountain's crest, I stayed in one of the beautiful brakes whose rhododendrons flush the air and the ground is soft with moss or bracken. It was like lying on a purple cloud above the dawn ('in the fields divine, and pastures blue of heaven'). You know that the mountain slopes: a little well or 'secret spring' freshened the middle of the ground which was islanded. Hazels, oaks, ashes and banks of bloom on the one side, rhododendron-covered rocks on the other – and rushes which had 'tufted' heads. I lay under a rhododendron and watched the midges dance like a fountain for joy of the sunlight. I mixed light purple rhododendron leaves in a girl's red brown hair – hair that becomes golden in the sunlight – you've heard me spout:

When the sun shines on Mary's hair
That splendour seems to own
That solid rays of sunlight there
Are blended with the brown;
And in the golden coils of it
A thousand little rainbows sit.
Then neither wonder that my sight
On her is wholly shed,
When she can take the heaven's light
To bind about her head;
Or that to her I captive fall
Who holds the rainbows in her thrall.

Well, this was she. Then we went up a sandy cliff road and whilst talking the foolish words more wise than all philosophies and watching the sunset on the waters and over the mainland I got an idea for an hymn or evensong, which later I must evolve – insist and spur me.

The same letter contains an amusing description of Joyce in which he records his delight in the quaint activities of his friend.

Joyce has written two pretty songs. I am disposing of 30 of his lyrics at £1 apiece or 5/- for one (Joyce's reckoning) to pay his digs bill. He was lately seen perambulating this tuneful town, with a large malay book made of palm leaves borrowed of Starkey (it looked like a Venetian blind) under his arm looking for a buyer. As he said to me, 'It aroused so much interest I think I was justified in telling the rabblement (his profane friends) that I got £7 for it'. 'How much did you really get, Joyce?' 'Two and sixpence'. Isn't Joyce delightful? As Thoreau says, 'Only with parity life is sweet, it's near the bone'. Joyce went to visit the 'Mummers', his name for Yeats' players in the Irish National Theatre, at practice. He being drunk fell 'the second time' as he said and two or three ladies passed over him lying. I called one morning about it. It was just after this escapade and he woke with a black eye – the gift of an angry lover whose lady he had importuned being ignorant of her lover's presence. His handkerchief was full of blood and drawing it from his pocket at the breakfast table he said: 'This reminds me of Veronica'. The 'Shy one' of his heart is perhaps not generally considered shy. He always quotes Yeats parodied, to heal or endorse his deeds. 'And little shadows come about her eyes' – this his black eye. Yeats won't give him the address of the lute maker so he cannot tour Margate and Falmouth as he intended, singing old English songs. The Mummers have gone to the Rosses, west Sligo: Yeats country. Joyce wishes to follow and horrify them on their holiday by bringing an holy woman or blessed damozel. His last parody – of O'Sullivan this time

The Sorrow of Love
If any told the blue ones, that
mountain-footed move,
They would bend down and with batons
belabour my love.

The original, you may remember, is Starkey's.

The Sorrow of Love
If I could tell the bright ones that
quiet-hearted move,
They would bend down like the branches
with the sorrow of love.

When he had returned from Oxford, Gogarty and Joyce decided to remove themselves from the madding crowd and take up residence in a Martello Tower which was situated near the sea on the outskirts of Dublin. These towers had been built round the coast of Ireland as a protection against invasions in Napoleon's time. A century later some official in Dublin Castle hit upon the idea of conditioning them and letting them out to private citizens as dwelling-places. To Gogarty and Joyce it seemed an ideal retreat in which to practise their craft.

In a letter written to Bell about the middle of July, Gogarty outlined his plans to help Joyce:

Joyce is to hold his estate at the Tower. The rent will be about £19 a year and as he won't have to pay it the scheme is feasible. He must have a year in which to finish his novel.

On the 22nd he writes to say that he and Joyce are to go into the Tower in a week's time:

I shall furnish the Tower with Chippendale sticks, no pictures. The Bard Joyce is to do the housekeeping. He is to Watts-Dunton me also.

A Bash in the Tunnel

After he had installed himself he wrote to Bell describing his new domicile:

> In the tower there are four rooms. One large one above, and three below. Two of those below are only pantries, one containing a well; the other is copper-sheeted and was a magazine when the place was used as a fort. The upper chamber in which I now write, and where the apostles assemble on occasion, is reached by a ladder stairway and is about twenty feet off the ground. The walls are nine feet thick and the door is massive. The view is splendid. Howth, to the North. The mountainous arm of the Bay, changing with every cloud and affording wonderful successions of colour in pink on a hot and sunny day. Purple or cerulean on clouded days. And, on days when there is an intermittent sunshine, the hill gleams yellow as if clothed with fields of corn. 'The barren steeps in ferny fields of corn.' To the South, that is behind one looking to Howth – Killiney stands; a tricipetal hill the middle head of which is cursed by an obelisk – a beauty blasting sight: conformity petrified. Some night I may blow it up. It's coming out of that when I have collected sufficient dynamite for the purpose; but it may take months as I shall have to spread my purchases over a long period to avoid the suspicion which would arise if I bought a lb. at once. This is a grand place to work in: the sea-blue air and green trees all around me, no dust, noise or cars nor civilized people to trouble.

In the same letter there is an example of how a single occurrence could trigger off in Gogarty's mind a rapid series of images.

> I bought a lobster today alive, and when I put him in a little pool his marvellous colours reappeared freshly so that I resolved to restore him to the 'great sweet mother' and I took the twine off his claws and sent him seaward. I suppose they'll catch him again if he has not taken his experience to his ganglion. I am without him to supper now but perhaps it is better to have had him feed whatever little of the idea is in me with the beauty of his colouring than to supply my more transient need with the muscles inside his skeleton. Surely I'm not a Christian? No, the Galilean incidents around the lake: filling nets with fish and actually increasing other lakes prove that I have not imitated. My lobster is now wandering in the weird submarine moonlight which they say is emitted night and day by the animalcules at the

sea-bottom and stretching his stiffened joints and (if he could) wondering has he been to Hades and gained a rebirth. Yesterday I saw shoals of mackerel swimming waveringly in the dim green depths their backs all marked with dark waved bands as if the shadow of the ripples had fallen upon them and remained. Many people were pulling them out momentarily with lines and hooks from boats and chucking them into the bottom of the boats. They couldn't eat them all, I suppose they rotted. It's awful. Fishermen, real ones, have no poetry, nonchalant, heavy louts as a rule. The poets put the glamour on them . . . the tunny fishers in Theocritos shall fish for ever, yet they would have cheated Theocritos to the last obol, or taken too many tunnies for their wants or their market if they got the chance.

One can visit this Martello Tower today. It has not changed in fifty years. You approach the metal steps which lead into the Tower through the garden of Mr Michael Scott, a Dublin architect who has built his house beside the Tower. Inside is the main room where Joyce and Gogarty used to sleep; downstairs are well-built ovens which were installed to enable the garrison of the Tower to cook their meals. Once up on the roof, the panorama of Dublin city unfolds itself. To the left, a crescent of Georgian dwelling-houses, painted in pleasant blues and yellows, fits snugly into the gentle curve of the bay. At the end of the crescent lies Dun Laoire, known in 1904 as Kingstown, with its huge Edwardian hotels and nineteenth-century Gothic church towers. The mailboat pier creeps out in a long spine from Dun Laoire sea front.

In the Tower Joyce and Gogarty lived in remote content for a while. How long exactly they were there together it is difficult to say. While they undoubtedly quarrelled, there is no reason to believe that Joyce quitted the Tower immediately as a result of a quarrel. He left Ireland on 12th October, and between the beginning of August and that date he probably stayed intermittently at the Tower, with a constant period from the beginning of August until near the end of that month. Mr Oliver Gogarty, Gogarty's eldest son, has suggested that his father and Joyce did not enter the Tower until 17th August, his father's birthday, but the letter of 22nd July would seem to indicate that they may have been living there before that date.

Joyce taught in a nearby school in the daytime and returned every evening to the Tower. The money he earned helped to pay for the food and drink of the occupants of the Tower. Foodstuffs were cheap and easily obtainable. Lobsters could be bought for twopence, and milk for a penny a pint. This left money for glasses of Guinness in Murray's bar and for the vellum paper on which they used to write their verses.

One evening Dermot Freyer, son of Peter Freyer, the surgeon who invented the prostate gland operation, visitated the Tower and found poems for Joyce's volume, *Chamber Music*, which Joyce had thrown behind him in a drunken fit of despair as he staggered into the night.

Gogarty used to swim two or three times daily in the forty-foot bathing pool which was directly below the Tower. He specially liked to swim in the sunset when the water became soft and crimson-flecked. Joyce, though he hardly hints at this in *Ulysses*, was quite an adequate swimmer and sometimes accompanied Gogarty on his swimming trips. Gogarty recollects seeing Joyce one day deliberately staggering on the strand at Howth carrying a sweeping brush on his shoulder. 'Jesus wept and when he walked he waddled,' was what Joyce replied when questioned about his curious pose. It was while they were living at the Tower that Joyce and Gogarty had their first quarrel. Gogarty was to complain later of an increasing seriousness in Joyce's demeanour, of his silences, and of being unable to rally him from 'being sullen in the sweet air'. He began to notice also that his friend was adopting a conscious artistic pose.

Joyce had collected his pose when he was in Paris. There Rimbaud became his model. Rimbaud influenced him so much that he sent Gogarty a picture of himself dressed in imitation of the master in broad-brimmed hat and flowing cape. The French poet's conception of the artist's function suited Joyce perfectly. Under the new dispensation he could become a high priest in the service of beauty instead of the priest of God he had wanted to be in the God-intoxicated periods of his youth. But Gogarty, who had no liking for priests anyway, was unwilling to accept Joyce in his new sacerdotal role. When Joyce started to adopt Rimbaud's custom of deliberately reviling those who had helped him, Gogarty found himself unable any longer to stomach his friend's Latin posturing. 'I have broken with Joyce,' he writes to a friend in Oxford on 16th August 1904. 'His want of generosity became to me inexcusable. He lampooned Yeats, A.E., Colum, and others to whom he was indebted. A desert was revealed which I did not think existed amid the seeming luxuriance of his soul'.

The quarrel between the two did not, as Joyce's brother suggests, mean the end of their friendship. It might have blown over in a few weeks if Joyce hadn't left Dublin hurriedly in October with a servant-girl whom he later married. Gogarty described Joyce's flight in a letter to Dermot Freyer. The play on the place-name is a typical Gogartian touch. 'The Bard Joyce has fled to Pola, on the Adriatic. A slavey shared his flight. Considering the poet's preaching and propensity the town he has chosen for the scene of his future living is not inappropriately named'.

It is necessary to advance slightly in the narrative in order to observe the course of the friendship between the two.

A year after Gogarty's note to Freyer was written Joyce and Gogarty had made up their quarrel. A request from Joyce to Gogarty that the latter might visit him in Trieste drew an enthusiastic reply from Gogarty, whose letter was forwarded from the Waldorf Astoria in New York, where he was on holiday. He wrote that he hoped to make a world tour and would certainly visit Joyce in the course of it. He missed, he said in the letter, 'the touch of a vanished hand and the sound of a voice that is still'. America promised great financial rewards for Joyce's singing voice, he added, if only Joyce could go over and try his fortune there. Whether Gogarty did visit Joyce in 1906 is not known. But in 1907 he and Joyce were corresponding on their old familiar terms. Gogarty spent that year in Vienna on a postgraduate course in ear, nose and throat surgery under Hajek and Chiari. Joyce was by then working as a bank clerk in Trieste. Gogarty had become so keen to have Joyce with him again that he offered to pay his expenses in Vienna for three weeks and get him some work teaching German there. He suggested a summer tour of the Mediterranean by steamer, on which they would write verses together in the old familiar fashion while Gogarty would undertake to pay the fares. Joyce agreed to Gogarty's plan for publishing in Trieste 'Ditties of No Tone', a collection of Rabelaisian verse by Gogarty and his friends which Joyce had been urging Gogarty to publish for some time. Joyce, however, must have failed to do as he said, for Gogarty wrote to Dermot Freyer, one of the contributors, that 'the Diminutive Dante', Joyce, had let him down over the publication of *Cockcrows*, which had been Joyce's suggested title for the work.

Joyce's brother, Stanislaus, has claimed that it was he who persuaded Joyce against going to Vienna on Gogarty's invitation. Stanislaus regarded Gogarty as a tempter who would wean his brother away from the cause of art. He believed that his brother's temperament necessitated his being kept free from the carefree, convivial company of his countrymen if he was to achieve an important place in literature, and he felt that a visit to Gogarty might undermine Joyce's purpose by arousing in him nostalgic memories of Dublin and making the circumstances of his exile seem unbearable. There may have been less altruistic reasons for Stanislaus's dislike of Gogarty. Gogarty had rebuffed him by telling him that there was only one freak in Joyce's family and he had no relish for any others. Perhaps Stanislaus may have been jealous of the fascination that 'burly, bustling Gogarty' exercised over his brother. Whatever the cause, Stanislaus, as he has stated himself in print, set out deliberately to destroy the association between his brother and Gogarty.

Joyce returned to Dublin for a holiday in 1909. He had been five years absent. Gogarty, who was now established as a young surgeon, hearing that Joyce was in town, sent him a note asking him to come and see him and proposing that they have lunch at the Dolphin together.

31. VII'09   11, Ely Place,
                                                   DUBLIN.
Dear Joyce,
    Curiosis Cosgrave tells me you are in Dublin. Before trying to get you to come to Lunch at Dolphin on Monday next at 1 o'c. I would like to have a word with you. My man will drive you across (if you are in). I leave town at 5 each evening; but there can be changes if you turn up.
    He will call about 3.20. Do come if you can or will. I am looking forward to seeing you with pleasure. There are many things I would like to discuss and a plan or two to divert you. You have not plumbed all the depths of poetry; there is Broderick the Bard! of whom more anon.
                                                        Yours
                                                        O. G.

Joyce seems to have accepted this invitation, but before the date for lunch came around, Gogarty, finding himself involved in a surgical consultation, wrote and asked Joyce if he could come on another date.

2 VIII.'09   15, Ely Place,
                                                   Dublin.
Dear Joyce,
    I find that at 1 o'c. tomorrow there is a patient coming who cannot come at any other time. I will be glad if, in view of this, you will forgive a little postponement of the lunch. I will let you know.
                                                        Yours
                                                        O. G.

There are two accounts of their subsequent meeting, one Joyce's, the other Gogarty's. Gogarty has written that Joyce came along to Ely Place and, after sitting in the dining-room for some time, looked out of the window at the roses in the garden and said enigmatically: 'Is this your revenge?' After he had made this remark he rose and left the house. This was the last Gogarty saw of his contrary friend.

Joyce gives a somewhat different account of the affair in a letter to Stanislaus dated 4th August 1909:

> Gogarty met me in Merrion Sq. I passed him. He ran after me and took me by the arm and made a long speech and was very confused. He asked me to go to his house. I went. He made me go in and rambled on. To everything I said: 'You have your life. Leave me to mine.' He invited me to go down to Enniskerry in his motor and lunch with him and wife. I declined and was very quiet and sober. He offered me grog (?), wine, coffee, tea: but I took nothing. In the end he said, blushing: 'Well do you really want me to go to hell and be damned?' I said: 'I bear you no ill will. I believe you have some points of good nature. You and I of six years ago are both dead. But, I must write as I have felt.' He said: 'I don't care a damn what you say of me so long as it is literature.' I said: 'Do you mean that?' He said: 'I do. Honest to Jaysus (sic). Now will you shake hands with me at least?' I said: 'I will; on that understanding'.

Joyce's account would appear to contain at least some inaccuracies if we look at it in relation to the evidence contained in the two letters referred to above. There is no reference to the fact that Gogarty had written to him or to the fact that he had seemingly accepted the invitation to lunch. It is probable that Joyce was, as usual, on the defensive when writing to his brother about Gogarty and was anxious to impress on him his obdurate resistance to the siren-lure of Dublin life. Whichever account is true, Joyce's or Gogarty's, this was to be the last occasion on which the two writers met.

But Joyce never forgot Dublin and it is probable he never forgot Gogarty either, whose personality embodied so much of the spirit of that Norman-Norse and Celtic town. Joyce decided that the carefree convivial atmosphere of Ireland was unsuited to his purpose as an artist. But he often expressed regret at his enforced exile from the city whose conscience he had articulated into literature. 'When I die,' he told an Irish friend in 1939, 'Dublin will be written on my heart'.

Joyce sacrificed race, religion and friends in his unswerving devotion to the cause of art. His sense of dedication acquired from the religious training of his youth stood him in good stead for his vocation as an artist. It gave him the strength of purpose to retire from life into a cell of his own making for the purpose of giving expression to his particular vision. Gogarty as much as Joyce did believe that the artist should 'pour into the mould of art' all that his heart would hold. But he felt it was by 'loving life and using it well', and not withdrawing from it, that he would have revealed to himself the inner harmony which is the poet's vision. Influenced by Mahaffy and Tyrrell, he would have regarded asceticism whether in the cause of art or of religion as a medieval degeneration from the Attic belief in the development of personality in every aspect. He had never acquired the penitential habit as Joyce had, when the hell-fire sermons of the Jesuits terrified him with visions of damnation. We can see from a remarkable letter written by Gogarty to Bell in January 1905 how repugnant the whole concept was to him and how he favoured instead a Graeco-Christian synthesis which laid its emphasis on the supreme necessity of personality.

I read Huysman's *En Route* the other day and read therein his appreciation of the very plaint that made me miserable. I felt, and I suppose I did justice to, the standpoint from which he looks – the music is very impressive certainly. Perhaps the calm that asceticism brings is bought at too great a cost: it makes Man miserable. It is not 'the still, sad music of humanity' but Man's unmanfulness and whinging *(sic)*. Surely not the least part of the cross each man must take up and bear is the knowledge that life is at best a burden; a knowledge that our greatest, from Sophocles to Matthew Arnold, have not shirked?

I cannot but think that religious people who live in ostrich holes and let their reason atrophy have disobeyed the very injunction they fancy they are following – they have not taken up their cross. Abstinence from luxuries – even when it is not accompanied by abstinence from work – does not constitute a cross for anyone but licentious millionaires or brainless lordlings. Certainly I find it a greater trial to gaze calm-browed at the inevitable end and, standing alone, support my own soul than to look at life communing with saints, through the windows of a cathedral. They too 'stain the white radiance of eternity'. Stoic and Epicurean alike kept unenslaved by luxuries, to reach mental contentment; the monk pleads that God's pleasure is manifested to him by the peace of mind which he enjoys. They are all alike: the Stoic for fortitude denies himself and does his duty; the Epicurean for the sake of ease has a care that no passion enslaves him; and the Monk in order to please God gains peace of mind. They all seek their own comfort and the monk is the least unselfish – he lives at the expense of the community. His good deeds consist in distributing things which he does not earn. He merely transfers property and gains in charity. He succeeds most of all and at the greatest cost to others in pleasing himself.

If I were to please myself I would like to live alternately at the sea and in the country or town: to travel a little, dabbling in literature on the plea that I sought beauty in order to confer it on mankind. This scheme might work were it not that tradition is otherwise: God is more popular than uranium mines. Or I might believe in a Deity less rational than myself who would be worshipped best by my reducing myself in a convent to a condition that he would punish me for, anywhere else in the world. Ah, well! though I worship nature yet I realize the ethical necessity of Personality and for His sake think it better to knowingly serve to the best of my power than, shirking the responsibility of His godlike gift reason, sleep it out in a cell.

This letter indicates that Gogarty's insatiable appetite for so many different forms of human activity was not merely the result of an emotional urge but of a carefully worked out philosophy of living. Motivated by a 'belief in the ethical nature of personality', he had become by middle life a champion athlete and swimmer, a surgeon, a senator of the Irish Free State, a dramatist, poet and aviator. Could there be a bigger contrast to Joyce's policy of monk-like withdrawal from reality? This passion for living not only may not have interfered with Gogarty's progress as an artist but may actually have helped to give his verse its special character. A.E. considered that it was Gogarty's refusal to separate art from life that brought a fresh, joyous note into his work. 'Oliver Gogarty has never made a business of beauty, and because he is disinterested in his dealing with it, the Muse has gone with him on his walks and revealed to him some airs and graces she kept secret from her other lovers, who were too shy or too awed of her to be natural in her presence'. Yeats was perhaps thinking of a similar quality when he wrote: 'Gogarty never stays long at his best, but how beautiful that best is, how noble, how joyous.' When he compiled the *Oxford Book of Modern Verse*, Yeats included seventeen of Gogarty's poems, to Joyce's three.

One wonders what Joyce must have thought as he learned of the high praise accumulating around Gogarty's poetic achievement. He had once referred to Gogarty and Yeats as the 'backlegs of literature'. But as he matured he must have realized that there was another path to Parnassus besides the Calvary-like one he had chosen for himself. Yeats he came later to recognize as one of the great poets of the twentieth century, and perhaps in middle life the intolerance of his youth may have diminished sufficiently to allow him to see Gogarty's genius in its correct perspective.

By a coincidence, when he died in Zürich in 1941, the two books found on his desk were Gogarty's recently published life of St Patrick and a Greek Lexicon, presumably there in order to translate Gogarty's Greek quotations. Those were sad years for Joyce when the world seemed to be breaking in pieces around him. One wonders if, as he read through those pages typically Gogartian in their witty discursiveness, he recalled again the gay companion of his youth, and regretted their broken friendship – broken by his own will in his unswerving purpose 'to forge in the smithy of [his] soul the uncreated conscience of [his] race' with weapons of 'silence, exile and cunning'.

The Bud

Stanislaus Joyce[1]

My brother went up to Clongowes Wood College when he was six and a
half years of age, and during his first year there was nicknamed 'Half
Past Six'. When my parents brought him up to Dublin to buy the list
of things the college required him to be provided with, and a trunk inscribed with his initials J. A. J. to put them in, I, almost three years his
junior, was attached to the group two or three times as a usual though
unnecessary appendage. Going to college was a new experience for my
brother, and though he must have had some presentiments, he welcomed new experiences even at that age. There may have been some
weakness at the moment of saying goodbye in the hall of the college (I
was not there), but my recollection is that when my father decided to
send him to Clongowes, he was eager enough to go and enjoyed being
the centre of such important preparations, including visits to shops up
in Dublin and lunch and tea in town. Unlike me in this, too, he always
liked new adventures, new scenes, new people. The illusion of stability
never seduced him.

I was taken down to Clane a few times on visiting day to see him.
Clane is a little town on his much-loved Liffey near Clongowes, 'the
meadow of the smith'. There was a drive of a few miles by old-fashioned
jaunting-cars to the college. Of course he was happy to see us, but the
impression that has remained on my mind is not that of a boy who was
lonely or felt out of place. He seemed to be perfectly free of his surroundings, a boy amongst boys. There was no reason why he should
not be so. He was always at the top of his class and always in good health.
His letters home usually ran: 'Dear Mother, I hope you are very well

---

1 From *My Brother's Keeper* (Faber & Faber), 1958

and Pappie also. Please send me . . . .' During his second or third year at the college he was chosen for the honour of serving as an altar-boy at Mass. Even in sport he distinguished himself. When after four years or so he left Clongowes we had at home a sideboard full of cups and a 'silver' (electro-plate) teapot and coffee pot that he had won in the school hurdles and walking events. He disliked football but liked cricket, and though too young to be even in the junior eleven, he promised to be a useful bat. He still took an interest in the game when he was at Belvedere, and eagerly studied the feats of Ranji and Fry, Trumper and Spofforth. I remember having to bowl for him for perhaps an hour at a time in our back garden in Richmond Street. I did so out of pure goodness of heart since, for my part, I loathed the silly, tedious, inconclusive game, and would not walk across the road to see a match.

In running he had a turn both for speed and endurance. Pat Harding, a friend of my father's, who was Irish champion for the 110 yard hurdles at the time when the American Kranzlein was champion of the world, offered to train my brother for the hurdles when he was in his last year at Belvedere, but my brother had already other fish to fry. They remained friends, and after my brother's elopement to Trieste my father wrote: 'In the whole city of Dublin you have only two friends, Pat Harding and Tom Devin'. In the story *Grace* Tom Devin appears as 'Mr Power', but the down-at-the-heels trainer in *Stephen Hero* is not Pat Harding, who was a lively young solicitor. As for training, the most Pat Harding himself ever did was a week or two before a meeting. My brother was very fond of swimming too. He was a splashy swimmer but fast. Over a short distance he could beat his burly friend Gogarty, who was, of course, a far stronger swimmer. And he was an indefatigable walker. On one occasion he wished to go to Celbridge to interview an Irish-American millionaire, who had bought an estate there and was reputed to have the intention of playing the part of Maecenas to young Irish geniuses. As my brother had not the train fare, he walked from our house in Cabra to Celbridge[1] to propose himself as a suitable subject, but he was repulsed at the gates by the lodge-keeper, who was unsympathetic and slow of wit. My brother went to the post office and wrote a letter to the Irish-American millionaire, whose name was Kelly, and then on the same day walked back to Dublin. I hope on the Day of Judgment to find out definitely whether it was stupendous cheek on the

---

[1] A distance of about fourteen miles each way

part of my brother or bad business on the part of the Irish-American millionaire. At the time I took the former view, my brother the latter, but now I am inclined to think that my brother may have been right. At any rate the Irish-American, who was not responsible for the repulse, wrote to my brother an apologetic letter, and getting no reply, wired to know whether his letter had been received. I have both the letter and the telegram.

My brother detested rugby, boxing and wrestling, which he considered a training not in self-control, as the English pretend, but in violence and brutality. When most of the newspapers of America and England and even of Trieste carried five column banner headlines on their front pages about Jeffreys, 'The White Hope', in that epoch-making event, the Johnson-Jeffreys boxing match at Reno for the heavyweight crown, his ironical comments were a rough draft of the description of the Myler-Keogh-Bennett fight in the Cyclops episode. There, however, it is used not to express personal bias but to associate violence and brutality with patriotism. Moreover, his first interest as a boy in the figure of Ulysses was aroused when his class was reading Lamb's *Adventures of Ulysses*. The boys were asked to say which of the heroes they admired most. My brother chose Ulysses in reaction against the general admiration for the heftier, muscle-bound dealers of Homeric blows.

My father had, no doubt, begun with the intention of giving his promising young son the best education the country had to offer a boy of his class and religion, but after a very few years that good intention, unfulfilled, formed just a minor item of the wreckage in the gradual ruin of his affairs. His office hours were short, from ten in the morning to half past three or four in the afternoon, and his work was light and easy, but such as it was he neglected it. To judge from his own reminiscences, he seems to have spent his time in the office drinking and telling 'good stories' with convivial companions of the same kidney whom he found there. They even played practical jokes on respectable old gentlemen who came to protest about their rates and taxes. If his work took him out of the office, the brief fiction of business soon ended in the bar of some hotel. Urgent work, such as the sending out of final notices to taxpayers, was neglected, and at the last moment he would have a couple of unemployed old clerks scribbling in his house from morning till midnight to help him to catch up on his arrears of work. When, finally, he succeeded in getting the notices out in time, he would lean back and take things easy again. Then, being an excellent mimic, he would tell his friends at home and in bars good stories about the poor devils he had got in to help him: about the boozy one, whose wife used to beat him, who turned up one morning with a black eye and a scratched face, and told a stale lie about colliding with the door of a cupboard in the dark (story in dialogue: sympathetic question and circumstantial answer with running commentary); or about the other who, owing to the high cost of handkerchiefs, used to blow his nose in sheets of tissue paper.

I dare swear that government work could be done in that way only in Ireland, or perhaps somewhere in the Balkans, or in some place at the back of God-speed in Tsarist Russia before the Inspector-General paid his surprise visit. Nor was the brown leather bag in which he carried the taxes he collected always inviolable, though he did defend it against two thieves who set upon him one night. He succeeded in beating them off with his blackthorn stick, and so had another story to tell over and over again in after years. His own borrowing from the bag, however, became more and more frequent and made it necessary for him to have recourse to money-lenders for fairly large sums at short notice. His property in Cork was gradually covered with mortgages, the interest on which ate up most of his rents. The end was already in sight when my brother was withdrawn from Clongowes and we moved up to Blackrock, a little nearer Dublin.

I liked the house in Blackrock – 'Leoville' was its name because of a stone lion over the porch – better than the one in Bray. It stood in Carysfort Avenue next to the garden that surrounded the Protestant church. I had been at an infant's school in Bray, and at Blackrock I was sent to a nuns' school, Sion Hill Convent, but so far as I can remember my brother was left to his own devices at home. Nobody in our house ever cared whether the children studied or not, though Dante[1] and Uncle William were still with us. The latter, however, used to read us fairy stories, working his way steadily through Grimm and Andersen, and when the story was of the misadventures of some beautiful princess, he would interpolate pathetic asides which escaped us, but were intended for my mother, sewing in another part of the room.

My brother was not among his listeners. He had begun to read very much for himself, and was eager to study. He used to ask my mother to

---

[1] 'Dante' was the name given to Mrs Hearn Conway who acted as governess to the Joyce children when the family lived in Bray, Co. Wicklow.

give him lessons to learn in the books which he had brought back with him from Clongowes and examine him on them. My mother did so, giving him long lessons which she hoped would keep him busy for a couple of hours so she could get on with her housework. But in half the expected time my brother would come back to be examined and to ask for more. The habit of examining him on his homework at his own request continued until much later, when we were both at Belvedere and he was in the junior grade between thirteen and fourteen.

I believe his first essays to write were made here at Leoville, Blackrock. He began to write a novel in collaboration with a Protestant boy, Raynold, a year or two older than himself, who lived next door. I have no idea what strange adventures were to form the plot of the book, which was soon abandoned, but I remember the two boys discussing it and my brother writing in the afternoon till tea-time at the big, leather-covered desk in the corner of the dining-room. He tried poetry, too, in the style of the drawing-room ballads to which he was accustomed ('My cot, alas! the dear old shady home'), but the most successful was a piece on the death of Parnell, which I see mentioned, apparently with my brother's sanction, by the title of 'Et Tu, Healy', though I do not remember that it bore that title. It certainly was a diatribe against the supposed traitor, Tim Healy, who had ratted at the bidding of the Catholic bishops and become a virulent enemy of Parnell, and so the piece was an echo of those political rancours that formed the theme of my father's nightly, half-drunken rantings to the accompaniment of vigorous table-thumping. I think it was in verse because of the rhythm of bits of it that I remember. One line is a pentameter. At the end of the piece the dead Chief is likened to an eagle, looking down on the grovelling mass of Irish politicians from

> His quaint-perched aerie on the crags of Time
> Where the rude din of this . . . century
> Can trouble him no more.

The production was much admired by my father and his circle of friends, whose judgment, in questions of literature at least, was as immature as the budding author's. My father had it printed, and distributed the broadsheets to admirers. I have a distinct recollection of my father's bringing home a roll of thirty or forty of them. Parnell, however, died when we were still at Bray, so the piece must have been written some months or a year after Parnell's death, because I am positive that the broadsheet was printed when we were living at Blackrock. My brother was, therefore, between nine and ten years of age when his ambition to be a writer bore its first timid blossoms. The lines I have quoted have stuck in my memory because 'the dear old shady home' and the blandly appropriate 'quaint-perched aerie' were standing jokes between us as late as when we were living at Trieste. Moreover, in the first draft of *A Portrait of the Artist,* now called *Stephen Hero,* the poem was assigned to the period I have indicated, and, further, describing a hasty packing up and departure from Blackrock, my brother referred to the remaining broadsheets, of which the young Stephen Dedalus had been so proud, lying on the floor torn and muddied by the boots of the furniture removers.

In Blackrock, the disintegration of our family set in with gathering rapidity. Dante left us and went to live with other friends. In the few years that still remained to her before she died, she changed frequently from one friend's or acquaintance's house to another's, and I conclude that she could not find again a family so tolerant of her dictatorship as we were. She had adopted my elder sister, now a nun, then a little girl going on for nine, as a kind of apprentice lady's maid, and succeeded, as only thoroughly embittered religious people can, in making her life a ceaseless round of tedious duties. While Dante remained with us we still had the Rosary and the Litany of the Blessed Virgin, at which she presided seated, every evening in the conservatory at the back of the house. The least I can say is that these two words Rosary and Litany do not mean for me what they mean for sentimental Protestants who have sojourned in Catholic countries. Yet when she had gone, perhaps in her sour way she missed the children. Uncle William left us, too, and went back to Cork.

I have a few scattered but significant memories of that brief interlude between relative prosperity and real poverty. I remember, for instance, returning with my father to Blackrock in the train from Dublin. In the third class compartment the only other passenger was a red-coated English soldier. My father, being in the quarrelsome stage of drunkenness, began to mutter quite audible curses at him. The soldier looked hard at him and edged nearer to us. I was on tenterhooks between them, fearing a row, and tried to distract my father's attention from him by asking childish questions, but the soldier said: 'I see you don't remember me, Mr Joyce.' My father, mollified, said: 'No, faith, I don't.' The soldier then explained that he was the boy whom many years before my father used to pay to look after his boat, and told a story of the time when, during a storm in the bay, he had begun to cry to be put ashore. My father had dropped him somewhere near Ringsend and sailed the boat back to Dalkey alone. My father, now very friendly, pretended not to remember, but when we got out at Blackrock, I was sent on home, and the rebel and the red-coat adjourned to a pub to talk about old times.

It was still less agreeable when, coming back in the evening from playing with other boys along the foreshore at Blackrock, I caught sight of my father, quite drunk but still elegant and with his eye-glass fixed, playing a piano-organ in the main street of the town and crooning 'The Boys of Wexford'. Meanwhile, the Italian organ-grinder stood looking at him, with legs crossed and one hand resting on the organ, wondering at what he no doubt called mentally 'questi matti d'inglesi'. We passed discreetly – the other boys as discreet as I – on the other side of the street, and I hurried on to bring the joyful tidings of his homecoming.

I wish I could see now, or could have seen then, the funny side of such happenings, as my brother did. And yet in *A Portrait of the Artist* he writes that 'any allusion to his father by a boy or a master put Stephen Dedalus's calm to rout and the smile waned on his face'. It did not seem so, but, of course, Stephen Dedalus is an imaginary, not a real, self-portrait and freely treated.

In the Jesuit schools he attended, the masters used to dwell rather heavily on the dangers of 'human respect', by which they meant doing something or leaving it undone against one's conscience for fear of what people might say or think of you. Their vague words were clearly understood. They desired to put their pupils on guard against a certain inferiority complex that might invade them when, in the little world of Dublin, they came in contact with a dominant Protestant class. In my brother they found an apter pupil than they expected, or, indeed, wished for. It is no idle boast to say that at that time there were very few youths, not only among the second-rate middle class of Blackrock but in Europe, destined to go their way so unperturbed as he, so callous against obloquy, or so determined to set completely at nought any praise or blame that might come to them for the work they considered they had to do.

I had neither such moral courage nor such love of my father. On the contrary, my antipathy to him seemed to have been born with me. There are some wise people who derive great benefit to their health and peace of mind by sleeping with feet and head in line with the earth's rotation. Conversely, I believe most firmly that when the heart feeds on hatred and contempt, the human being is facing the wrong way. But how is one to blink facts and maintain one's honesty? When my brother read Hardy's story, *A Tragedy of Two Ambitions*, which is about a drunken millwright and his two serious, clerical sons, he animadverted almost petulantly on Hardy's 'incredible woodenness'. But I, having our own case in mind, attempted a generalization. I said that it was a proof of Saxon earnestness and Celtic frivolity that a situation that suggested tragedy to an Englishman produced only low comedy in Ireland. My brother received the quip in silence, because he liked neither generalizations nor the implied reference. But he probably chewed upon both.

It is not surprising that the usefulness of a public office served by employees of the kind I have endeavoured to describe should sooner or later be questioned by the higher authorities on whom it depended. Furthermore, it was under hybrid control, partly governmental, partly municipal, and hardly destined to a long life. In 1891 or 1892 the office was abolished and the clerks pensioned off. Because of his bad record, it was at first doubtful whether my father would be granted any pension, but on the personal intercession of my mother, the people at the top, whoever they were, assigned to him a pension equal to about one third of his salary, and amounting to eleven pounds a month. At about the same time his house property in Cork, or what was left of it, was sold, apparently to make good defalcations, but it was so heavily mortgaged that little or nothing came to him from the sale. We left Blackrock abruptly and moved up to Dublin.

My father was still in his early forties, a man who had received a university education and had never known a day's illness. But though he had a large family of young children, he was quite unburdened by any sense of responsibility toward them. His pension, which could have taken in part the place of the property he had lost and been a substantial addition to an earned income, became his and our only means of subsistence.

The wish to shuffle off one's mortal load of responsibility is one among a number of common, human, quite unrealizable wishes. That, however, does not invalidate it as a literary theme. One of the world's masterpieces – *Faust* – is based on such a longing. In *Ulysses* Simon Dedalus, for whom my father served as model, is a battered wreck in whom even the wish to live carefree has become a vague memory, but if the facets of his character that are presented make the figure an effective and amusing literary creation, that is only possible because the tolerance of literature greatly exceeds that of actual life.

In Dublin the steps of our rapid downhill progress, amid the clamour of dunning creditors on the doorstep and threatening landlords, were marked by our numerous changes of address. I have before me a list of nine addresses in about eleven years, though I cannot be sure of the order. In the beginning two furniture vans and a float were required for the moving; in the end it was just a float. The bourdon of these recollections is my father's tipsy boasting.

I'll show them a trick. Just you wait. I'm not dead yet. No, by God, not half dead. Who-op! What do you think?[1]

The weariness of it was partly relieved for his children by that unquestioning acceptance of all things which is the grace of childhood and by a capacity for simple happiness that could be satisfied even with fine weather, but under the strain his wife aged rapidly.

According to my reckoning we moved up to Dublin in 1893. For the first months of our stay in lodgings there was no question of our attending school. We had a long vacation which my brother enjoyed exploring Dublin, with me at his heels. Then my father took a large sombre old house in Fitzgibbon Street, off Mountjoy Square, at that time quite a good residential quarter for well-to-do families. To judge by the size of the rooms the house had seen better days. Our subsequent changes of address were due to my father's thoroughly Irish repugnance to paying any rent. I do not know what kind of landlord he himself had been in his time, except that during the Split, as it was called, when the overwhelming majority of the eighty-three Irish nationalist members, egged on by the clergy, turned against Parnell and left him with only eight followers, my father quitted his office without leave during an election, and travelled down to Cork to persuade his tenants to vote for 'the Chief'. It was one of the things held against him when the office was closed down. The nine addresses which I recollect over a period of, at most, eleven years, besides representing a descending step on the ladder of our fortunes, are each of them associated in my memory with some particular phase of our gypsy-like family life. From Fitzgibbon Street, after a few months at a Christian Brothers school, we were sent,

---

1 " 'I'm going to show you a little trick,' Mr Dedalus said. 'I'll leave you all where Jesus left the Jews.'" *Ulysses*, p. 225 (Bodley Head, 1947)

free of fees at the invitation of the Jesuit Father Conmee, to the Jesuit School, Belvedere College, in Denmark Street at the other side of Mountjoy Square.

My vague memory of the Christian Brothers school is that my class was so large that I felt lost in it, and sitting in a back bench, I heard little and understood less. In any case, it did not matter. At Belvedere the classes were much smaller and surveillance closer. Before I had been there long, I was startled and awestruck to see our Jesuit teacher turn a boy of about nine across his knees and whack him with a leather pandy-bat for writing the 'Our Father' at dictation in pencil instead of ink. But after all, priests have so few pastimes. He had other simple pleasures in which a sporting spirit was blended with his religious zeal. Then he would come up to a group of boys, rubbing his hands, and announce breezily:

'A great day for the Catholics! The ladies of the North Side beat the ladies of the South Side at hockey. A great day for the Catholics!'

Otherwise he was mainly bored. One evening when I was taking a walk with some other boys, towards the Phoenix Park, we met him returning from it. He stopped to talk to us about the lovely evening and our nice little walk, and then suddenly opened his mouth wide in a hearty yawn. Quite unperturbed, he bade us good evening with yawning tears glistening in his eyes, and strolled off. There was a humorous allusion to him in the first draft of *A Portrait of the Artist*. This was the same man who, at my First Communion in their private chapel in Belvedere House, began the Mass by blessing himself in English. I suppose God understood all the same, although, of course, as all Catholics know, Latin is the proper diplomatic language to use in conversation with God; or perhaps he got Adrian IV, that great friend to Ireland, to interpret for him. He corrected his mistake, and then got on with his day's work, but I wonder, was anybody waiting outside for scatter-brained Father Farrelly after Mass with a pandy-bat?

Unfortunately, there was a boy in my class who lived at Blackrock and came into school by train. He informed our classmates that my father had run away from Blackrock because he had gone bankrupt. I considered myself in duty bound to call him a liar (though I knew I was) and to challenge him to fight me after school. The venue given was a quiet spot behind St George's Church, and we were beginning to have quite a set-to when a woman, shocked at such precocious barbarity, began to shout from a window overlooking that side of the square and to call to a man who was passing to stop us. We scattered; but after that encounter my adversary, whose name I don't even remember, kept to himself whatever other first-hand information he had about our family.

Our stay at the Fitzgibbon Street address must have been short, for we were already at our second address when my brother won his first exhibition in the Intermediate Examinations, a prize of twenty pounds in the Preparatory Grade. He was twelve at the time and I was nine and still young enough to wonder how on earth he could prefer to stay at home with a book on a fine afternoon in summer rather than come out to play. I have, again, a distinct recollection of his refusal, absolute trifles having an exasperating habit of sticking in the memory while important events escape it. Before we left Fitzgibbon Street, however, my mother had time to get scarlatina and the youngest brother, Georgie, to catch it from her. They were isolated after a fashion, in a large bedroom on the second floor, but the rest of the family, except two very young children, remained in the house. I do not remember that any special precautions were taken during the dangerous period of convalescence, the undeclared principle of large patriarchal families being that there shall be an ample margin to allow for losses while the tougher or the luckier ones survive.

Our new house was a small semi-detached villa at Drumcondra in the outskirts of Dublin. I liked it, because it was almost in the country at the foot of a low hill, and just near it were fields with a weir into the Tolka and woods where my school friends and I could trespass at pleasure. Our neighbours in Millbourne Lane, except in the other half of the villa, were farm-hands and navvies who lived in dilapidated cottages. Though there were certainly no signs of wealth about the children of our family, the infant proletarians from the cottages were unfriendly, and displayed their hostility by name-calling in chorus and stone-throwing. It was quite unprovoked, due solely to that innate animosity, observable everywhere in the lower classes, to anybody who is not yet quite so lousy as they are. Our house was well down the lane and we had to run the gauntlet of the unwashed every evening coming home from school. In the end, I had a fight with one of the most active of the catcallers, a little red-headed rough-neck, who rejoiced in the sobriquet of Pisser Duffy. It was late in the afternoon, and the loungers from the cottages, and even the women, stood around without interfering. In the imaginary portrait for which I served as model, 'A Painful Case', my brother has given me the name of Duffy.

After my modest skirmish with P. Duffy, I used to go about with a little group of boys from my class. One evening, when we were about to engage an enemy group of street arabs, we saw the rector of our college, Father Henry, coming towards us. At the sight of a priest the street arabs made off. We saluted him and he returned our salute, looking at us keenly from under his dark, bushy eyebrows, but did not stop. I fully expected trouble the following day. We had Father Henry for Latin and Greek, and as soon as the lesson began he called out my name. I stood up.

'What were you doing when I saw you last evening?' he asked.

I gave the usual stupid answer:

'Nothing, sir'.

'Do you call it nothing to go fighting ragamuffins on the canal bank?'

'I wasn't fighting, sir'.

In fact we had only got as far as the preliminary 'angry parle'.

'Oh', said the rector, 'I suppose you don't call it fighting unless you have a black eye or a bloody nose'.

Then he trailed off into the usual warnings and threats, but I could see that he was not altogether displeased. He was literary-minded, and imagined me to be a typical schoolboy. That was far from being my description. I was a scraggy, underfed boy with arms like the shins of thrushes, and too conscious of my weakness to be quarrelsome, but there is hardly any way out of it when you have been grazed by a stone.

Even my brother, in spite of his poise and unruffled temper as a boy, could not escape the aggressive jealousy of his companions. The discussion about Byron and heresy and the tussle with three of his classmates in *A Portrait of the Artist* is neither invented nor exaggerated. He must have been thrown heavily against barbed wire, for my mother had to mend the rips in his clothes so that he could go to school the following morning. It was one of the unpleasant memories of Millbourne Lane.

A boy was born there, who lived long enough to be christened Frederick, and then, after a few weeks, died, leaving in me at least a sense, though not yet the idea, of futility. The infant had been in the care of a certain Dr Tuohy, the father – so my mother told me – of the artist Tuohy, who long afterwards painted an excellent portrait of my father as an old man. It was at Millbourne Lane, too, that my father made a vague attempt to strangle my mother. In a drunken fit he ran at her and seized her by the throat, roaring that 'Now, by God, is the time to finish it'. The children who were in the room ran screaming in-between them, but my brother, with more presence of mind, sprang promptly on his back and overbalanced him so that they tumbled on the floor. My mother snatched up the two youngest children and escaped, with my elder sister, to our neighbour's house. I remember that a police sergeant called a few days after this pretty scene, and had a long talk in the parlour with my father and mother. We were, at last, on the same level as the navvies and farm-labourers around us. Nothing else came of it except that there was no further actual violence, though we lived amid continual threats of it.

My brother was less affected by these scenes than I was, though they certainly influenced his attitude towards marriage and family life. Half-hushed-up stories reached us of somewhat similar happenings in the families of friends of ours, whose material position, at least, was assured and normally comfortable: poverty cannot, therefore, have been the root of the evil. The main struggle of the various Mrs This-bodies and Mrs That-bodies, with whom we were acquainted, was to conceal care-fully what went on at home, but not more than a couple of years later it became my brother's set purpose to reveal it. The first short stories he wrote at school – *Silhouettes* – were neither adventurous nor romantic. They were already in the style of *Dubliners*. But that attach-ment to his father, which was to be one of the dominant motives in his character, remained unchanged. When he went up to Clongowes, the home he left was moderately prosperous and happy. He came back to it when a holiday atmosphere prevailed at Christmas and, so well as I remember, at Easter, and during the long summer vacation. Summer is always a boon, and 'The wild freshness of morning' clings about early memories. As he remained at college until he was almost ten, he knew only the more gracious aspect of our family life, the more amiable side of my father's character, and the image of him formed in those years was never to be effaced. Moreover, he could escape from it all into the domain of fiction. A little later he noted a memory of his reading of novels by Erckmann-Chatrian – *L'Invasion* at school, *L'Ami Fritz, Le Juif Polonais* and others for himself – in which these collaborators do not seem to have produced the effect they desired:

No school tomorrow: it is Saturday night in winter: I sit by the fire. Soon they will be returning with provisions, meat and vege-tables, tea and bread and butter, and white pudding, that makes a noise in the pan . . . I sit reading a story of Alsace, turning over the yellow pages, watching the men and women in their strange dresses. It pleases me to read of their ways; through them I seem to touch the life of a land beyond them, to enter into communion with the German people. Dearest illusion, friend of my youth! . . . In him I have imagined myself. Our lives are still sacred in their intimate sympathies. I am with him at night when he reads the books of the philosophers or some tale of ancient times. I am with him when he wanders alone or with one whom he has never seen, that young girl, who puts around him arms that have no malice in them, offering her simple abundant love, hearing and answering his soul he knows not how.

In those days my brother used to study so eagerly that, when we went picnicking to Howth or to the Bull, he would bring with him little note-books with summaries of history or literature or lists of French or Latin words so that my mother could examine him after lunch. It did not spoil the outing, though I sometimes protested. Before lunch we had a swim and in the afternoon a stroll round Howth Head or along the North Strand, and in the interval the examination occupied half an hour or so of a warm and lazy summer noon. The weekly English composition was his strong point. A.M.D.G. – 'Ad Majorem Dei Gloriam' – was piously inscribed at the top of two leaves taken out of the centre of a copy-book, and then there followed four pages of bright ideas on such inspiring subjects as Love of Country, Independence, or Make Hay while the Sun Shines. He was never at a loss what to say, but wrote quickly without making a rough copy beforehand. Then came the conclusion – L.D.S., not an anagram of L.s.d. but a Jesuit motto 'Laus Deo Semper', 'praise to God always'. His English teacher, George Dempsey, 'Mr Tate' in *A Portrait of the Artist*, soon noticed his turn for composition. He pointed him out to the Prefect of Studies as a boy with 'a plethora of ideas in his head', and when my brother passed into the higher classes, Dempsey used to read his compositions to the class to serve as models. In the end he took it for granted that 'Gussie', as he jocularly called him from his second name Augustine, would be a writer. My brother seems not to have been unmindful of his encouragement, for I have heard that from Paris he remained in correspondence with the old man until his death. The rector showed less appreciation. What caught his attention was the signature at the end – 'Jas. A. Joyce' with a whirligig of a flourish underneath – on which he commented ironically. He would have appreciated modesty and submission. Well, he just didn't get them.

My brother was never subject to the moodiness or plain tantrums that so often impelled me to go up to my room when my father came home, followed by his sarcastic parting shot, 'What a loving son!'[1] Much more than his reputation for being clever, his good humour and gaiety made him a favourite with his many sisters and relatives. And neither bawling in the home, nor tireless political ranting to cronies, nor the near imbecility of tipsiness ever spoiled his accord with his father. The full twenty pounds that he won for his exhibition in the Preparatory Grade was handed over by his father to the young boy to do what he liked with it. My brother had no idea what to do with the money, for twenty pounds, in purchasing value equivalent to at least twice that sum today, was too much pocket money for any boy to handle. He bought presents for all of us, practical presents, a pair of boots for one, a dress for another; and there were frequent visits, in which I was occasionally included, to the cheaper parts of theatres, to see Edward Terry in his comedy parts, or Irving or Tree if tickets could be had, or the lesser lights, Edmund Tearle as Othello, or Olga Nethersole. Clever as he was, my brother was still little more than a child, and liked to play with the money. He opened a bank for the family in order to play at issuing receipts and making up accounts. I had unrequested loans of an odd sixpence or so pressed upon me, but his parents were the principal and most assiduous customers, and the money soon melted away in 'dribs and drabs'. Yet even so, at the beginning of those years of squalor, he could still be happy in the satisfaction of effort crowned with success.

My brother accompanied my father on a few rare trips out of Dublin, and seemed to enjoy travelling with him. At least he went willingly. When the property in Cork was sold, he had gone with my father on what I think was his last visit to his native town. In *A Portrait of the Artist*, the visit takes place later and awakens in Stephen a raw sense of unrest and spiritual discomfort, but my brother's letters home at the time were written in a tone of amusement even when he described going from one bar to another. While we were living in Millbourne Lane, there was a further visit of a few days in summer to Glasgow, at the invitation of the captain of one of the Duke liners, who was a friend of my father's. The great joke of the visit, which was spoiled by rain, was

---

[1] 'By God, you're a loving pair of sons, you and your brother!' *Stephen Hero*, p.207 (231). Page references to *Stephen Hero* are first to the English edition (London: Jonathan Cape, 1944), and then in parenthesis to the American edition (New York: New Directions, 1944)

that my father, soused to the gills on the return trip, had a heated and noisy argument about politics with the captain, an anti-Parnellite. Fortunately, the captain was a teetotaller on board though not one on shore. 'By God, man', my father would conclude in telling this wonderfully good story, 'if he had been drinking he would have thrown me overboard'.

I can picture my brother as a handsome young boy, all eyes and nerves, traipsing about in the muggy drizzle of Glasgow after his tipsy father. In Dublin I have more than once seen children, younger than my brother was at that time, trying to lead a staggering mother home. Why, I wonder, seeing that people pretend to hold by the decalogue, has it never been thought fit to add a postil, enjoining some kind of consideration for children, to the fourth commandment? Can Moses have forgotten it, in the hurry of jotting down more important matters such as the commandment not to covet one's neighbour's house, nor his wife, nor his man-servant, nor his maid-servant, nor his ox, nor his ass?

I do not know how long an indulgent landlord allowed us to occupy the house in Millbourne Lane, but it was long enough for me to find out for myself the fascination of books. It was there I first read a whole book alone, though it took me about six months to do so. The book was *David Copperfield*. Much of the novel was beyond my comprehension, but its sentimentality and oddity were within my reach. More than half of it was vivid; it awoke and satisfied some longing in my imagination. In the attempt to cast the parts among the people I knew, the one about which it seemed to me there could be no discussion was that of Steerforth for my brother. But my brother never cared for Dickens. Before we moved out, the big, bony father of Master P. Duffy called to say goodbye. He was received in the dismantled parlour, and over a bottle of stout expressed his regret for past misunderstandings and offered the good wishes of the cottagers, so that we left in a halo of pecae re-established.

I have a clearer recollection of our next house, as I was already about ten years of age when we moved into it. It was the house in North Richmond Street described in 'Araby'. It stood in a quiet neighbourhood, 'North Richmond Street being blind', and, as my brother says, 'an uninhabited house of two storeys' (really of two storeys and a large basement storey) 'stood at the blind end, detached from its neighbours in a square of ground' – a garden with apple trees. The rest of the story of 'Araby' is purely imaginary. In the preface to the American edition of *Dubliners*,[1] Padraic Colum says that this story and 'The Sisters' are, evidently, recollections of childhood. This is a mistake. In fact, only two of the stories – 'An Encounter' and 'A Mother', describing a concert at which my brother sang with John McCormack – are based upon his actual personal experience. The remaining stories are either pure fiction or elaborated at second-hand from the experience of others, mostly from mine, as I shall show later.

In 'An Encounter' my brother describes a day's mitching which he and I planned and carried out while we were living in North Richmond Street, and our encounter with an elderly pederast. For us he was just a 'juggins'. Neither of us could have any notion at the time what kind of 'juggins' he was, but something funny in his speech and behaviour put us on our guard at once. We thought he might be an escaped madman. As he looked about fifty and had a military air, I nicknamed him 'the captain of fifty', from a phrase I had seen somewhere in a biblical quotation. My brother did not write the story until after he had come to Trieste. I was still in Dublin, and when he sent me the manuscript, as he always used to do when he completed a story, I suggested my nickname for the fellow as the title for the story, but my brother preferred his own title for it.

It was one of the stories to which great exception was taken when, in 1912, the tug-o'-war began with Roberts, the shifty manager of the Dublin publishing firm, Maunsel & Co. My brother's solicitor in Dublin, George Lidwell, pleading with him for a less rigid attitude in respect to changes in his work, said to him: 'You see now, your father, who has read that story and is a man with experience of life, has no idea what kind of individual you are writing about'. I was in Trieste then, keeping the Triestine end up. I wrote back suggesting that my brother should have replied: 'Neither do I, but I have my suspicions, and I put them into the story'. Tom Kettle, a man whose opinion my brother valued because his Catholicism was an intellectual conviction, not just a phase of nationalism, also declared against the book. He kept saying: 'Oh, I'll slate that book when it comes out. I'll slate it!' That was a fair fight that my brother accepted and that Kettle, by the by, would have lost had the First World War not claimed him as one of its wasted victims. My brother pointed out that it was an actual experience, but Kettle waved the reply aside. 'I know', he said, 'we have all met him'.

---

[1] New York: The Viking Press, 1925

I think it was Kettle's words that decided my brother to keep his own title for the story. He wrote to me that he would like to dedicate it to the author of 'The Voyage of the Ophir'.[1] But why pitch on poor George Meredith as a typical exponent of English educational methods and their suspected effects? Why not the author of *Ralph Roister Doister?*

My father now became, or had already become, an easygoing canvasser for commercial advertisements in the employment of the *Freeman's Journal*. (My brother has used this financial background for the make-up of Leopold Bloom.) He also did odd jobs in connection with the revision of voting lists, and got a few guineas now and then for acting as presiding officer at municipal elections. But these small additions to his pension made still smaller difference in satisfying the most urgent needs of his large family. My brother's prize money from the Intermediate Examinations, nominally left at his disposal, went in what it is far too dignified to call domestic expenses, and served only to confer on the household a month or so of effortless ease, in which my father bloomed again like a wilting flower in the rain.

He was always looking for a job, one suitable, of course, for a man that does not want to work, and now, during spells of sobriety, for it must not be imagined that he was not occasionally sober, he would make optimistic calculations of how much he could earn 'between hopping and trotting'.

During these halcyon days when he was temporarily, though not bigotedly, 'on the water wagon', Sundays and holidays were spent, weather permitting, in taking long walks in the lovely surroundings of Dublin. My brother and I were always in the group, which usually included a friend or two of his, for whom he was better than a guide, though they were truer Dubliners than he was. We would stop to look in at the gates of a country house.

'A delightful spot,' my father would say enthusiastically, 'I wouldn't mind ending my days there'.

'Whom does it belong to, John, do you know?'

'Well, it used to belong to old So-and-so.'

'Is it the solicitor in Dame Street you mean?'

'Yes, that's the man.'

---

[1] Meredith's poem written for the voyage around the Empire taken in 1901 by the Prince and Princess of Wales

Then would follow the life, death and miracles of old So-and-so; or it might be scraps of information regarding more important people, the place where Addison used to walk, or Swift's supposed residence, or the house of the infamous 'Sham Squire', Francis Higgins, on Stephen's Green,[1] or Surgeon Wilde's house (Oscar was never mentioned) on Merrion Square. He had an inexhaustible fund of Dublin small talk, and my brother shared with him this interest in Dublin lore, which distance and the lapse of time served only to increase.

When friends dropped in on Sundays or of an evening during the week, my father was unaffectedly delighted to see them and unwilling to let them go home even when the night had worn on: 'Why, man, the night is young yet.' He was genial, amusing, hospitable. He had more talk, more stories, more reminiscences than the rest of the group, and they seemed to look up to him. Of course, they asked him to sing. His voice was still good, mellow and rather dark in colour with resonant high tones.

Many of the songs he sang were rubbish, such as that insufferable 'Yes, let me like a soldier fall' (from which perhaps Verdi got the idea for 'Di quella pira', though the Irish aria will not stand the comparison), sung, not quite seriously, however, for the sake of the high C at the end. But ballads he sang well and many operatic airs in English but known by their Italian names – 'M'appari' (very well), 'Ah si, ben mio', 'Salve dimora', 'A te, o cara', which I liked best though he did not think much of it and rarely sang it. My brother, also, was beginning to have a voice, and singers of the past were often discussed, as in 'The Dead'. In the first years at Trieste, my brother found the same atmosphere in the Tuscan family with whom we lived. The wife of his friend Francini had been on the operatic stage before her marriage and had sung 'Sonnambula' and other light soprano parts. She always urged my brother to have his voice trained as a sure solution of his difficulties.

In the course of these evenings at home we became acquainted, through my mother, with a good deal of romantic piano music: Chopin, Mendelssohn, Liszt, Schumann, Schubert. The interest in these moody

---

[1] Higgins (1746–1802), an attorney's clerk in Dublin, married a respectable young woman whom he led to believe he was a country gentleman. He was prosecuted and imprisoned, and afterwards owned gaming houses and got possession of the *Freeman's Journal*, in which he libelled Henry Grattan and other patriots. He received £1,000 for revealing the hiding place of Lord Edward Fitzgerald

men, once the idols of the élite, was not so strange for our family as might at first appear. Indulgence in moodiness is one of the cheap luxuries of youth. I understood the spell of their melancholy perhaps better than I do in these crude days, and my brother was evidently not immune to the 'maladie du siècle' either, for 'Moods' was the title which he gave to the first volume of poems which he began to write about this time or a little later.

Towards the end of the summer holidays that were to furnish either the idea or the emotional environment for the few stories of childhood I have mentioned, two Dominican priests called to see my father. They were shown into the parlour, and when my father appeared they soon declared the purpose of this visit, couching it in a few words of flattery to his paternal vanity. The results of the Intermediate Examinations had just been published, and it appeared from them that my brother had again won an exhibition, this time in the Junior Grade. The two Dominicans had come to offer him free board and tuition in a college belonging to their order in the country. My father called my brother into the room, and, after explaining the proposal to him, told him that he was to decide for himself. My brother did so without hesitation. He rejected the offer. 'I began with the Jesuits', he said, 'and I want to end with them'. Whether the decision in itself was good or bad, my father did right, I think, to leave it to his son, for he believed such decisions tempered the will. My brother learnt to come to a decision without regretting it. My father called it 'making a man of him'.

The Dominicans, for their part, were not above engaging in a little underhand, clerical competition with a rival order; and they were certainly very alert businessmen. The addresses of students were not given in the lists published by the Board of Education, only the names of the colleges they attended. To find us out so quickly, especially since my father's traces were not easy to follow, they must have had an informant in the offices of the Board, where names and addresses were registered when the trifling entrance fees for the examinations were paid.

A later rector of Belvedere College seized the opportunity afforded by an interview with Patricia Hutchins, the author of *James Joyce's Dublin*, to assert with some emphasis that my brother was given his breakfast at the college. Some other anonymous source adds also his dinner. But so far as I can recollect, in all the seven or eight years I remained at Belvedere College, breakfast was never served there for anyone. 'It was a mistake', said the same misinformed spokesman of his order, 'although well meant by Father Henry at the time, to educate a boy here when his background was so much at variance with the standards of the school, cultural and religious'. (The suggestion was Father Conmee's, not Henry's; we were then at one of the Christian Brothers' schools, and Father Henry didn't know us.) I remember my classmates. If by 'cultural background' he means independent, out-of-school interest in literature, music, painting, religion, history or even politics, my 'cultural background' – not to speak of my brother's – was considerably higher than that of my classmates and by a complexity of causes as much a result of our kind of family life as theirs was of their kind. In fact, this is a very cheap boast, for their cultural background hardly went beyond tennis and dinner-jackets. To me at least it seems that there is a reasonable suspicion that this is just the 'cultural background' that the rector of Belvedere College had in mind.

Clerical orders, the most unabashed beggars in the country, exposed a little later by Michael McCarthy in his *Priests and People in Ireland*, monopolize secondary education, thrive on it, and yet consider it a favour if they impart it. That, at least, is the attitude of the Jesuits of Belvedere College towards the most brilliant pupil their school had produced in over 100 years. Even as a boy, he won three exhibitions, and twice, in the Middle and Senior Grades, he won the prize for English composition. In any civilized country in Europe, the son of a large and impoverished family (we were ten at the time) is admitted free of school fees to the State schools as a right, not as a favour, and it is high time secondary education was in secular hands in Ireland, too.

About the time when we moved into the house in Richmond Street, and so when I was between nine and ten years of age, an incident took place which was typical of Jesuit educational methods and had considerable influence on my 'religious background'. One day the rector, Father Henry, sent for me without any reason that I have ever been able to imagine. He began by asking me questions about my work in class, which aroused some forebodings, but soon changed to more intimate questions. Though he was a priest and there seemed to me to be nothing unusual in the turn his questions had taken, I was a good deal bewildered. Then, changing again, he began to question me about my brother's morals; and such was (and is) the dominance of the priest in Irish life that it never entered my head that he had no right to do so. At any rate, I could not answer because I did not know; and I said so.

It was something new that I had not thought of. He seemed to suspect that I was evading his questions, for he warned that it was 'as in the confessional', and that the lips of the priest are sealed. He was a sallow-faced man with jet-black hair and a deep voice. It was rumoured amongst the boys that he suffered from heart disease, and might drop dead at any moment. Looking at me with the searching suspicious eyes of a fanatical convert from Protestantism, and laying his fingers solemnly on his lips, he promised that 'no word of what I might say shall ever pass them'. He spoke earnestly – and he was reputed an eloquent preacher – of the most terrible of all sins, the sin of telling a lie to the Holy Ghost. I was impressed. I tried conscientiously to remember something in the Holy Ghost's line, but could think of nothing but some horseplay between my brother and a hoydenish young servant girl we had then, a kind of catch-as-catch-can-cum-spanking match. So I hawked that out for the Holy Ghost's benefit, hoping it would be enough on account. The rector evidently thought it was, for he dismissed me, and sent me back to my classroom. Another hour was already half over, but the teacher, a Jesuit of course, asked me no questions either about my long absence or about the lesson for the day. I sat there with my head in a maze, almost oblivious of the curious glances of my companions, and much more upset than I had been during the cross-examination.

The following day the rector sent for my mother, and, without alluding to any specific fact or mentioning me, gave her clearly to understand that she should watch her elder son who was inclined to evil ways. My mother was astonished and shocked, but at the same time incredulous. On her return from the college she said only that the rector called her to speak to her about Jim. Floundering in doubt whether or not it was a sin to speak, I told her about the long interrogation of the day before, omitting nothing; but though in the course of my account I mentioned the pledge of secrecy 'as in the confessional', it was still only remotely, and in the vague background of my mind that I felt, not so clearly as words express it, that I had been put upon and that there had been some breach of faith. I was too young to appreciate the subtle but useful difference between 'in the confessional' and 'as in the confessional'; and in any case at that time there could be no shadow of a doubt in my mind that in such a matter a priest, especially the stern and devoutly pious rector of the college, could not be wrong. But my reactions lose nothing by being slow.

My mother was certainly not pleased with what she had heard, but in a way she was relieved, for from the rector's earnest admonitions she had been led to fear worse things. Of course, she blamed the servant, who was a girl of twenty-three or twenty-four, and so about ten years older than my brother. She had already left us, and we never had another. My mother had long before that time ceased to confide in my father about anything, but he observed that something was amiss, and inquired what all the hugger-mugger was about.

'I am under a cloud at school,' said my brother.

'What about?' asked my father.

'I don't know,' said my brother. 'You had better ask the rector.'

My father went to the college, but again the rector limited himself to solemn but vague warnings.

'That boy will give you trouble,' the rector told him.

'No, he won't,' said my father, 'because I won't let him.'

Neither of them knew whom he had to deal with; but for years after, intermittently, until my brother left Dublin, my father would rehearse the story of the rector's thrust and his own clever parry. Nobody seemed to think that I had done anything at all open to criticism, but I was uneasy and brooded on the trouble in which, under duress, I had been an unwilling agent.

As for my brother, he just laughed at me and called me a fathead. His imperturbability, not only at home, but in various interviews with the rector, was far beyond his years, and deeply angered the rector, who considered it a mute challenge. It is true he had just won a second exhibition and was studying hard to win a third. My father, apparently guessing nothing in spite of his reputed shrewdness, cursed the rector's 'tawny soul' roundly every night for 'putting the boy off his studies'. The boy, however, was not put off his studies; he applied himself to them quite regularly. My brother never undervalued himself. That is certain, but it is not a sufficient explanation of his calm. To judge by his unaffected imperturbability, he might have been assisting at a badly rehearsed comedy that did not concern him. That 'cold lucid indifference', which, he says, in *A Portrait of the Artist,* reigned in the boy Stephen's soul after his first sexual experiences, seemed never to forsake him. But I fancy there was a further reason. I fancy he grasped at once what I understood only long afterwards by brooding on it, that the rector had gone parlously near a breach of the vowed secrecy of the confessional, and that he had the rector in the hollow of his hand. He knew he was the victim of a Jesuit intrigue, and was coldly determined to out-Jesuit the Jesuit. Even at that early age the rumpus could not throw him off his balance. He gave proof even then of that wariness in defence that later stood him in such good stead in his struggle with hostile authorities in various lands and in times of upheaval.

The storm blew over as unexpectedly as it had sprung up because, of the two people who had the matter in hand, one had already said too much and the other kept her counsel. But it was the beginning of an almost open hostility between the rector, Father Henry, and my brother which lasted until my brother left Belvedere. The hostility, however, was mainly one-sided. I find no trace of it in the portraiture of the rector in the Belvedere chapters of *A Portrait of the Artist*. My brother considered him the victim of his own fanaticism; and in any case, justice towards the characters of his own creation, or imaginative re-creation, became an artistic principle with him. That year or the next my brother won an exhibition in the Middle Grade, as well as the coveted first prize for English composition, but though the other teachers were smiling and congratulatory, the rector was silent. It is interesting to note that in the Middle Grade his marks in mathematics were high – he was placed about thirteenth in Ireland, so well as I remember. He detested mathematics; it was his weakest subject, but he tackled it resolutely because he wanted to win an exhibition, and he succeeded. He had, in fact, the kind of cleverness which is supposed to be distinctive of successful lawyers, that of acquiring at short notice, when necessary, a temporary mastery of some subject in which they have not a particle of personal interest.

Before we left North Richmond Street my brother and I were often invited to go on Sunday evenings to the house of school fellows of ours, the Sheehys, who lived not far from us in Mountjoy Square, a locality which seems to have declined as a residential quarter. This friendly relationship lasted some years and was practically the only experience of what might be called social life that my brother had in Dublin. The father was a member of Parliament, and the family consisted of two clever brothers and four clever sisters, one of them a really handsome girl. David Sheehy, the father, was a vigorous-looking man, who lived to be about ninety. I liked him, but my brother thought him pompous and inclined to lay down the law. He preferred the mother.

I must still have been a young boy when we first went there, for I remember a girl student, a university friend of the eldest sister's, who took possession of me, and talked to me almost all the evening about gymnastics and sport. I was a minor member of the college team which had won the inter-school shield for gymnastics, and she, a pretty girl with a lithe figure, was keen on sport too. To me she appeared to be a young woman, but I was captivated, and disappointed time after time not to meet her again. On another occasion, after I had been partnered with his youngest daughter in a dance by Mr Sheehy, we both sat, when the dance was over, on separate arms of a large armchair, she looking west-south-west, and I looking east-south-east.

My brother, for his part, never lost his poise and, though generally rather distant in manner, he was treated with easy familiarity as between successful students by the Sheehys, brothers and sisters, all of whom were then or later university students. The eldest son was professor in the University of Galway when he died. My brother was not only the most brilliant pupil in the college, and, at that time at least, of exemplary diligence, but also an omnivorous reader in English and French. His heterogeneous and mostly unorthodox reading often surprised them and was the subject of good-natured raillery. To improve his French he corresponded with some student in Vire, Calvados, whose name he had got from one of the many societies for improving Anglo-French relations. As the second daughter, Margaret, was just then beginning to make a name as an actress in amateur theatricals, charades were frequently arranged. My brother, too, almost always took part in them and discovered a real talent for mere clowning, unsuspected in so serious a youth. Besides which, his voice was already developing, and though the Sheehys were not musical, he was often asked to sing.

Until his fourteenth or fifteenth year he studied regularly according to the school curriculum, and altogether was in danger of becoming the model of a serious schoolboy in the higher classes, were it not that the works he borrowed from the Capel Street Lending Library sometimes seemed to the librarian open to question for a boy of his age. One of the books against which Old Grogan, the librarian, solemnly warned my father was *Tess of the D'Urbervilles*. My father had no notion what kind of book it was, or who the author might be, his own taste in literature wavering among *Tom Burke of Ours, Frank Fairleigh* and, for breath-taking interest, *The Moonstone*.

'What kind of books is this I hear you are reading?' he asked my brother.

'I have read many. Which do you mean?'

'Old Grogan was saying something about the last book you took out,' said my father.

'What! *Tess of the D'Urbervilles*. It's by Thomas Hardy. So I have to ask Old Grogan what I am to read. The ignorant old clod-hopper! He'd be much more at home in his native bog than in a library. I've a good mind to write a letter to the Corporation about him.'

'Well, if you say it's all right,' said my father, easily convinced.

As my father had often made Old Grogan, who had just the cut of a hedge-schoolmaster, the butt of his mimicry, the librarian was sacrificed conversationally on the altar of freedom of thought. But I, too, very nearly became involved as another comic victim in this first brush with a censor. The Capel Street Public Library was at a mile or so from where we lived, and my brother, with the excuse that he could not spare time from his studies, used to send me to change books for him, giving me a list of books in order of preference in case the one he wanted should be out. Second or third on the list he gave me, after the librarian's ineffectual attempt to act as censor, was the name of another of Hardy's works, *Jude the Obscure*. I did not know the book, and when half way to the library I glanced at the list, I could not read the name aright. In my brother's scribbled handwriting, it looked like 'Jude the Obscene'. I puzzled it over, but there seemed to be no doubt about it. The more I looked, the surer I was that that word was 'obscene'. At first I thought that I would say the book was out, but even in my own eyes I did not wish to be found wanting in the rebellion declared against the librarian. Fortunately, the first book on the list was in, for I had screwed my courage to the sticking point and was quite determined to call for 'Jude' boldly by the title as I read it. When I came home and told my brother about my dilemma, he shouted with laughter. He was sorry, he said, that I did not have to ask for it. He wished he could have been there to see Old Grogan's stupid face and my stupid face when I asked for 'Jude the Obscene'.

By this time we had already moved once more. The new house was in Windsor Terrace, Fairview, near the road that winds round the wide, shallow mouth of the Liffey to Clontarf. It was the second last house on the left at the top of parallel rows of two-storeyed houses, bordering on the rather extensive grounds of some invisible suburban villa, and belonged to a young clergyman named Love, a long-suffering Christian, who, it is to be hoped, had other sources of income. He makes a brief appearance in *Ulysses*. We remained for some years near the sea, our next two removals being in the immediate neighbourhood. Clontarf, the scene of one of the most famous battles in Irish history, was within easy reach by tram. The name Clontarf means 'the meadow of the bull', and the Bull is the long sandbank, which at high tide is completely cut off from the coastal road by a narrow channel of water. The uneven green turf of this sandy islet, overgrown with bushes and bitter-tasting bent-grasses, had attracted golfers, who built a little club house, putting greens and artificial bunkers on the Bull stretching out for more than half its length. Seaward a breakwater, partly submerged at high tide, ran far out to the river-mouth. Here as before we used to spend the long summer holidays, bathing almost every day when the weather was fine and the tide served, the whole family often picnicking at the end of the Bull or on Howth Head, which we could reach on foot from the tram terminus at Dollymount. Haunting memories of this wild, little frequented strand, with its tang of sunbaked seaweed and stinging sea-breezes, occur in various places in my brother's work, but chiefly in *A Portrait of the Artist*, where it is the scene of Stephen's sudden resolution to live his life as an artist freely and boldly.

Until fourteen or fifteen years of age, as I have said, my brother had been a docile and diligent pupil, but from this age onwards his systematic studies, which had followed the prescribed curriculum obediently, gradually gave way to a line of reading, as my father generally preferred to call it, of his own choice. The last examination for which he studied regularly was the Middle Grade. He used to go up to our room a couple of hours after our return from school at about three and remain there until ten o'clock, when he would come down in high good humour for some light supper before going to bed.[1] Meanwhile, on four or five nights a week, I had the pleasure of my father's drunken company in the kitchen or in the parlour. I had succeeded somehow in winning a book prize in the Preparatory Grade (a small credit with a bookseller of which a student could avail himself) but it was considered unworthy of any mention at home. My own private impression at the time was that the examiners had given me some other fellow's marks by mistake. In spite of the book prize, I went through that school year (and others) without some of the principal textbooks. I had a rather good memory and used to cram during the brief intervals and even during the lessons,

---

[1] (His mother to Stephen) 'Get Dilly to make you that boiled rice every night after your brain work.' *Ulysses*, p.548 (Bodley Head, 1947)

and generally succeeded in getting the smattering that was sufficient unto the day like the evil thereof. I had a special grudge against a Greek grammar by a Jesuit, Father Brown. I remember too that the rector, Father Henry, who was our teacher for Greek, altogether disregarded the accents. With my classmates I earned the reputation of being a 'hard case', an adept at cribbing exercises under the teacher's very nose, and unblinking under exasperated tirades and threats when I did not succeed in getting away with it In the end I managed to scrape ingloriously through examinations.

The school hours were the hours of high tension, and there was little relaxation at home. It does not facilitate a boy's study to have a drunken man at the other side of the table asking him:

'Are you going to win?'

'Well, I'll try.'

'That'll do. That's all I want.' (Repeated about a dozen times)

And then again 'da capo':

'Are you going to win?'

'I'll try.'[1]

How long the third degree examination continued with the same question and answer, I do not remember, but certainly long enough to seem incredible to people who are not familiar with the imbecility of drunkenness, that malodorous mixture of partial paralysis and semi-insanity. In the end the 'Chinaman' and 'hard case' collapsed in tears. Afterwards, my mother arranged that I was to study in the room I shared with my brother.

Another more boisterous interlude to homework comes back to my memory, the evening when my father and the skipper of a fishing smack, both very drunk, brought each other home. This sea-captain was reported to be the one who had taken James Stephens, the Fenian organizer, away to France in '65 after his escape from Richmond Prison. The story was that he had brought Stephens, dressed as a woman and disguised as his bride, aboard his fishing smack. The vessel was stopped and searched by an English cruiser in Dublin Bay shortly after setting sail. With presence of mind Stephens, apparently in great distress, clung to the captain, who appealed to the officer in charge of the search party not to frighten his newly married bride, and that gallant officer and

---

[1] 'Ho, boy! Are you going to win? Hoop! Schatt! . . . Head up! Keep our flag flying! *Ulysses*, p.540 (Bodley Head, 1947)

gentleman apologized for the trouble he had given them and let the vessel proceed on her way. Unfortunately, my admiration went not to the quick-witted Irish skipper, but at least equally to the gallant English officer and gentleman.

At the time I speak of the captain was a stocky man with a pointed grey-white beard, who walked steadily even in his cups, but seemed to be invaded by a kind of 'rigor vini' that made it necessary for him to move all of a piece when he turned this way or that. I have in my mind's eye the picture of him sitting stiffly on my father's knee, like a ventriloquist's stooge, while they crooned in unison: 'I dream of thee, sweet Madeline.' Every now and then my father would interrupt the duet to pluck the captain's beard and shout: 'Who-op! You're the best bloody man that ever scuttled a ship', until the rickety chair gave way under the double weight and they fell sitting on the floor. After this abrupt end to the concert, the captain took his leave with dignity, without forgetting his umbrella, which he had stood in a corner of the room.

I observe that it is usual in the pseudo-scientific jargon of our days to classify such people as weaklings. But if the story about the captain was true – and it probably was true, though he himself always avoided speaking of it – he had risked a long term of imprisonment in a minority cause and shown presence of mind in the face of danger. My father, for his part, had been a more than average all-round sportsman, an amateur actor and singer immune from stage-fright. He lived to be eighty-three and had more than a dozen children. If such people are weaklings, the word must have very elastic connotations.

In such circumstances, I had little wish to study, and even my brother's inflexibility of purpose seemed to weaken. I used to read a good deal, for the most part plodding my brother's tracks. He devoured books, while I was a slow reader. It sometimes surprised me, however, to find both that my brother remembered little or nothing of most of the books he read so voraciously, and that at need he could make good use of the one or two things he did remember from his reading. He read quickly, and if the book or the author did not appeal to him he forgot them both. If a book did, on the contrary, make some impression on him, he tried to read as many by the same writer as he could lay his hands on. Whenever I struck out for myself, I always felt a little guilty, as if I were indulging an inferior taste. That questionable taste included Scott and Dickens, whom my brother could not stand. In fact, I read ten or twelve of the Waverley Novels running and only cried 'Hold, enough!' when I reached *Count Robert of Paris*. This habit of reading in tandem continued when we were in Trieste; not, of course, for all books (he read far too much for me), but for many, and even for some foreign authors. My reading, which had to serve instead of regular study, may have been useful to him as a kind of revision, for occasionally in our endless discussions I happened to point out things he had passed over and to re-arouse his interest. He said frankly that he used me as a butcher uses his steel.[1]

There is an example of this revision in *Ulysses*. Stephen Dedalus sends Malachi Mulligan a telegram which runs: 'The sentimentalist is he who would enjoy without incurring the immense debtorship for a thing done.' My brother had paid no particular attention to the epigram when he was reading *The Ordeal of Richard Feverel*. To me, struggling to understand the sentimentalists by whom I was surrounded, one of whom wept when he sang 'The Bells of Shandon', it seemed far too superficial to dismiss their sentimentalism, in such bewildering contrast with their conduct, as mere silliness. Meredith's epigram was a sudden illumination, and I drew my brother's attention to it. At least I could think I now understood why I detested 'The Bells of Shandon', as well as those other old favourites 'The Lost Chord', and 'Thou'rt Passing Hence, My Brother'.

I cannot, of course, remember the religious crisis which is the central theme of *A Portrait of the Artist*. The impression it leaves is that it was an actual experience, and I have a vivid memory of many outward signs that confirm this impression: the long talks at the college, not with the rector, but with the preacher of the Lenten sermon, Father Jeffcott, who had known my brother at Clongowes College, and with Father Conmee at Gardiner Street, a brief interview of friendly admonition with the Provincial, the early morning Mass which he attended with my mother after which he would stay on in the silent chapel, where Mass had come and gone so quietly, to say another prayer, while his mother whispered to him that breakfast was ready, as well as the self-imposed abstention from sweets, newspapers and theatres during Lent.

I watched these mild austerities with surprise, but without admiration and without any inner urge to emulation. At that age (I was getting

---

[1]'Where is your brother? Apothecaries' Hall. My whetstone.' *Ulysses*, p.199 (Bodley Head, 1947)

on for fourteen then) I still went to confession and Communion twice or three times a year at Easter, at Christmas, and perhaps once more at some other time, but always with distaste. I was always more upset by a blunder or a 'gaffe' than by sin. The offence to the Godhead never troubled me, but faults in my relations with others did. When at Low Mass on Sunday, to which I always went because it is shorter, the celebrant went into the pulpit to denounce the perils of 'serious mortal sin', his words fell flat and echoless on my ear. I felt that they really meant nothing to the preacher either, that they were so much gospel gibberish, and that the twenty minutes' sermon, which bored me into the fidgets, was for him what the weekly English composition was for me, the squeezing of a dry lemon. But I just thought to myself, 'Father Reynolds is a bad preacher', and that for the moment was the end of it.

Neither had I ever been able to work myself up into anything like religious fervour in regard to Holy Communion. For me the host was a thing like tissue paper with a curiously tasteless taste, that stuck to the palate and had to be dislodged carefully with the tongue. The prayer to be read after Communion, which contained the quotation, 'Lord, I am not worthy that thou shouldst enter under my roof', puzzled me like an ill-timed pun. The roof of my mouth or the roof of somebody's house? Some people are born hypocrites, and some have hypocrisy thrust upon them. The latter was my case then. Of course, it was the body and blood of Jesus. Oh, of course! And then the idea that it was an act of cannibalism came into my mind to be bundled in horror out of the door and come back through the window for an answer. It had always been dinned into my ears that Jesus Christ was true God and true Man, and that as Man he had a human body of flesh and blood. At Mass the host was converted miraculously for the hundred millionth time into the flesh and blood of Jesus. Those were their words. When I, together with other boys, was being prepared for my First Communion they had taught us that the feast of Corpus Christi, one of the greatest festivals of the Catholic Church, had been instituted in the Middle Ages after a doubting priest had found blood dripping from the host over his hands and the altar linen. I could not get away from the conclusion that to deny in the teeth of such common doctrinal instruction that Communion was an act of cannibalism, at least in intention, at least in imagination, was downright lying. And there was always the danger of dying suddenly and going to Hell if one did not believe, that permanent blackmail for vacillating believers. Of course, one was permitted to doubt, provided it was honest doubt and one had taken the utmost care to find out the truth of such a supremely important matter. So, I supposed, after a lifetime of study, at fifty or sixty, one might venture to harbour doubt about the Real Presence. Meanwhile, I was in a cleft stick, forced to tell myself, lyingly, that I believed what in my heart I disbelieved even with a certain disgust.

Although the Lenten sermons preached by Father Jeffcott stirred up no such brain-storm of terror and remorse in me as they did in my brother, I remember that retreat well. I listened to them with something akin to irritation as one does to a story which one feels to be an invention but which one cannot disprove. In order to illustrate God's horror of sin and how much it offended Him, Father Jeffcott told us that if all the natural catastrophes and all the wars and all the ills and evils of mankind could be avoided by deliberately committing one venial sin, it would be far, far better not to commit that sin. With a start of anger that deafened me for a while to the rest of his sermon, I thought, 'A lie! A thumping falsehood!' and later, when my anger ebbed, 'Do the sufferings of men not matter?' When I began to listen to him again, what he said did not matter, for another thought amused me. Approximately it was this: if it is true that sin offends God so much, considering the amount of sin that is committed per minute per square mile, He must be in a constant state of divine apoplexy quite inconsistent with celestial bliss. My scepticism regarding the things revealed to 'one of our fathers' had one immediate effect; it startled out of his apathy our lay teacher, Dempsey ('Mr Tate'). When we came up from the College Chapel, the boys were discussing the latest sermon. One of them told him that Father Jeffcott had said that it had been revealed to a Jesuit saint that the damned were pouring into Hell like hailstones. Master and pupils were silent for a moment, awestricken.

'Hailstones fall pretty quickly,' said I. 'That must be about the rate at which people are dying all over the world.'

'I suppose so,' said Dempsey, with the indifference of a man who does not realize what he is admitting.

'And that means,' I concluded, 'that in the war between God and the Devil for man's soul, the Devil is winning all along the line.'

Dempsey had been chewing his moustache and listening half be-mused to the talk about a religious question that he took for granted. Now he woke up. He was very angry to find that he had walked into a trap.

'I don't want to discuss religion with you. That's not my business,' he said sharply. 'You should ask whoever teaches you Catholic doctrine.'

But it was the rector that taught us Catholic doctrine and I had no intention of asking him anything. So I hedged.

'I don't believe,' I said, 'that we are obliged to accept the visions of the saints as gospel truths.'

It was not exactly hedging either, for at the time my groping doubts about Catholic doctrine hardly went beyond that point.

The reverent landlord of Windsor Terrace must have been as largely endowed with Christian charity as his name betokened, for our residence at that address appears to have been somewhat longer than elsewhere. I cannot be certain how long my brother's conversion lasted, rather more than a year I should say, for we were still at Windsor Terrace when the reaction set in and he came under what was to prove one of the dominant influences of his life, the influence of Henrik Ibsen. It seems to me little short of a miracle that anyone should have striven to cultivate poetry or cared to get in touch with the current of European thought while living in a household such as ours, typical as it was of the squalor of a drunken generation. Some inner purpose transfigured him.

One afternoon comes back to me distinctly, the afternoon when Ibsen's *Master Builder* arrived from Heinemann's in William Archer's translation with his excellent preface, a slim volume in yellow paper covers with a vignette of Hilde Wangel, alpenstock in hand, on the outside. It was an event; and my brother stayed up that night to read the play. In the morning I must have been the first to come down for I found the large armchair pulled near to the extinguished hearth and the table to the armchair. The lamp had been pulled to the edge of the table so that the table-cover dropped on the floor. The whole room bore witness that he had read late into the night. My brother had been keeping vigil to hear the message from Norway of the younger generation that sooner or later comes knocking at the door.[1]

---

[1] Professor Joyce is echoing his brother's words at the end of 'The Day of the Rabblement': 'Elsewhere there are men who are worthy to carry on the tradition of the old master who is dying in Christiania. He has already found his successor in the writer of 'Michael Kramer', and the third minister will not be wanting when his hour comes. Even now that hour may be standing by the door.'

Joyce Without Fears:
A Personal Journey

John Jordan

There still exists in Ireland a body of opinion which tends towards reductive comment on the labours of foreign Joyce scholars. I have heard derisive comment even on Richard Ellman's by now classic biography. These people pride themselves on their first-hand information on, and intimacy with, Ireland, with Dublin, with the Roman Catholic Church. Yet only three full-length studies of any aspect of Joyce have been written by Irish people to date: J. F. Byrne's *Silent Years: An Autobiography with Memoirs of James Joyce and Our Ireland*, 1953, *Our Friend James Joyce* by Padraic and Mary Colum, 1959, and Constantine P. Curran's *Joyce Remembered*[1], 1968.

The acknowledged Irish Joycean mandarins, Niall Montgomery and 'Andrew Cass', have not found it worth their while to assemble their findings in book form. It would be comic if it were not disgraceful that Maurice Harmon has had to say recently: 'It is . . . significant that the two Irish contributors to this collection of essays take Joyce seriously, concerned as scholars everywhere are with the literary achievement, its modes, relationships and sources.'[2] Now, admittedly, there is a considerable quantity of shale in the Joycean academic machine. But on the native side there is also, I suggest, a burden of resentment that good American dollars, especially, should be lavished on a local who started off little better than many another middle class Irish boy, an education by the Jesuits and a B.A. from University College, Dublin as his equipment. My countrymen veer between extravagant praise and

---

[1] There are also Charles Duff's *James Joyce and the Plain Reader*, 1932, and L.A.G. Strong's *The Sacred River*, 1947.
[2] *The Celtic Master*, ed. Maurice Harmon, Dolmen Press, 1969, p. 7. This is the first scholarly book about Joyce to be published in Ireland.

snide depreciation of those of their fellows who have been successful by international standards. And a fair share of the depreciation goes to the intellectual and the artist.

In fairness, half-baked attitudes to Joyce and his monument more lasting than gall have diminished, and diminished rapidly, over the last fifteen to twenty years. In 1947, I recall, my lay schoolmaster in English at the Christian Brothers, an estimable man on many counts, spoke briefly of Joyce in hushed tones. I will never forget the sepulchral, monitory tone of his last words: 'He died blind.' One had to resist the impulse to chirp: 'So did Milton.' Book One of *Paradise Lost* was part of our curriculum.

Nineteen forty-seven, that was the year I first read *Ulysses* and what follows is an account of how it was possible for an Irish boy to become acquainted with and grow to love Joyce, before ever he had heard of Homeric parallels or had read even a paperback translation of the *Odyssey*. In some particulars my experience may have been singular but I believe that on the whole many of my generation (late 'twenties, early 'thirties), whether or not they had the good or ill fortune to take a university degree, followed comparable paths. For all my grateful acknowledgement of foreign scholarship I never read a book about Joyce, not even Herbert Gorman's biography, until I had graduated. As for Homeric Parallels and analogues, I knew nothing of them until I began my training as a university lecturer.

In the years immediately after puberty (1945-6) Joyce, for me, was only one of a stellar system waiting to be explored. But as a Dubliner and a Catholic, and disposed to literature, I was ready for him. At least for *Dubliners* and *Portrait*. Reading *Dubliners* at fifteen, Emerson's phrase about seeing our own thoughts reflected back in alienated majesty, which I had picked up somewhere like the jackdaw I was, came back to me. But it was not 'thoughts' that were reflected, but objects, details of living, the fabric of my life. A few examples will suffice to show how easily the book could find a slot in my mind. And perhaps, after all, the Dubliner in terms of sense-experience, and if exposed to Joyce at an early age, must have a *kind* of pleasure that can only be acquired by an imaginative extension on the part of foreigners (and to the true Dubliner, I am afraid the historic Pale is still in some measure a reality). For me, forty years after *Dubliners* was written, the idiom of my childhood sprang out on the page bright as fresh paint. In the first story 'The Sisters,' the narrator's uncle remarks of their lodger:

'Mr Cotter might take a pick of that leg of mutton now.'[1] I recognized immediately the language of shabby genteel euphemism. Like the narrator of 'An Encounter' I 'miched' (the Elizabethan word is still current as we move into the seventies), but it was not far from my own home and out of school-hours that I encountered a local tramp who talked to me of what I later learned to be perversion. And 'An Encounter' synthesized innumerable incidents in my school-life from eight onwards: for instance, the jovial Christian Brother who slapped the bottoms of little boys as they were changing into ducks for the Annual Drill Display at Iveagh Grounds. It has always been a source of wonder to me that children can retain their innocence so long in such matters.

'Two Gallants' came alive for me because one of the heroes pretended he had worked in Pim's, a now extinct emporium, and for years I had gone there with my mother or aunt to see Santa Claus and receive from him a bauble costing one shilling. I could still pass it every day on my way down town and reflect, 'That's where Corley chose to have been employed.' Pim's was regarded as a very respectable firm, and that is why Corley picked it to deceive the poor 'slavey' (the term is virtually gone now, but in 1945 was still quite common) from Baggot Street. And Joyce's 'gay Lothario' used to go with 'girls off the South Circular Road.' This was the territory of all my schooldays, from five to eighteen, when all of Joyce except *Finnegans Wake* (but for fragments) would have become part of my mind. The poetry of urban street names Joyce taught me: Nassau Street where I tried to buy and sell second-hand school-books; Kildare Street where I was mortified in the National Library when the Assistant Librarian, these days a Professor in the Institute of Higher Studies, looked me up and down disdainfully and refused to issue me a Reader's Ticket; Hume Street where a mysterious body known as 'The Department' functioned, and had final control of our destinies. Stephen's Green, Grafton Street, Rutland Square, Capel Street, Dame Street, Westmoreland Street: they were all in 'Two Gallants', and surely no normal boy could fail to be electrified at finding his own city, the setting of his works and days, enshrined in a book peopled by familiar persons speaking in a familiar idiom.

But if the topography of *Dubliners* was mine so also were the forms of its dialogue, whether direct or reported, and, of course, its peculiar phraseology. It took a Vatican Council to eliminate from Dublin speech

[1] *Dubliners*, Modern Library, 1954, p. 9

that popular institution known as 'the short twelve'. In 'The Boarding House' Mrs Mooney intends to catch this convenient Mass at Marlborough Street the Sunday morning she decides to have it out with Mr Doran. I have not, that I recall, seen any reference in the Joyce critical literature pointing to Mrs Mooney's exemplary Sunday morning: half an hour spent in settling the destiny of her daughter and Mr Doran, and twenty minutes of mandatory worship. In 'Clay' I found infinite poignancy in one particular fragment of indirect speech. Maria the laundress is duped while blindfolded into putting her finger into a saucer of clay. 'There was a pause for a few seconds; and then a great deal of scuffling and whispering. Somebody said something about the garden, and at last Mrs Donnelly said something very cross to one of the next door girls and told her to throw it out at once: that was no play.' In the speech of my childhood the word 'angry' was never used, it was always 'cross'. And every phrase at that Christmas party given by Aunt Julia and Aunt Kate, which was to lead to the anguish of Gabrial Conroy, had the authenticity not only of brilliantly selected speech but of *heard* speech. This, of course, is not really surprising when I realize that Joyce had died only four years before this year 1945, and the idiom of Dublin is tenacious, though fading fast. It should be remembered, of course, that the idiom of 'The Dead' is itself a sub-species: the idiom of gentility, of a class that in Joyce's time was still vigorous and even in my own. Consider this summation of the mode of life of the Miss Morkans and their niece Mary Jane: 'Though their life was modest, they believed in eating well; the best of everything; diamond-bone sirloins, three-shilling tea and the best bottled stout.' How exquisitely Joyce indicates the line between frugality and luxury. Balanced quality-buying is here more than a token of good housekeeping. It is a banner of class. So long as they can afford three-shilling tea, the Misses Morkan can claim their status.

But, of course, it was years later before I learnt the true greatness of 'The Dead.' The story that made most impact on me was 'Ivy Day in the Committee Room.' The extraordinary fact is that I managed to get through ten years of schooling without ever hearing the name of Parnell. (Even more surprising is the fact that my teachers gave up teaching Irish history altogether after the age of twelve.) Anyway, I first learnt of the reality of that monument by Gaudens at the end of O'Connell Street from Joyce's chancers and codgers drooling over a dozen of stout sent in from the 'Black Eagle.' It was many years later that I read the words Joyce wrote about Parnell in the Triestine paper *Il Piccolo della Sera*.

In his final desperate appeal to his countrymen, he begged them not to throw him as a sop to the English wolves howling around them. It redounds to their honour that they did not fail this appeal. They did not throw him to the English wolves; they tore him to pieces themselves.[1]

Nor had I read, at that time, Yeats' *Last Poems* (1939). 'Ivy Day', however, had done the job: at fifteen Parnell was, for me, the very type in Irish politics of the tragic hero. The Chief, as he was known to the cronies of John Aloysius Joyce and their contemporaries, came before, and for long overshadowed, the signatories of the document proclaiming the Irish Republic, and Sir Roger Casement.

By Holy Week of 1946 I was reading *A Portrait of the Artist as a Young Man* for the second time. I will always associate it with the elaborate and dirgeful ceremonies of Holy Week. Three great sections of the book struck immediate and plangent chords, and indeed they form almost the whole of it.

My pre-university education was wholly given by the Christian Brothers (Joyce had them for a few months when the cupboard was bare)[2] while Joyce had the Jesuits at Clongowes and Belvedere. None the less I could identify. The education provided by the Christian Brothers had, by my time, reached an unquestionably high level. I would even say that little nuggets of Jesuitical lore had found their way into the Brothers' classrooms. For instance, somewhere along the line I had picked up the solemn pronouncement overheard by Stephen in his last year at Belvedere: 'I believe that Lord Macaulay was a man who probably never committed a mortal sin in his life, that is to say, a deliberate mortal sin.'[3] It may well be that one of my teachers had actually read *A Portrait* but even the youngest of the Brothers, good souls with a taste for the 'leather', did not appear to have progressed beyond the Chesterbelloc. (This, of course, was over twenty years ago.)

What I may call the school identification went further of course. Stephen's Retreat Sermon is still, I know, the common experience of

[1] *The Critical Writings of James Joyce,* ed. Ellsworth Mason and Richard Ellmann. New York. 1964, p. 228
[2] Richard Ellmann, *James Joyce,* New York, 1959, p. 35
[3] *A Portrait of the Artist as a Young Man.* New York: The Viking Press, 1964

Irish Catholic schoolboys, perhaps even schoolgirls. 'Hell lay about them in their infancy,' wrote Graham Greene of his classmates, in sombre parody of Wordsworth.[1] What Stephen heard, my fellows and I heard, not only at Retreats, but in the daily half-hour of what purported to be 'religious instruction.' I have it on unimpeachable evidence that as recently as the early sixties the baroque types of Joyce's sermon were in use in one of the most progressive of the Christian Brothers' schools. As my informant put it, 'the time-span of Hell measured in terms of the sands of the desert and the drops of the ocean'.

A second section I was prepared for was, of course, the 'Christmas' dinner scene where the *passio* of Parnell is re-enacted. And when the next year I finally came to *Ulysses,* what I was later to know as the 'Hades' episode was to pivot about the Parnell exchange between Hynes and Mr Power.[2]

At sixteen, I never dreamed that two years later I would be entering University College, Dublin, the lineal descendant of Joyce's Jesuit-run University College, nor that I would spend much time in the rooms where Joyce had been lectured, now known as Newman House and the students' recreation centre. None the less, I followed closely in *A Portrait* the moves of Stephen and Cranly and Davin and the others because I knew the outside of the building and had envied these seemingly carefree students as they came down the steps, scarves flying in the wind. As it happened, I was not to see them on the steps of the National Library until I became a student myself, for that Assistant Librarian had made it for me a place of shame.

In point of direct influence, the ruminations and conversations of Stephen bore odd fruit for me. It will be recalled that in his interchange with the Dean, an English convert, he reflects:

The language in which we are speaking is his before it is mine. How different are the words *home, Christ, ale, master,* on his lips and mine! I cannot speak or write these words with unrest of spirit. His language, so familiar and so foreign, will always be, for me, an acquired speech . . . [3]

Later Stephen explicitly rejects the Irish language. Now whether I felt about English what Stephen felt, *before* I read *A Portrait,* is not relevant. The fact is that Joyce planted in me his particular kind of

---

[1] *The Lawless Roads,* Penguin Edition, 1947, p. 10
[2] *Ulysses,* Bodley Head Edition, 4th Impression, 1964, pp. 142–143
[3] Ed. cit., p. 189

'unrest of spirit.' And I began to read Irish outside my school curriculum and I owe it, in fact, to Stephen that I can read modern Irish with genuine pleasure, and when necessary speak and write it with moderate proficiency. I often wonder whether this experience of mine through Joyce has been uncommon.

Foiled by the Assistant Librarian of the National Library, my extra-mural education continued weekly at the tea-table of Lady Longford, who lived around the corner from me at 123 Leinster Road.[1] It was she who lent me *Ulysses* at the beginning of my last year at school. I began it in a quite preposterously romantic setting. A friend's parents had taken a farmhouse in Woodenbridge, County Wicklow, for the month of September. My friend, Donal O'Farrell, invited myself and two others, one of them the painter, Patrick Swift – who now lives in the Algarve, but was then twenty and a clerk in the Dublin Gas Company – to camp in the garden of the farmhouse. I came armed with Christine's *Ulysses* and a little book of translations from Lorca by J. H. Gili and Stephen Spender. Swift, who was to influence me until our ways parted and I went to the university, had already familiarized himself with extracts from *Finnegans Wake* and had worked up an uncanny rendition of Joyce's own recording of the last pages of Part II. If anything, I found his recital more moving than Joyce's when, at the drop of a hat, he would begin, in a high, clear voice, and an accent which though like Joyce's was also reminiscent of Shaw's: 'Ah, but she was the queer old skeowsha anyhow, Anna Livia trinkettoes.'[2] He had also by heart the last pages of the novel, and I too committed them to memory one time, but I have not read them aloud since asked to do so by one of my lecturers in English, for his own pleasure and that of the Professor of Greek. That was twenty years ago and little did I know then that the same lecturer would, many years later, become my implacable enemy. For I know little of 'their little warm tricks' and 'their mean cosy turns'.[3]

But to return to *Ulysses*. By the light of oil lamps, and sitting about a great deal table, we pored over the precious text. We all knew the Tower, of course, and we had all walked along Sandymount Strand. We knew beforehand also that 'stately, plump Buck Mulligan' was derived from

---

1 Since the death of her husband, the Earl of Longford, in 1961, Christine, Countess of Longford. Their home has been razed by building speculators.
2 *Finnegans Wake*, Faber, 3rd Ed., 1964, p. 215
3 *Finnegans Wake*, Faber, 3rd Ed., 1964, p. 627

Oliver St John Gogarty, whose delicate neo-classical and neo-Eliza-
bethan lyrics we cherished, and I certainly still do. I can recall being
shocked by Mulligan's parody of the Mass, but unlike some of my
elders, I was sensible enough to recognize that the blasphemy was
Mulligan's, not Stephen's, and that Joyce was the tenacious recorder.
What came home to the heart most is the section I was to learn years
later to call 'Telemachus.' Stephen's bitter comment on Mulligan's
shaving-mirror: 'It is a symbol of Irish art. The cracked looking-glass
of a servant.'[1] Mulligan's recalled comment, *O, it's only Dedalus whose
mother is beastly dead;*[2] and above all that extraordinary interchange
between Haines and Stephen:

> I am the servant of two masters, Stephen said, an English and an
> Italian.
> Italian? Haines said.
> A crazy queen, old and jealous, kneel down before me. And a third,
> Stephen said, there is who wants me for odd jobs.
> Italian? Haines said again. What do you mean?
> The Imperial British state, Stephen answered, his colour rising, and
> the Holy Roman Catholic and apostolic Church.[3]

The 'third' is the 'crazy queen, old and jealous'.

Commentators have not noted the abnormal emotiveness of that
description of Ireland, for the Irish at least. I have indicated that
Stephen's attitude drove me to rather than from the Irish language. At
this stage, I saw more than Yeats's Cathleen Ni Houlihan behind the
image of the 'crazed queen.' I was aware of a thousand years of Gaelic
literature and all its innumerable personifications of Ireland. At this
time I was reading the Irish Texts Society's edition of Aogán ó Rathaille
and, of course, at school we were inundated with Gaelic Jacobite verse.
I knew the dark centuries' dream of a queen rescued by the Stuarts or
by the progeny of the exiled Earls of Ulster. Joyce, of course, knew
Mangan's 'Dark Rosaleen',[4] and must have been aware of the long
tradition of Ireland personified by her poets as a queenly beauty. Did
he know the ninth century poem 'The Hag of Beare?' Whatever, his

---

[1] *Ulysses*, Bodley Head, New Edition, 1960, p. 6
[2] Ibid, p. 8. Robert Martin Adams has pointed out that the epigram is based
on one of Wilde's in *The Delay of Lying*. See *Surface and Symbol*, New York,
1967, p. 124
[3] Ibid, p. 24
[4] See C. P. Curran, *James Joyce Remembered*, 1968, pp. 14–17

'crazed queen' cut to the bone. It must be realized that my generation came to puberty in a neutral Ireland. At seventeen I had already seen the bomb sites of London. I had known guilt over neutrality, since the Brothers had failed to infect me with their singularly unpoetic brand of Nationalism.

Donal O'Farrell slept in the farmhouse that week-end. We others adjourned to a tent in the garden and read by torchlight from *Ulysses*. I have mentioned the Gili-Spender volume of Lorca. We read from that also. And one of those nights I pondered bitterly Buck Mulligan's contemptuous 'snotgreen sea' and the 'green' of Lorca. 'Green, how much I want you green.'

The imaginative engulfment of *Ulysses* had been well and truly initiated. When we got back to Dublin, Swift and I finished the book in a few weeks. It did not strike us that it was a very difficult book. We knew and recognized the kind of superstitious anti-Semitism evinced by Mr Deasy in 'Nestor'. And we knew the poor Jews of Dublin who lived on the South Circular Road. Coming from school during Yom Kippur, I would be accosted by poorly dressed Orthodox Jews who would offer me a penny or maybe even a threepenny bit to light their fire or their gas-stove.

We knew intimately the setting of 'Proteus'. As for 'A hater of his kind . . . his mane foaming in the moon, his eyeballs stars'; one had lived all one's life less than a mile from St Patrick's Cathedral and the imminence of Swift was in all that area.

It would require a much weightier essay than this to itemize the points of contact between my experience and the experience of *Ulysses*. But there are some responses I would single out. The kind of jumbled and pinchbeck erudition possessed by Leopold Bloom was not unlike that we ourselves possessed as schoolboys. A reflection such as Bloom's on the woman outside the Grosvenor Hotel, 'The honourable Mrs and Brutus is an honourable man,' struck home immediately, for *Julius Caesar* was one of the first Shakespeare plays we read on entering secondary school. Though we knew little or nothing of the Victorian theatre in Dublin, at school we had sung 'The Croppy Boy' and got the effect of Martin Cunningham's 'pompous' comment on Ben Dollard's singing of the ballad. We knew the funeral trains and the funereal gossip of Glasnevin and Mount Jerome, for members of our families lay in those cemeteries. For me one passage in 'Hades' had a peculiar poignancy. 'A tiny coffin flashed by. "Sad", Martin Cunningham said.

A Bash in the Tunnel

"A child." " Poor little thing," Mr Dedalus said. "It's well out of it." '
At four or five, I had overheard my mother speak of an infant sister:
'Yes. Baptized and buried in Mount Jerome.'
'Aeolus' and 'The Lestrygonians' were plain sailing, and also a
revelation. We found that we were living in a work of art. The familiar
treat of Lemon's Sweets, even, was now a detail in the vast tapestry.
We followed Bloom up Grafton Street[1] and knew nothing of the vast
research machine that was cranking into action. Yeates and Son, and
Brown Thomas, were and are still there, and Combridge's the book-
sellers, but by then Davy Byrne's 'Moral Pub' in Duke Street had
changed character completely. And we were with him when he led the
'blind stripling' across Dawson Street to Molesworth Street, and when
he turned into Kildare Street and then turned into the Museum to
avoid Blazes Boylan. For reasons I have given, I did not follow him
into the Library. O! If I had known that the episode in the Library had
been described as 'Scylla and Charybdis'! But I did fancy that I had
been humiliated a year or so previously in the very room where Stephen
is closeted with A.E., John Eglinton and the Librarian, T. W. Lyster.[2]
But 'Scylla and Charybdis' is an education in itself for a boy of seventeen: Goethe, Milton, Shakespeare, Ben Jonson, Shelley, Aristotle,
Plato, Hyde's Lovesongs of Connacht, Mallarmé, the minor Elizabethan
Robert Greene, Villiers de l'Isle Adam,[3] Padraic Colum, James Starkey
('Seamus O'Sullivan'), George Moore, Edward Martyn, George
Sigerson, James Stephens, Brunetto Latini, Drummond of Haw-
thornden, Ernest Renan, Sir Philip Sidney, Coleridge, Boccaccio,
Meredith, Dumas père et fils, Maeterlinck, Oscar Wilde, not to mention
Professors Georg Brandes, Sidney Lee, Edward Dowden and Mes-
dames Marie Corelli and Helena Blavatsky. Of all those then living, I
was to meet only Seamus O'Sullivan, who quoted Verlaine to me when
I proclaimed the greatness of Patrick Kavanagh, and later Padraic
Colum. And one other. 'George Roberts is doing the commercial part.'
This was the Roberts of Maunsel and Roberts, whom Joyce was to re-

---

[1] Harry Blamires, The Bloomsday Book, 1966, p. 69, makes the curious error
of writing 'He wanders down Grafton Street.'
[2] Lyster died in 1922, the year of Ulysses
[3] I read Axel the following summer in H. P. R. Finberg's translation. The copy
was lent to me by a lady who claimed to have been an intimate of Gogarty. I
learned years later that Christine Longford had met her husband in H. P. R.
Finberg's rooms at Oxford. So the wheel had come full circle to a point years
before my birth.

144

gard as his enemy, and lampoon in 'The Holy Office'. When I met Roberts in London in December 1948, he looked like a leprechaun, tiny, rubicund, white-whiskered and bearded. He was more than kind to me and although he spoke with reverence of A.E., who published him in *New Songs*, the volume discussed in 'Scylla and Charybdis,' he would never speak of Joyce.

I must jump ahead to 'Circe,' the episode in *Ulysses* furthest removed from my experience, except in so far as Dublin was, and still is, a city of picturesque and foul-mouthed speech. As one who might be described then, superficially at any rate, as a devout Catholic, 'Circe,' of course, shocked me. It also left in me a profound sense of the piteousness of unsatisfied sexual desire. When the Bawd in 'nighttown' spits after Stephen and Lynch, 'Trinity medicals. Fallopian tube. All prick and no pence', I was less shocked by the moral squalor of commercial sex than by the fact that people have to seek it out. Strangely I was moved too by the wrangle between Stephen and the two English private soldiers, Compton the *provocateur* and Carr the poor, dumb ox with his blind loyalty to Edward VII: 'I'll wring the neck of any fucking bastard says a word against my bleeding fucking king.' For all Carr's bravado and brutality, he has pathos when faced with the cocksure Dedalus. Stephen is struck down but does he not deserve it?

After the nightmare of 'Circe,' Part III of *Ulysses* was easy going, except, very naturally I think for someone without academic assistance, the catechetical interrogation of the second last episode 'Ithaca'. And what of Molly Bloom's soliloquy? So far as I was concerned for exact literal meaning one needed only the addition of punctuation and some conjunctions. I was less dazzled by its technical virtuosity than by its gross and poignant poetry. I cannot recall the approximate date of my first acquaintance with Yeats's *Last Poems* (1939). But for me Molly's soliloquy was epitomized in Yeats's phrase 'the foul rag and bone shop of the heart.'[1] Molly is often 'foul', her reflections are miscellaneous junk, but 'the heart' was there as surely as in *Hamlet* or the Odes or Keats. And I had to begin to read Villon after D. B. Wyndham Lewis's biography had impressed me.[2] Poor Molly's fantasies could not shock me with *La Belle Heaulmière* in mind. If anything, I was most moved by the singular sweetness of Molly's novelettish notions of high Romance. I failed to understand how a great prose poem could be disedifying.

---

[1] 'The Circus Animals' Desertion', *Collected Poems*, 1961, p. 392
[2] *Francois Villon*, 1945

I will leave *Ulysses* there and my garnerings of how it affected me twenty-two years ago. About 1949 Patrick Kavanagh told me he had read *Ulysses* twenty times. I disbelieved him. But I will give him the third last word; he is writing about 'that readjusting of one's values which is common in regard to one's enthusiasms.' He says: 'It often happens in the case of a person with whom we were in love.' The second last word to Graham Greene on discovering *Ulysses* in 1923: it was *comme une bible et aussi riche que elle.*[1] And the last word to P. S. O'Hegarty:

> Ireland is all through him and in him and of him; and Dublin, its streets and its buildings and its people, he loves with the whole-hearted affection of the artist . . . He may live out of Dublin, but he will never get away from it.

---

[1] *Le Figaro Litteraire*, 2 Mai 1959 (Interview with Georges Adam)

Father Conmee and his Associates

Eoin O'Mahony

Clongowes (1814) – *Tullabeg* (1818) – *Belvedere* (1841)

After forty years' seclusion in Russia, the Jesuit Order was universally restored by Pius VII on 7th August, 1814, and the Irish Jesuits purchased Castle Browne, or Clongowes Wood, Co. Kildare, from the Wogan-Browne family, whose ghosts still haunt the school in a friendly way. It was one of the old Castles of the Pale which had guarded the Anglo-Normans – ancestors of the Joyces – against the native O'Tooles and O'Byrnes. With the blessing and active advice of Daniel O'Connell, the college was established twenty miles from the capital as an academy for the sons of the landed gentry, professional and mercantile classes. There was nothing quite like it for Catholic higher education. Carlow College, the oldest Catholic residential school in Ireland, was nearer to the ideal of a seminary. Maynooth, founded in 1795 by a British Government, fearful of the consequences of the French Revolution on the education of Irish priests in France, concerned itself almost exclusively with clerical education. In the nineteenth century Clongowes produced the polyglot and poet Rev. Francis Sylvester Mahony ('Father Prout') (1804–66); The O'Gorman Mahon, M.P. (1800–91); Thomas Francis Meagher (1804–66), Deputy Governor of Montana; and the great jurist, Christopher Palles (1831–1920), Lord Chief Baron of the Exchequer for over forty years. Statesmen included John Edward Redmond (1856–1918), the Chairman of the Irish Parliamentary Party; his brother, Major William H. K. Redmond, M.P. (1861–1917); and John's son, Captain William Redmond, D.S.O., M.P., and Member of Dail Eireann. In our own century the tradition of public service was nobly maintained by Kevin Christopher O'Higgins, first Vice-President and Minister for Justice in the Irish Free State Cabinet

(1892–1927), assassinated in 1927. Count Henry Russell and his brother mapped the Pyrenees. Three Clongowians who shone in literature were also educated in Belvedere, the Dublin day school which the Jesuits founded in 1841. These were, in chronological order, Conal Holmes O'Riordan (F. Norreys Connell), Director of the Abbey Theatre after Synge's death, Oliver Gogarty and James Joyce. Until 1886, when there was a major alteration of policy, the school was largely for the sons of comfortable country gentlemen, who vegetated on their farms and contributed nothing to literature or the arts.

Within a few years of the founding of Clongowes, the Jesuits purchased Rahan, or Tullabeg, near Tullamore in the King's County, now Offaly, from a wealthy family of Athlone woollen manufacturers of landed background, thus excluding from the succession Florimond Comte de Basterot (grandson of the French general and statesman Comte de la Tour Maubourg), friend of Edward Martyn, Yeats and Lady Gregory. It was at his house, now a youth hostel, at Kinvara, Co. Galway, that Yeats and Lady Gregory planned the Abbey Theatre, after lunch, on a wet September afternoon in 1897.

The two schools led parallel and undistinguished lives, and were hardly moved by the struggle for higher Catholic education which came to a head when Sir Robert Peel founded the 'godless' Queen's University and its three Constituent Colleges of Belfast, Cork and Galway in 1845. These were condemned by the Irish bishops by only one vote, and by the failing Daniel O'Connell; but they were supported enthusiastically by Thomas Davis, his patriotic newspaper the *Nation*, and the Young Irelanders, nearly all of whom were graduates of Trinity College.

The Irish bishops' reply to the Queen's Colleges was to ask John Henry Newman to found a Catholic University (1851). With the exception of his Professor of Theology, Father O'Reilly, Newman got no help from the Jesuits, whose policy then was rather to flood Trinity College, and this aloofness continued for nearly thirty years, until the Irish Hierarchy handed over the Catholic University to the Irish Jesuits in 1882, when they changed its name to University College Dublin. Newman's most famous alumni were Captain William Henry O'Shea, M.P., first husband of Mrs Charles Stuart Parnell, who was also on the books of T.C.D., and the Irish-American patriot, John Devoy.

With the Jesuits and the bishops still sulking in their tents, it remained for a Jesuit (who had not been educated by the Jesuits) to cut the Gordian knot. William Delany (1835–1924) was educated at Carlow College, and studied theology at Maynooth. At twenty-one he entered the Jesuits at St Acheul, near Amiens, and completed his theology at Rome. He served as chaplain to the Irish Zouaves in the Pope's fight against Garibaldi, and returned to Ireland.

His ten-year rectorship of Tullabeg is an epoch in the history of Irish Catholic higher education. To compete at games on equal terms with the English and Irish Anglican public schools and older universities he widened the Grand Canal at Tullabeg for rowing, and brought Father Wishtoff from Germany to lay down, with German thoroughness, the finest cricket crease in Ireland. He trained his pupils like greyhounds for the public examinations of London University. It was said that Delany got more out of a man than was in him, and got it without asking. He was convinced that the time had come to let people know that the work done in Irish schools was as good as the best elsewhere, and he 'steered the ship boldly into the waters of English competitive examinations' with the active support of Parnell and the Irish Parliamentary Party. Unfortunately, the Irish Catholic leaders quarrelled foolishly with Gladstone over his Irish Education Bill of 1874, and defeated him, largely by abstentions, a circumstance which finally led him to ignore the Catholic landed gentry, the Whiggish clergy and the Liberal, Whig and Catholic commercial and professional classes, and to trust the peasantry, all of which had momentous consequences as evidenced by his Land Acts, and his conversion to Home Rule in 1886. John Stanislaus Joyce's patron, Dr Spencer Lyons, M.P., was just such a Catholic Whig as Parnell and Gladstone were glad to see depart from public life in the General Election of 1885.

With the active co-operation of the Vicereine the Duchess of Marlborough, Sir Winston Churchill's able grandmother, the Jesuits and Father Delany had a big say in drafting Disraeli's Intermediate Education Act of 1878, and the Bill which set up the examining body known as the Royal University in 1879, all of which had been conceded by Gladstone five years before. The Royal University gave the Catholic schools a chance to prepare pupils, by private study, for the higher posts in the Home and Indian Civil Service, and there were generous funds for secondary schools of all denominations. When the Irish bishops handed over Newman's Catholic University at 86 Stephen's Green in 1882, to co-operate with the new Royal University, Father Delany became vice-rector. In 1883 he became rector, a post he held for a quarter of a century, until the establishment of the National University in 1909. His work by voice and pen for the establishment of that university cannot be sufficiently appreciated today. He was President of University College during all four of James Joyce's years at the college (1898–1902) and naturally they quarrelled. The Jesuits honoured him by making him Provincial of the Order from 1909 to 1912.

William Delany had set his mark on Irish higher education, but the price for Tullabeg, the Jesuits and Clongowes was a high one. To compete on equal terms with the best Protestant schools and older universities in England and Ireland, the college had gone into debt. Now it was the Newfoundland-born friend of the Joyce family, Father Thomas P. Brown (1845–1915), not Father Delany, who had to solve the problem. Like Delany, he was educated at Carlow College, and studied at Jesuit houses in Paris, Roehampton, Stonyhurst, Innsbruck and St Bueno's College, St Asaph, North Wales. He taught for a year at Tullabeg under Delany, and was ordained in 1880. He served as Provincial from May 1883 to February 1888, and was Minister at Clongowes when James Joyce arrived at the school in September 1888. Father Brown is responsible, as Provincial, for the decision, arrived at in 1886, to close Tullabeg, and saddle Clongowes with all the debts incurred by Father Delany in the service of higher Catholic education. Clongowes was paying off the debt until 1922. Father Brown is described as 'big in stature, big in heart and sympathy, big in ideas and of unflinching fortitude'. In 1889, at the end of James Joyce's first year in Clongowes, Father Brown left for Australia, where he survived for twenty-six years, being successfully Rector of Xavier College, Kew, Melbourne, and Superior of the Irish Jesuit Mission in Australia from 1908 to 1913.

Apart from Father William Henry, Rector of Belvedere from 1894, and Joyce's Clongowes master in elements, and choir master in Clongowes, Father William Power, the biggest influence on James Joyce in Clongowes and Belvedere was his mother's family friend and possible kinsman Father John Conmee of Kingsland, Athlone (1847–1910), who was at school in Clongowes from 1863 to 1867, Prefect of Studies there from 1883 to 1887, and Rector from 1885 to 1891, a rare combination of offices in a Jesuit house. Conmee studied rhetoric at Roehampton, philosophy at Stonyhurst and theology at St Bueno's College, St Asaph. He taught for five years under Father Delany's brilliant rectorship at

Tullabeg, where he had much to do with the formal education of the students, who competed in the London University examinations for the first time in Ireland, and obtained important posts in the Indian and Home Civil Service. The outstanding Indian Civil Servant whom Tullabeg produced was Sir Michael Francis O'Dwyer, K.C.S.I., G.C.I.E., Balliol College, Oxford, Lieutenant Governor of the Punjab, 1913-19, born 1864, assassinated 1940. Tullabeg was also responsible for the great soldier, writer and Irish patriot, Lieutenant General Sir William Francis Butler (1838-1910).

Teachers complained that the boys devoted too much time to Mr Conmee's studies, and that the balance of power was thus disturbed. The school plays produced at Tullabeg and Clongowes became famous, and for these he poured out topical prologues and epilogues. It was said that if W. S. Gilbert were to die, his work could still be carried on by John Conmee. He ran the school debates on parliamentary lines and had the debating hall ringing with questions that made the boys think, and consequently read, carefully, and talk well. He encouraged the musicians by taking an instrument in the college orchestra.

Prefect of Studies at Clongowes in 1883-87, and rector from 1885 to 1891, it was Father Conmee who was given the heavy task of carrying out the amalgamation of Clongowes and Tullabeg as planned by Father Brown in 1886. The decision to merge the schools was a serious one. The difficulties in the way of a successful fusion of the two sets of boys were many. The Tullabeg boys had been trained like greyhounds for the London University Examinations with a view to high office in the Home and Indian administrations. The Clongowes boys were intellectually lazy. Father Conmee, assisted by his new Prefect of Studies, Father James Daly (1847-1930) – the Father Dolan of the *Portrait* – decided to change all that.

'As for the pedagogical part, the shortest rule would be, consult the Jesuits; for nothing better has been put in practice.' Thus Lord Chancellor Bacon on the old Jesuit system of education, the Ratio Studiorum, a curriculum predominantly humanistic and philosophical in content, which had been carefully developed over a period of two hundred years, and was now to be sacrificed on the altar of Irish Intermediate Education.

Born at Daly's Grove, Co. Galway, James Daly was educated with the Jesuits in Belgium and at Tullabeg. Two of his brothers were also Jesuits. He studied rhetoric at Roehampton, philosophy at Stonyhurst and taught at Clongowes for five years under Father Delany (1868-74).

From 1879 to 1883 he taught at the Crescent College, Limerick, where he remained as Prefect of Studies for three years. Then began his devoted but misguided career of preparing boys for the public examinations, which became too much associated with cramming and which threw overboard overnight the old Jesuit system. Richard Ellmann is in error in stating that James Daly was low-bred.[1] If there is anything in blood, breeding or a pedigree, the Dalys of Daly's Grove had it. But that did not prevent James Daly from being more than eccentric. He came to Clongowes as Prefect of Studies in 1887 and directed the cramming operations for thirty most successful years. It is a great tribute to Clongownians that the school survived. His abiding service to the school is that he made the boys work hard at their books, a habit hitherto confined to Tullabeg. Clongowes rapidly came to the front in the Intermediate Examinations, and has ever since maintained an honoured place in a system which has been condemned by Patrick Pearse as the 'Murder Machine'.

John Conmee had a great love for 'things softened and beautified by the hand of time, especially mediaeval times and tales'. Of Continental cities he loves Assisi and Prague best. His Catholic Truth Society pamphlet 'Old Times in the Barony,' which deals with his native Athlone, is well known and long overdue for reprinting. The most fortunate thing for James Joyce's academic career was that Father Conmee was transferred from Clongowes to Belvedere in 1891, and remained there as Prefect of Studies barely long enough to induce the impecunious John Stanislaus Joyce to remove James from Clongowes and send him to Belvedere in April 1893, along with his brother Stanislaus. If not a blood relation, he seems to have known Joyce's mother's family in the Athlone-Mullingar area of Co. Westmeath. As Rector of Clongowes he had Joyce under him for three years, from 1888 to 1891. He would have been aware of the boy's ability, and of his father's increasing irregularity in the payment of school fees. It can safely be said that it was John Conmee who induced John Stanislaus Joyce to transfer his son from Clongowes to Belvedere, where he remained for five years from April 1893 to June 1898, distinguishing himself all along the line in the Preparatory, Junior, Middle, and Senior Grade examinations of the Irish State Board of Intermediate Education.

---

[1] See *Burke's Landed Gentry (Ireland)*, 1899, 1904, 1912, 1958, sub tit, and *Daly of Castle Daly and Daly's Grove*.

On ceasing to be Prefect of Studies at Belvedere in 1892, John Conmee remained at the school for another year, when he taught Latin and directed the School Sodality. From 1893 to 1895 he acted as Prefect of Studies at Newman's old university at 86 Stephen's Green. In 1895 he was transferred to the then Jesuit Headquarters in Ireland, St Francis Xavier's, Upper Gardiner Street, Dublin, then the residence of the Provincial, and only round the corner from Belvedere. He served as rector of this house for ten years, from 1895 to 1905. In 1905 he was appointed Provincial of his Order and held office for four years when he was succeeded by his old friend and Tullabeg colleague, William Delany. He died in a Leeson Street Convent Nursing Home in May 1910. John Conmee administered the Last Rites to Mrs Dillon, wife of the Irish Leader, John Dillon, M.P., in May 1907.

It is still a matter of dispute as to who preached the famous Retreat Sermon of the *Portrait*. Professor Kevin Sullivan in *Joyce Among the Jesuits* identifies the preacher with Father James A. Cullen, who was technically on the staff at Belvedere, but who never taught in the school. He was Editor of the *Messenger of the Sacred Heart*, Director of the League of the Apostleship of Prayer, and founder and head of the Pioneer Total Abstinence Association, all religious and pious organizations radiating throughout Ireland from their Belvedere headquarters. On the same page Professor Sullivan also suggests that the Director of the Retreat may have been Joyce's former Clongowes teacher, Father William Power – Father Arnall of the *Portrait*. If this be so, Father Power may have been an even bigger influence in Joyce's life than has hitherto been suggested. Father Power's seven-year absence in Australia (1889–96) would seem to exclude him as the giver of the Retreat.

There is, however, a strong case for Joyce's Belvedere rector, friend and Latin teacher, Father William Henry, who came as rector in 1894. Herbert Gorman in *James Joyce*, page 43, suggests that he was 'a fanatical Roman Catholic convert who wore whiskers'. He was born a Catholic of strong Unionist politics from Draperstown, Co. Derry, and was brother of the First Lord Chief Justice of Northern Ireland, the Right Hon. Sir Denis Stanislaus Henry, Baronet. Both brothers were educated by the English Jesuits at Mount St Mary's College, Chesterfield, near Derby. There is a well-founded tradition among the Irish Jesuits that, having read the Retreat Sermon in *Portrait*, Joyce's old friend and teacher said that it was a very fair paraphrase of one of his sermons. If the preacher was Father William Power, the association between the two began in the class of elements, the lowest class in Clongowes and in all the old Jesuit schools, in September 1888.

William F. Power (1848–1931) was born at Ardee, Co. Louth, but had some unexplained connection with Kilmacthomas, Co. Waterford, where the Norman names de la Poer, le Poher and Power are indigenous. He was educated, apparently, at Tullabeg and Clongowes, studied at St Acheul, near Amiens (like William Delany), and at Louvain, and taught English in a Jesuit house in Antwerp. He taught in Clongowes and Tullabeg. Ordained in 1881, he completed his theology at Jersey, in the Channel Isles, taught for the next four years at Tullabeg, Belvedere and Galway, and completed his tertianship, or third year after ordination, at Tronchiennes, in Belgium. From 1887 to 1889 he taught in the two lowest classes in Clongowes, rudiments and elements, and was choir master. After two years' association with James Joyce in choir and class, Power was sent to Australia, then part of the Irish Jesuit Province, where he remained for seven years, returning to Clongowes as choir master for four years, from 1896 to 1900. From 1900 to 1915 he lived at Tullabeg, the Novitiate of the Order (1886–1930). From 1915 to 1917 he taught at a Jesuit house in Malta, and in the latter year he returned to Tullabeg where he remained for fourteen years, until his death in 1931. A younger Jesuit who knew him in his last years at Tullabeg, when he was a very old man, says that he had done brilliantly in his ecclesiastical studies, and was a Scripture scholar, with special knowledge of the Psalms. 'In addition to his perfect command of French, he was also a musician of parts, violin and piano, and, I believe, wrote some music. He was known to have spent much of his time composing verse, most of which has been lost. One small book has survived. It is *The King's Bell, and Other Verses*, published in Belgium in 1910 by Zech and Son, Braine le Comte. He seems to have been a very indifferent teacher, in spite of his learning and wide reading. While his intellectual ability was unquestioned, he seemed to lack any very practical bent. He was a happy bookworm, with little interest in the outside world.'

The fact that Father Power was in charge of the two lowest classes in the school is a tribute to his ability to deal with little boys. Usually, in Jesuit schools, those lowest classes are put in charge of one patient master who devotes all his time to the one class, instead of moving from one class to another as a specialist. In his classes at Tullabeg and Clongowes he stimulated the interest of the boys in their work by dividing the class into two rival camps of Romans and Carthaginians, 'pitting one against the other, and awarding or deducting marks according as lessons were known or missed'. There was keen rivalry between the camps, and each side watched for a mistake, with consequent loss of marks. 'What angry looks greeted him who, by a mistake in gender or declension or conjugation, risked the loss to his side of the much-coveted tin of biscuits.'

When in Father Power's class of elements in 1888-9, James Joyce must almost certainly have been a member of Father Power's Army which made forced marches across the fields and through the surrounding country. There is a photograph of that army in an early number of the *School Annual,* drawn up in double line, with wooden musket, bandolier and forage cap, 'standing beside the Colonel-Master, tall-hatted and frock-coated'.

In his letter to Joyce dated 3rd October, 1921, Father Charles Doyle of Belvedere, who was on the staff of the college during Joyce's fifth year at the school (1896-7), does not deal fully with Mary Molesworth, first Countess of Belvedere. By no stretch of the imagination can Gaulstown, Co. Westmeath, be said to be near Belvedere House, on the shore of Lough Ennel, or Belvedere Lake, near Mullingar. Robert Rochfort, first Earl of Belvedere, locked up Mary Molesworth, his countess for thirty years, in his old family mansion at Gaulstown, miles away from Belvedere House, which he built for himself on the shores of Lough Ennel. Gaulstown passed later by purchase to the Barons Kilmaine.

Drums and Guns, and Guns and Drums. Hurrah! Hurrah!

Patrick Boyle

On the first page of the first story in *Dubliners* – 'The Three Sisters' – there occurs this passage:

> (Old Cotter) began to puff at his pipe . . . Tiresome old fool! When we knew him first he used to be rather interesting, talking of faints and worms.

Taken in conjunction with the opening paragraph, where the emphasis is on disease and death, it would be safe to assume that Joyce is, here, referring to swoons and endoparasitic helminths.

At any rate, that is what I took for granted when many years ago I first devoured the story. Subsequently, I discovered that the clue to the meaning of these two words lay in the final section of the quoted passage:

> but I soon grew tired of him and his endless stories of distilleries.

The *Oxford English Dictionary*, I found, defined 'faints' as 'the impure spirit which comes over first and last in the process of distillation' and 'worms' as 'long, spiral or coiled tubes connected with the head of the still, in which the vapour is condensed'.

From this initial encounter with a Joycean booby-trap sprang a love-hate relationship that has lasted over the years. His work has influenced me profoundly and I believe him to be the major literary figure of the century. For that very reason I felt that manners should be put on this foxy joker. Who did he think he was, this supercilious nail-parer, who juggled with words as he sat aloft on his silent, cunning and exiled arse? Maybe he could cod the troops with his 'faints' and 'worms' but there was never a joker yet that couldn't be caught out once in a while himself. So there was nothing for it but to put *Dubliners* through the grinder.

Rereading my notes after all these years, I can only wonder at the delight I felt at the results – meagre enough, God knows – of my labours. Still, there must have been a measure of comfort in the knowledge that Joyce, so invulnerable, so precise in his choice of words, with such a highly trained ear for the music of language, could drop the occasional clanger.

In 'An Encounter,' he describes a hunted cat escaping across a wall. To clear this obstacle, the domestic cat to which we are all accustomed would climb, clamber or scramble. Maybe leap, jump or spring. It might even bound. But these methods of upward propulsion are not good enough for Joyce's cat. Oh, no! It *escalades*. Regardless of the fact that no cat, of whatever size or species, age or ability, can escalade a wall without a scaling ladder.

The night porter in 'The Dead' points to the 'tap' of the electric light. Why not the *switch?* This word, in its technical sense, has been current in the language since around 1860.

A passage from 'The Sisters' details the snuff-taking procedure of an old, retired priest.

> It may have been these constant showers of snuff which gave his ancient priestly garments their green, faded look, for the red hand-kerchief, blackened, as it always was, with the snuff-stains of a week, with which he tried to brush away the fallen grains, was quite inefficacious.

Here is a piece of prose marching along with dignity and discipline, only to fall on its mouth and nose at the very last word, 'inefficacious' – a pompous, discordant, five-syllabled abomination that hurts like a dentist's drill. Perhaps it has the exact meaning Joyce wished to convey. Still, there is such a word as 'useless' – short and simple and carrying the same meaning, but with a little euphony thrown in.

Sometimes too the contrived elegance of Joyce's style can cause grating of teeth. One of his favourite devices is the deliberate repetition of the same words, either at the end of one sentence and the beginning of the next, or recurring at short intervals as in the famous last paragraph of 'The Dead':

> Snow was general all over Ireland . . . snow . . . softly falling
> . . . falling softly . . . falling faintly . . . faintly falling . . . upon
> the living and the dead.

Besides its hypnotic effect on the reader, the muffled drumbeat of this particular passage succeeds in spotlighting both the central image and its awesome background. Time and again he employs this rhythmical reiteration with brilliant effect. Even where, as in the concluding sequence of 'A Painful Case,' Joyce uses eight short sentences each beginning with 'He,' you discover this to be the right and only way that the paragraph could have been written.

But then passages occur in which he will repeat, word by word, complete phrases. An extreme case of parrot disease can be found in 'Clay'. Maria, the protagonist in this story, is a very tiny person, long nosed and long chinned. Her age is indeterminate and we are told that when she laughed 'the tip of her nose nearly met the tip of her chin.' There is no need to harp on such a strikingly unforgettable idiosyncrasy. Whether she had an india-rubber face or had no teeth or was a mini-witch, we would all recognize Maria if we met her on the street. Yet every time the poor little angashore laughs, Joyce keeps telling us that 'the tip of her nose nearly met the tip of her chin.' An unsophisticated reader might well expect the story to climax inevitably in 'Maria's Last Laugh,' a hysterical outburst causing the long delayed meeting of nose and chin, in a welter of snot, saliva, broken bones and bruised flesh.

If the foregoing strictures appear captious, there can surely be no doubt about the verdict on Joyce's description of Father Keon in 'Ivy Day in the Committee Room'.

He opened his very long mouth suddenly to express disappointment and at the same time opened wide his very bright blue eyes to express pleasure and surprise.

Ignoring the irritating repetitions of 'opened' and 'very' and 'express' it should be obvious that three conflicting emotions, such as disappointment, pleasure and surprise, cannot be displayed on one face at the same time, no matter how wide the eyes and mouth are opened. Yet Joyce, intent on endowing Father Keon with plastic features capable of expressing multiple emotions, falls back on the hackneyed formulae of the flashing eye, the flaring nostril and the curling lip – phrases no doubt dear to the heart of Paul Nicenamehehas de Kock, the author of that famous classic, 'Sweets of Sin'.

The invasion of an author by one of his characters intent on creating discord and disturbance is not so rare an occurrence as one might suppose. Joyce appears to have been peculiarly susceptible to the ravages of literary poltergeists like de Kock. The most striking example of this phenomenon can be found in 'A Painful Case.' On two adjoining pages he describes Mr Duffy and his lady friend, Mrs Sinico.

Mr Duffy abhorred anything which betokened physical or mental disorder. A mediaeval doctor would have called him saturnine. His face, which carried the entire tale of his years, was of the brown tint of Dublin streets. On his long and rather large head grew dry, black hair and a tawny moustache did not quite cover an unamiable mouth. His cheekbones also gave his face a harsh character; but there was no harshness in the eyes which, looking at the world from under their tawny eyebrows, gave the impression of a man ever alert to greet a redeeming instinct in others but often disappointed. He lived at a little distance from his body, regarding his own acts with doubtful side-glances. He had an odd autobiographical habit which led him to compose in his mind from time to time a short sentence about himself containing a subject in the third person and a predicate in the past tense. He never gave alms to beggars, and walked firmly, carrying a stout hazel.

This is one of the finest vignettes in *Dubliners*. It is authentic Joyce – austere, abrasive, lucid, ruthless, discerning. After reading it, what more could you possibly wish to know about the physical, mental or spiritual make-up of Mr Duffy? How different from the description of Mrs Sinico, some thirty lines further on.

Her face, which must have been handsome, had remained intelligent. It was an oval face with strongly marked features. The eyes were very dark blue and steady. Their gaze began with a defiant note, but was confused by what seemed a deliberate swoon of the pupil into the iris, revealing for an instant a temperament of great sensibility. The pupil reasserted itself quickly, this half-disclosed nature fell again under the reign of prudence, and her astrakhan jacket, moulding a bosom of a certain fullness, struck the note of defiance more definitely.

In this passage, with its flabby prose, its rickety construction, its coy and sugary sentiment, its incredibly befuddled thinking, it would appear self-evident that demoniac possession has taken place, and that the poltergeist is none other than Mr Philip Beaufoy, Playgoer's Club,

London, who, it may be remembered, wrote a prize-winning story for *Titbits* entitled 'Matcham's Masterstroke' in which the opening sentence began 'Matcham often thinks of the masterstroke by which he won the laughing witch' and, no doubt, continued in the same vein 'by what seemed a deliberate swoon . . . revealing for an instant . . . a bosom of a certain fullness'.

And so, by a commodious vicus of recirculation, we are back where we started with old Cotter still sitting at the fire, puffing at his pipe and babbling away, as usual, about 'faints' and 'worms,' those impure spirits, first and last to be created, who prowl through the world seeking the ruin of souls: souls swooning deliberately and deliberately swooning as the fragrance of condensing vapour escalades from the endoparisitic helminth: escalades inefficaciously and inefficaciously escalades, like the ascent on the last day of the living and the dead.

F

A Short View of the Progress of Joyceanity

Denis Johnston

Gogarty slapped down a quarterly on the counter of the New York chophouse, and jabbed it with an indignant finger.

'That's what we've come to,' he said, 'The fellow once spent an evening with me in Holles Street Hospital. And now some character in Canada is probably getting a Ph. D. for analysing his profound knowledge of midwifery.'

I opened the periodical and glanced through the essay that had caused him such annoyance. Written by a Montreal attorney who combines poetry-writing with law, it proved to be an elaborate study of the Oxen of the Sun chapter in *Ulysses*, and was described in the poopsheet as the Appendix to a forthcoming critical examination of the whole book. Although it was obviously the flower of much learning, it could hardly be recommended as light and informative reading matter, as it was couched in that irritating jargon that prefers expressions like 'he essays no explication' and 'illustration seems to confirm the surmisal' to the simpler phraseology that you or I would use. And as if this were not trying enough, the author also had a way of putting the lay reader in his place by throwing out breezy asides such as: 'Joyce is illustrating Haeckel's fundamental biogenic law that ontogeny is a recapitulation of phylogeny.'

Nowadays scholars and critics have gone one better than lawyers in this trick of turning their job into a mystery by a powerful use of hard words, and this Mr Klein had obviously a peculiar advantage by excelling in both fields. Nevertheless, he had much of interest to say about this meaty chapter, in which he had found embryological and geological parallels relating to each of the nine months of pregnancy. And in his genuine regard for every syllable of our bad boy from Belvedere, he is typical of the present attitude of almost all literate North America. But what most fascinated me was the effect of all this on Gogarty, who went home in a tantrum, and wrote a scalding article for the *Saturday Review of Literature* striking an assassin's blow at an important industry. Joyce – he said in effect – was a phoney and his *Ulysses* a joke. As for *Finnegans Wake,* the whole thing was a colossal hoax, with no other purpose than to pull the academic leg of the entire world.

Need I say that the reaction was catastrophic! It was as if Gogarty had deliberately belched at Mass. No use in pointing out the ghastliness of his own position. All his life, Gogarty has been a celebrated wit in his own right, but now in his riper years he finds himself being regarded, more and more, merely as a character in the book of an early hanger-on whom he never liked. Would any man of spirit not be entitled to lose his temper, just a little, at being forced into such a role? What more degrading fate could befall anybody? But the bifocal lenses of Harvard only gleamed more glassily whenever I made this speech for the defence. Doubts had been cast on the integrity of the Textus Receptus, and for that there could be no forgiveness. It was, in short, in bad taste.

The intensity with which Joyce's work is being studied in these United States always arouses in me the same mild sense of surprise that must have been experienced by first century Galileans as they observed the growing excitement of the Gentiles over local matters. Not that Joyce's work is unimportant to myself. Indeed, *Ulysses* was the one book that I used to carry around with me during a somewhat fluid period of my career, when more than one volume in my baggage would have been frowned upon. But this was largely for nostalgic reasons. In my imagination I liked to walk again on Sandymount Strand – even in the company of a prize Wet, and to turn my attention to the topics under discussion on the North Quays.

To a Dubliner of my generation, the book must always be rather like an old box room or glory hole in which one can spend a delightful hour taking objects of no great significance out of trunks, and putting them back again. A rereading of it enlarges the present by re-creating the past – a past that is very clear to more Poldys than one. But what if this city and these sins for which I experience so comforting a fellow feeling were not mine also? If the contents of those trunks had no personal associations, would the book interest me then – after the first start of surprise at finding words in it that I have not heard in general conversation since I was a member of Leeson Park Church Boy Scouts (where they were all in current use)? Maybe as an exercise in virtuosity I would continue to study it; or perhaps I would read it because of the fact that it is extremely amusing.

On the whole, however, these are not the baits that are being offered to the sophomores as reasons for enjoying Joyce. As we have seen, they are being set to mull over the nine months of pregnancy, and to consider the significance of each. They are being told that Mr Bloom is a scapegoat, bearing on his shoulders the sins of the human race, and they are well out now on a limb of the Golden Bough, looking for anything else that can be found with whiskers and horns. They are busy writing papers on Bruno's ideas that all created things are the offspring of a Demiurge of Intellect and a Matrix of Necessity. And they are shaking their heads over Vico's picture of history as a sort of organ-grinder with only a limited number of tunes.

From a letter of Joyce to Frank Budgen quoted by Mr Klein, it is quite clear that most of this is just as Joyce intended. He did, in fact, write his Oxen chapter in nine parts, with (believe it or not) Bloom as a spermatozoon and Stephen as the embryo. Double-thudding Anglo-Saxon motifs are actually introduced to represent the bovine hooves of the beasts mentioned by Homer, and each progression of the embryo is linked back to some foregoing episode of the day, and also with the great periods of formal evolution.

So what? So the scholars have not just invented all this for themselves, and are evidently justified in going ahead with their analysis. If we presume to question the significance of these aspects of the chapter – except, perhaps, as an attack on birth control – it is the master we must attack and not the disciples. It is true that in some instances the latter have gone too far. For example, I have been present at a discussion that raged around a recent discovery that it is not possible to gaze upon 'the snout of Bray Head' from a roof overlooking the Forty Foot Hole, as described in the 'Telemachus' chapter; from which fact one commentator wishes to argue that the scene of this episode ought properly to be placed in the Martello Tower at Sutton, or else on Dalkey Island, with whatever consequences this change implies. One can see what complications this sort of thing could lead to, wherever it is not realized that the things that Joyce has forgotten about Dublin are often more remarkable than the things he remembered.

Meanwhile, a mass of misinformation provided by people like his brother Stanislaus, and by biographers who do not wish to tell us the whole story for reasons of good taste, is signposting the way down further blind alleys. For the present, however, most of the departments are having as much as they can do in disentangling the author's actual message. This is a task which he deliberately left to others, and it was a very clever move to have done so – unless we are wrong in our suspicions that Joyce's message is the least important part of Joyce.

There is actually no reason why the legacy of Dedalism to the world should be of very great weight once it has been discovered. It is only a coincidence when those who have the supreme gift of self-expression in any of the arts have got anything startling to express. The one does not in any sense depend on the other. The impression of profundity that we get from Shaw, for example, comes from his lucidity rather from any special merit in his plethora of half-truths. Compared with Goethe or Ibsen – who happened to have had both gifts – he is a very readable Smart Alec, with a good line of bull that smothers opposition. Swift was another case in point. What gallons of ink have been expended in endowing him with a meaning; when all that he needs is a biography.

Now, one only has to read Joyce's description of the movements of a dog to see what a consummate artist in words the man is – what evocation of all the dogs one has ever seen can be brought about in a few lines of prose! But is he more than an artist – if that is not sufficient in itself? What nuggets have the diligent workers in the quarry of Great Thoughts managed to produce so far?

Well, respectfully admitting that ontogeny is probably a recapitulation of phylogeny, we have the fact that all religion begins in a thunderclap; that the Liffey is female, while Howth Head is definitely male; that in the world of dreams, all time happens at once. This, I admit, is impressive enough, and may perhaps provide some clues to a new way of life. But it also must be admitted that the vast bulk of the clues from *Finnegans Wake* that we have been offered to date are concerned only with puns, chance resemblances of words, forced parallels from history or mythology, and (Joyce's greatest sin) an unabashed confusion of the subjective with the objective that makes it impossible to distinguish between the author's observation of his hero, the hero's observation of his past, or the reader's observation of any of them. In fact, there is an air of unreality about all the explanations that reminds me irresistibly of a commentary on the liturgy, and not of literary criticisms at all.

This should immediately put all good Irishmen on their guard, because if this exhausting evening with Mr Earwicker is in fact a liturgy, and we are going to avoid falling into the sin of superstition, ought we to enquire at once where or what is the religion to which it applies? Are Bruno and Vico all that it is going to offer us in the way of prophets? Because if so it is important for us to know what class of niche he sees himself occupying in the Hall of Fame, and how far his ambitions have really carried him.

The fact that there is any difficulty in answering these questions is entirely Joyce's own doing. Sometimes I wonder whether in days to come there will be anything left of Shaw except his explanations of himself. Joyce, on the other hand, says little or nothing about himself, and seems to have directed all his contemporary biographers away from the real facts of his life to a lot of dreary rows with Maunsel & Co. He even goes so far as to delete the chapter headings from his work, so as to make us find them out for ourselves.

If this makes us suspicious, it also has had the effect of making him God's gift to the English Departments. It is not always realized that scholarship is just as much a trade or profession as politics and religion. In the fields of learning there are many lectures that have to be given, and many, many theses that have to be written in the course of each academic year. And in this respect Joyce provides a widow's curse. I do not suggest for a moment that there are not innumerable teachers of modern literature who are not genuine lovers of Joyce as a brilliant craftsman and as an acute observer of life. But there is more in the present-day excitement than this.

Twenty-five years ago he had many readers whom he would not otherwise have had, because of a mistaken belief that he was pornographic. Now that is all past – except in his home – and he has become instead an enigma. A great many conscientious workers are professionally interested in the study of this enigma, and many reputations have already been committed to the hazard of the printed page. Herein lies the hub of Gogarty's offence. He has broken the Geneva Convention that is observed in all professions from barristers to bootleggers. Outsiders must not foul the pitch.

Joyce may be right or wrong, significant or unimportant. But he must not be a hoax. Too much depends on him. He has too many ideal readers suffering from the ideal insomnia. To have known him in the flesh gives one a right to a seat amongst the Fathers. Like Polycarp, I never had this privilege myself. But, like Polycarp, I have known the Fathers – which is the next best thing.

Childe Horrid's Pilgrimace

Andrew Cass

The literature on Joyce's life and work is growing apace but a large amount of it is inaccurate in biographical detail and uncritical in literary appraisal. Such writing is worse than useless for it tends to turn the man into a myth and to embalm his works in shrouds of speculative and unfounded commentary.

A major biographical error is the confusing of Joyce's own personality as a youth in Dublin with that of Stephen Dedalus, a fictitious character albeit presented as 'a portrait of the artist'. This character was the outcome of careful elaboration over the years from 1904 to 1916, when the first version was released in *A Portrait of the Artist as a Young Man*, and also as late as 1922 when we meet Stephen again in *Ulysses*. These versions portray a youth of twenty and twenty-two respectively with a fully matured artistic vision the expression of which he realized to be his life's mission, a cold, knife-sharp intellect emancipated from the trammels of faith and fatherland and a literary style which no sane reader can believe to be what it is held out to be – the spontaneous conversation of a young man expounding ideas to his cronies in their walks around the town or in the National Library. Our incredulity is confirmed in one particular, at least, when we read that the Hamlet interpretation was not in fact given impromptu in the National Library in 1904, but was carefully built up into its present form from a series of lectures on Shakespeare which Joyce delivered on the Continent long afterwards.

The circumstances of the flight into Europe have given rise to a series of further myths. One is that the youth of twenty, feared and envied by the uncouth islanders, 'the most belated race in Europe', was expelled from their 'inhospitable bog', as Joyce himself put it in a letter seven or eight years afterwards. No evidence of the alleged expulsion has been produced either by Joyce or by his biographers, nor is it likely that any more than a small proportion of his fellow townsmen was aware even of his existence.

An alternative reason for his departure to Paris in 1902 is given in *A Portrait of the Artist,* where it is suggested that the young man, realizing that he could not live a free intellectual life in Ireland, of his own volition shook the turf mould from his heels. Here again, it must be remembered that the statement of his youthful attitude, in the form in which we find it, is one composed long afterwards.

Stephen Hero, portion of a first draft of the *Portrait* and ultimately rejected by Joyce for publication, gives a more credible picture. It shows us a much rawer and more juvenile mind, much more uncertain of its destiny, than does the finished work of art on display in the *Portrait.* Mr C. P. Curran's snapshot, published in Miss Hutchins's *James Joyce's Dublin,* reveals a correspondingly gauche and seedy character.

In the 'definitive' biography, Mr Gorman takes the Dubliners of the time to task for ignoring the youthful Joyce and letting Paris and the four corners of the earth *(sic)* shelter the man who was not stamped in their pattern, but he apparently contradicts himself by admitting that 'there was a third element that was violently pushing him toward flight. It was Nora Barnacle, his present wife'. No further explanation of this 'third element' is offered. There seems to be more Bowdler than Boswell in biography of this kind.

Joyce himself long afterwards referred to his flight to the Continent as a 'wild goup's chase across the Kathartic ocean', and recognized the limitations of his subsequent life abroad, 'self-exiled in upon his ego'.

The myth-obsessed commentators, however, ignore the derivation of the 'wild goose' references from the name Barnacle and prefer to account Joyce with those who (also voluntarily, by the way) spread the grey wing upon every tide after the battles of the Boyne and Limerick and of whom Ireland has been made to say

> . . . I never called them sons,
> I almost ceased to breathe their name,
> Then caught it echoing down the wind
> Blown backwards from the lips of Fame.

Enough has been said to make it clear that Stephen Dedalus is not an accurate portrait of James Joyce as a young man. Accordingly, unless it can be treated as a study from which the writer had achieved an inhuman and almost schizoid detachment, it must be ascribed to the pathetic desire of a middle-aged man to dramatize his own lost youth and to exaggerate its intellectual capacity and promise. Such a petty pursuit is reminiscent of the father who writes his boy's prize essays or of the mentally retarded person whose conversation impulsively recurs to 'when I was in college twenty years ago'. Byron was taken savagely to task by the *Edinburgh Review* for, as alleged, extenuating bad poetry on the plea of youth, but he had published *Hours of Idleness* before he was twenty-one and he never attempted to antedate his mature work as if it had been written when he was a minor. Byron is also Joyce's exemplar in having borne through Europe the pageant of his bleeding heart while the impressed continentals counted every drop, but here again he is outdone by Joyce in bitter antagonism to the people whom he blamed for his exile.

As Joyce himself said, all this stuff was boiling inside him and he had to get it out of his system, but it is a pity that he did not rid himself of it quickly. If, for example, the *Portrait*, with the Stephen Dedalus portion of *Ulysses* included, had been written by 1907, it should have provided an adequate medium for the expression of his youthful resentments and he could then have redeemed his 1904 promise that 'in ten years' time I will give them a novel to talk about'. This threatened novel was not published until 1922 and then proved to be a mere continuation and elaboration of *Dubliners* and the *Portrait*, with the author of forty still preoccupied with the burnt-out passions and dissipations of twenty-two.

We know, of course, of the time-lags in writing due to the portentous tasks of progressive autobiography and politobiography having to be pursued in the intervals between grinding rounds of teaching and tuitions in Pola, Trieste and Zürich. We know also that the author's mind was not free from the bourgeois cares of domestic economy and all other impertinences incidental to a family ménage – he even brought out members of his father's family from Dublin after the manner of the Irish provincials coming to the Big City of that prime bourgeois, Napoleon Bonaparte. In wartime Zürich, as well, he had to be careful what he'd write or say: the long arm of British espionage was all around him. These were grave obstacles to composition.

In addition, when the material was ready for publication, there were the delays arising from what he regarded as the unaccountable, puritanical censorship of English publishers and printers (English, mark you, for the negotiations with Maunsel's did not take place until Grant Richards' procrastination had well-nigh broken the author's heart).

All these circumstances left the author in arrears with that programme of his, whether one calls it art, apologia or autobiography, not one tittle of which would he modify if it took him till Tibb's Eve to get it all down in black and white.

Slow rises worth, indeed, by such-like cares oppressed, but, surely, it was to escape such drudgery, household cares, spying and censorship, and the narrow intransigence of unappreciative book publishers, that the 'wild geese' winged their way from the thraldom of the 'rabblement', the Church and the Empire.

His 'definitive' biographer does not define precisely how or on the score of what achievement the Irish community should have intervened to keep the youthful hero at home. Should they have sought a stipend for him out of their British master's privy purse merely because he entertained some vague ambition to write books of undisclosed content with letters for titles, 'epiphanies on green oval leaves, deeply deep', copies to be sent if he died to all the great libraries of the world including Alexandria?

Mr Gorman thinks that it would be a worthwhile undertaking for some ambitious young student, 'in one of the greater universities' (no less) to base *(sic)* a painstaking thesis 'on the aesthetic reasoning and development' of Joyce as a young man. There is already far more exile than silence in all this affair but if we are to have such a thesis it would be well to conduct the research in sources other than those obligingly created for us long after that development had been completed.

Ulysses, with its interminable trimmings and its stuffed Odysseus promoted from a short story to balance the pretentious epic of Telemachus, enabled Joyce to get off his chest a great deal of juvenile resentments and self-pity. Like Iago, he had all those years been harbouring a motiveless malignancy against various Dubliners but the scarifying he gave them in *Ulysses* was also apparently a form of self-rehabilitation.

The literary standards of 1922 veered between pre-war conservatism and an uncritical post-war enthusiasm for novelty. The former was moribund but while it lasted it contributed to the bonfires with which *Ulysses* was greeted, and so unwittingly increased the significance of its advent. Considering it now even as a product of the general mental unrest of thirty years ago, its curious extravagances of obscenity and blasphemy quite definitely detract from its value as a work of art. The *monologue intérieur* was not, of course, a new literary form although it was developed considerably in the meditations of Mr Bloom. But what captivated while it shocked the 1922 critics was the novel treatment of the long, unpunctuated soliloquy in the last chapter, a magical record (they acclaimed) of the quintessential inwardness of femininity. The form of expression is certainly designed excellently to suit the representation of a stream of consciousness but the actual content is very far from such a representation. Much of it is dependent upon, and indeed intended to supplement, the preceding treatment of personalities and events.

It does not carry any conviction as a natural series of meditations, which would have much less sequence and more variety. The omission of punctuation marks is a mere trick designed to hide the fact that a great deal of the alleged run-on thinking is in fact nothing more than a characteristic piece of pungent Joyce prose. The whole chapter conveys the impression of a literary composition the words of which are intended for the eye and not for the mind. Who, for example, ever listened to the time chimed from a city clock in the small hours and thought of it as '¼ past 3'?

Ulysses demonstrated the author's inability to give forthright expression to his own mature personality. Stephen Dedalus is a dead youth taken from cold storage after twenty years, touched up and exhibited as a show-piece. This mental paralysis inhibiting direct self-expression continued, but side by side with it, there was an uncontrollable urge for some form of autobiography, some method of self-portraiture which would depict the ageing artist and his preoccupations. By this time he must have realized that his long years of exile had failed to divorce his mind from Irish themes and Irish modes of expression and that he had no alternative to Ireland as the scene of anything he might write. He was reading history, archaeology, mythology and philosophy but he seems to have been incapable of either making any reasoned contributions to these subjects or commenting on them without tying them up with his Dublin memories. He therefore wanted a medium of expression in which he could give vent to his Irish memories, be obliquely autobiographical and at the same time epiphanize himself as an all-wisest Stagyrite who could express all knowledge in the most intricate symbolic terms.

The dream-state regarded as a reservoir of personal and racial memories and a furnace for remoulding language provided the required medium. Complexity was achieved by puns, parody, portmanteau words and other modes of multiplying meaning. The philosophy of Giambattista Vico would provide historical universality for his characters. Giordano Bruno's ideas of life-force based on conflict and tension, coupled with certain eastern myths of creation and numinal power, would give him the framework of his symbolism.

While the primary themes of *Finnegans Wake* are, therefore, autobiographical and Irish, these incidental trappings have also been meticulously and inextricably worked into it and it is with them that we now find foreign commentators very seriously concerned. They are setting out on profoundly earnest exegeses of the references to Vico 'cycles', Bruno 'opposites' and mythological 'archetypes', notwithstanding that the theories in question have today no philosophical or scientific validity whatever and that the myths are a mere farrago of oriental refuse. *Finnegans Wake* is thus sending researchers down the weedgrown labyrinths of dead thought rather than to the actual local material on which it is primarily based.

It may be salutary to give one example: At the end of the second section of Book II there is a vertical column of numerals from one to ten, the spelling based more or less on Irish save that cuig is written 'cush' and deich 'geg'. Cush and geg carry footnotes and childish drawings – a hand thumbing a nose in profile, 'Kish is for antichrist . . .'; and a cross-bones, 'and geg is for skool and crossbuns'. An entertaining finale, one would think, to the children's evening homework in the Earwicker household. But no, the nose (we are told) is that of Makroprosopos (always, of course, represented in profile), and through it he emits the sacred breath which is the creative force of all the worlds. The hand is referenced to Cush or Kish to indicate the division at rung five of the descending numinal power into good and evil forces, Kish being the evil one and therefore spurned with the thumb. Geg down on the plain is the place of love and death (X) after which there is renewal in a new decade.

Another note may be given without comment. It is on: *Move up Mackinerny! make room for Muckinurney!* This is annotated: Move up you great Archetypal Man and make way for the local example!

Discounting its incoherences, nonsense and irrelevant repetitions and elaborations, *Finnegans Wake* is, indeed, a miraculous 'polyhedron of scripture', a palimpsest of anthologies. The literature of the world, particularly Anglo-Irish literature, has been ransacked and tortured to 'forge' this farraginous 'funferall'. Covetous of his neighbours' words, Joyce purloined them, transmuted them and synthesized them into the last word on everything. Here, as in most of his previous work, he does not create: he transforms. If the book can be termed art at all, it is the moonshine of art, the reflection of the art of others. The Four Masters are a comic quartette in *Finnegans Wake*. Joyce did not seem to realize that in writing what amounted to the literary and historical requiem of Western Europe, he was engaged on a task analogous to that undertaken by the Four Masters themselves as historical synthesists at the end of the Gaelic epoch in Irish history. Whether performed in the dry, trite style of the Four Masters, or in the florid, Joyce's complex Book of Kells style, synthesis is inevitably a post mortem on the cultural and civic life which it records.

Ireland is the real 'Joyce Country', the primary scene and source of inspiration for *Finnegans Wake,* and in no other work in the English language has the Irish accent ever been so authentically reproduced. In that portion of it which is derived from existing Anglo-Irish literature and ballad-poetry and transmuted to suit the author's purpose the Irish note has if anything been enhanced. His own original composition, even where it may seem nonsensical, is equally racy of the soil:

> For be all rules of sport 'tis right
> That youth be dowered to charm the night
> Whilst age is dumped to mind the day
> When wather parted from the say.

> His bludgeon's bruk, his drum is tore
> For spuds we'll keep the hat he wore
> And roll in clover on his clay
> By wather parted from the say.

Nor is he incapable of changing from the Dublin accent to that of other cities. The metallic accents of the shipyards and the linen factories of Belfast are equally authentic:

> And when ye'll hear the gould hommers of my heart, my floxy lass, bingbanging again the ribs of your resistance and the tenderbolts of my rivets working to your destraction ye'll be shivering wi' all yer dinful sobs . . .

Throughout the book there is a partially concealed but unmistakable desire, repeatedly discernible, to be understood and appreciated where these accents and turns of speech belong. There are, for example, reams of cover-up for the simple statement that *Finnegans Wake* was dedicated to Ireland. The contradictions as well as the camouflage around the expression of this intention of the author reveal a Hamlet-like vacillation, a bad boy's awkward embarrassment when he slouches back to the parental threshold. It was shown in the *Irish Times* in April 1947 how this book written by 'Shem' ('letter self-penned to one's other, that never-perfect, ever-planned') was to be delivered by his opposite number at home ('Shaun') to his mother, Anna Liffey, and (more grudgingly) to his father (Dublin).

In dealing with his spiritual mother, Anna Liffey, he shows his affection for the accents and the story of Ireland, her woods and mountains and plains and her rivers as symbols of eternal nature in their unceasing flow by bogs and bends and green hills and dark pools till, too full for sound, they approach at last the great dark-heaving sea and join the 'moyles and moyles of it'. The imagined night-waters of a place remembered from his youth are, therefore, symbolized in Alp in Joyce's dream-world, just as 'Alph the sacred river' was the approach to Coleridge's Xanadu.

While the living waters were dwelt on with nostalgic affection, there was no similar regard for the living people as symbolized by his brother (Shaun) and his father (Dublin). Indeed, if we pursue his own symbols of universality to their logical conclusion and take the personified Dublin to represent all men and all cities, we get the impression of a dull misanthropy pervading Joyce's mind even in his later years, milder perhaps than that which soured his youth, but still potent enough to bedevil his outlook on his fellow men. His closest friends tell of a wall of reserve beyond which none of them ever penetrated. Many friendships formed during the years crumbled suddenly, surely because his intimates were inevitably bound to sense the ultimate exclusiveness of that cold, introverted, antisocial intellect.

He could play with the idea of an alternative life's history for himself had he stayed at home in 1904 and participated in the developments which by the time *Ulysses* was published had crystallized in a new Ireland and a new concept of national destiny. 'Shaun' (i.e. 'brother Jonathan'), his twin, born like himself in 1882, represents in his political capacity this unrealized, mythical portion of his self. In other contexts he is a stage-Irish caricature, mercenary (da valorem) and shrewd, while Joyce himself (Sham) is portrayed, strangely enough, as a mere improvident grasshopper. This is rather unfair to our politicians of the present generation.

It is indisputable that Shaun is Eamon de Valera. Nevertheless Shaun is not invariably depicted in an unfavourable light. It is conceded that he is 'a genuine prime, the real choice, full of natural grease, the mildest of milkstoffs yet unbeaten as a risicide and, of course, absolutely unadulterous'. He is even permitted to pillory Shem for his moral and national shortcomings:

> You were bred, fed, fostered and fattened from holy childhood up in this two easter island . . . and now . . . condemned fool, anarch, egoarch, Hiresiarch, you have reared your disunited kingdom on the vacuum of your own most intensely doubtful soul. . . . You were designed to fall in with Plan as our nationals should . . . but you beat it . . . to sing us a song of Alibi . . . an Irish emigrant the wrong way out, sitting on your crooked sixpenny stile, an unfrillfrocked quackfriar.

The following are further references to 'Shaun' (page numbers of *Finnegans Wake* 1st Edition, in brackets):

> Man Devoyd of the Commoner characteristics of an Irish Nature. (72)

> There were some further collidabanter and severe tries to convert for the best part of an hour and now a woden affair in the shape of a webley (we at once recognize our old friend Ned of so many illortemporate letters) fell from the intruser who, as stuck as that cat to that mouse in that tube of that christchurch organ . . . (82)

> Xaroshie zdrst! – in his excitement the laddo had broken exthro Castilian. (91)

> (Of 'Brutus', alias Shaun): A king off duty and a jaw for ever! and what a cheery ripe outlook, good help me Deus v Deus! (162)

> Arouse thee, my valour! And save for e'er my true Bdur! (165)

> (Present of) a loaf of bread and a father's early aim for Val from Skibbereen. (In *Anna Livia Plurabelle* published in 1930 the recipient was 'Tim from Skibbereen.') (210)

> (Shaun) Candidatus, viridosus, aurilucens, sinelab . . . his smile likequid glue (receiving) neuchoristic congressulations . . . we thank

to thine, mighty innocent that diddest bring it off fuitefuite (234-5). (This obviously relates to the 1932 period.)

(Problem in geometry): Dolph (Shem): First mull amugfull of mud, son. Kev (Shaun): What the D. V. would I do that for? That's a goosey's ganser he is told, what the Deva would you do that for? (286)

Pardon the inquisition, causas es quostas? It is Da Valorem's Dominical Brayers. Why coif that weird hood? Because among nosoever circusdances is to be apprehended the dustungwashed poltronage of the lost Gabbarnaur – Jaggarnath. (341)

(Description of Shaun the Post) . . . a star-spangled zephyr with a decidedly surpliced crinklydoodle front with his motto through dear life embrothered over it in peas, rice and yeggyyolk, Or for royal, Am for Mail, R.M.D. hard cash on the nail (404). No mistaking that beamish brow. . . . Those jehovial oye-glances. . . . He was immense. (405)

(NOTE: The peas, rice and yolk signify green, white and orange, and 'hard cash' seems from other contexts to stand for 'da valorem'.)

(Shaun is eating) . . . and Boland's broth broken into the bargain . . . and in their greenfree state a clister of peas . . . a fingerhot of rheingenever to give the Pax cum spiritututu. (406)

('Boland's broth' suggests the pot of broth of the 1916 Rebellion, with special reference to Boland's Mills. The 'Pax' reference is to the League of Nations.)

I heard a voice, the voice of Shaun, vote of the Irish, voice from afar (4). (Shaun speaks, presumably, on the wireless) . . . (408) (Shem) looks rather thin, imitating me. I'm very fond of that other of mine. (Shaun, asked if he has painted our town a wearing greenridinghued): . . . I will confess to have, yes . . . Down with the Saozun ruze! (411)

The Ondt (Shaun) (Ant versus Grasshopper) was a weltall fellow . . . sair sair sullemn and chairmanlooking . . . (417) . . . a conformed aceticist and aristotaller (but when he had his work done he danced and). Never did Dorsan from Dunshangan dance it with more devilry! (416)

Regarding the length of the lost letter, Shem asks Shaun: Have you not . . . used up slanguage tun times as words as the penmarks used out in sinscript with such hesitancy by your cerebrated brother? (421)

Peax! Peax! Shaun replied in vealar penultimatum. (424)

Shaun weeps on departing as 'Embrassadar-at-Large', overpowered by the love of the tearsilver that he twined through her (Anna

Liffey's) hair, for, sure, he was the soft semplgawn slob of the world. (426)

His departure is bewailed. He is the 'Winner of the gamings, primed at the studience, propredicted from the storybooks, the choice of ages wise! Spickspookspokesman of our specturesque silentiousness! (427)

Life, it is true, will be a blank without you, ere Molochy wars bring the devil era. (473)

(Moloch, god of war; King Malachy, Malachi, Hebrew prophet and Saint Malachy, Irish prophet; Armageddon, Antichrist and future wars are all embodied in this short phrase.)

Commong, sa na pa de valure? (478)

Would you know a young Kevan or Evan Vaughan . . . that found the dogumen number one . . . an illegible downfumbed by an uneligible?

– If I do know sinted sageness? Sometimes he would keep silent for a few minutes as if in prayer and clasp his forehead and during the time he would be thinking to himself and he would not mind anybody who would be talking to him or crying stinking fish. (482)

James Joyce -
The Internationalist

Arthur Power

Joyce hated all manner of provincialism. It was the main reason for his continual residence on the mainland of Europe. Also it was the reason for his determination not to return to Ireland. Even a short visit to England, before his marriage, made him unhappy.

In that diary which ends *Portrait of the Artist as a Young Man,* under the entry 14th April, we read:

> John Alphonsus Mulrennan has just returned from the West of Ireland. European and Asiatic papers please copy. He told us he met an old man there in a mountain cabin. Old man had red eyes and short pipe. Old man spoke Irish. Mulrennan spoke Irish. Then old man and Mulrennan spoke English. Mulrennan spoke to him about universe and stars. The old man sat, listened, smoked, spat. Then he said, 'Ah, there must be terrible queer creatures at the latter end of the world.' I fear him. I fear his redrimmed horny eyes. It is with him I must struggle all through the night till day come, till he or I be dead, gripping him by the sinewy throat till. . . . Till what? Till he yield to me? No. I mean him no harm.

'Ah,' exclaimed Joyce contemptuously to me once when we were discussing the Irish literary movement, 'the bloody nonsense that has been written about Ireland! – parish froth! I intend to lift it into the international sphere and get away from the parish pump, and from "my dearly beloved brethren".' For the dogmatic provincialism of the Irish Roman Catholic Church enraged his own innate spirituality, and weighed down his searching soul with, to his mind, its absurd rituals, medieval restrictions, and fears of inhuman punishments which are to last forever. He wanted to be free of all this and to swim in the international waters of the Continent where no one would pry into his private life, nor censor what he wrote, or his thought even: a stranger among other strangers. It was the condition in which his genius could wax in strength.

Ireland at that time, still under the British rule, was a country of frustration. According to the English conqueror, nothing Irish could be any good, and this baneful influence lay like a heavy blanket over the entire nation.

Curiously enough, Joyce himself in a way subscribed to it for he constantly reviled her. 'I felt proud to think that my son . . . will always be a foreigner in Ireland, a man speaking another language and bred in a different tradition,' he wrote to Nora from Dublin in 1909. Also about the same time he wrote to her: 'Dublin is a detestable city and the people most repulsive to me . . . .' All of which was, in truth, but a reflection of the English propaganda at that time. Indeed, I remember calling in on him at his flat in the Avenue Charles Floquet. There was some sort of Irish art exhibition being held in Paris at that time: also it happened that the streets were placarded with blood-red posters advertising an agricultural show, 'Exhibition des animaux reproducteurs'.

The opportunity was too easy, and as I entered the darkened room where he lay on the bed stooping his eyes, he looked up with a grin that was half sardonic and half humorous.

'I see the Irish have arrived in Paris,' he quipped.

Even as late as 1930 in Paris I would try to interest him in the new Free State which was in being. But no, he would obstinately cut across my conversation to ask details about some old building or shop he knew in his day. Indeed, I remember when once I was extolling the beauty of the West to him, he cut me short by repeating the supercilious, and in my opinion stupid, remark an American woman had recently made to him at a dinner. 'Have you got a West?'

All this was to show his hate of provincialism, for he was determined to be the universal or, to put it more accurately, the Continental man.

It was the reason why he had originally left Ireland. For he revelled in Continental life, in the flowing in of so many diverse rivers, and in the scintillating beauty of the Paris of his time. New art, new ideas, new forms were appearing everywhere of which he, strangely enough, was a leader. Also, as a foreigner, he had no local or nationalistic attachments, and so he was freer than any. In fact, no one but himself could call him to account, so he could follow to the full his own bent in creating the avant-garde and prophetic literature of our time; in which he used words as the advanced painters used paint for the pleasure of the material itself; to become in the end, as Wilde had said of himself, 'a lord of language'.

Also to sex, which has become so intensified in this present day, more than any other writer he gave a new dimension. What men and women had always thought and done in secret, and kept secret, he now wrote out in detail, minimizing nothing.

Indeed, it was hard, sitting before the fireplace with him in the evening, as he quietly sipped his white wine, guiding the conversation on to literature, to realize how he had, with his realistic sex details, shocked civilized society to the bone. His insouciance was disarming, as were the conditions of his daily life. How different were they, for example, from those of his great French contemporary, Proust, who had also given a new dimension to sex in literature by his exploitation of homosexuality. Proust, who subsidized a homosexual brothel in a hotel of the Champs Élysées where he used to show the photographs of his aristocratic girl-friends, and even that of his adored mother, for the butcher boys to make gross remarks about them. Also he watched the sewer men demonstrate how they tortured the rats they had caught by sticking them with long hat-pins.

Such excesses would have revolted Joyce, who was essentially kind and human; Joyce who, putting aside the selfish ferocity which marks some of Proust's characters, preferred to look on the sexual aberrations of men and women with humour and tolerance. It was an attitude, one may remark, which would have been impossible if he had remained under the care of Mother Ireland. In fact, he even objected to the social restrictions of English life, for when he was staying in Camden Grove in Kensington (or 'Camden Grave', as he called it) to fulfil the conditions for his legal marriage, he was very discomforted as I remember him, only longing to set his wings for the Continent, never to leave it again.

His purpose in staying in London at that time he kept secret, as no doubt he hoped that his marriage would remain a secret too: his name lost among the thousands of other names filed in the marriage registers of that day.

But no – it was not to be. All over London the streets were placarded: 'James Joyce married.'

I knew where he lunched every day, at Slater's on the High Street, Kensington, so I called in. There he was, sitting at a table with Mrs Joyce, with his straw boater – the last in London – on the chair beside him – this man of habit who, even on the day of his marriage, lunched where he always lunched.

I sat down at the table, though I do not think that at that moment I was particularly welcome, but in my impishness I decided to get some fun out of it – not that I cared a damn whether he had been legally married or not.

'What will I say to my friends now,' I bantered, 'when they ask me questions? I thought that you were married in Trieste twenty years ago. What excuse can I make?' I implored most earnestly.

But Joyce was in no joking humour.

'If you want any information,' he remarked severely, 'I can give the address of my lawyer'.

Mrs Joyce, however, seemed more good-humoured about it, and re-marked: 'I felt such a fool!'

Also it was during this stay in London he told me he had been at a party – probably with some well-known literary personality – and how, during the evening the men, or at least he, had been shown into a separate room to be given drinks. This procedure was past his under-standing: he who, at his parties, had his drinks on the table, free for any-one to help themselves. No, it was all part of the provincial puritanism, an attempt at moral management, to be found on these islands, which he hated. In England there is a legal freedom which perhaps does not exist on the Continent, but in revenge everyone is a censor of their neighbour. Abroad, a foreigner, anyway, can do as he likes and live as he likes pro-vided he does not annoy anyone. And that last sentence can be repeated.

Also food – for having apparently given up other sensualities, he now concentrated on food and wines. It is why every biographer who knew him personally talks about the 'Trianon' restaurant, and later Fouquet's on the Champs Élysées, for dining, to Joyce, was a serious and carefully chosen ritual. It was his one form of relaxation in the tradition of many other literary men living city lives. Undoubtedly he lived softly and in-dulged himself. There is that photograph of him in Paris, paying off a taxi in the street. It was taken not long before he died, and in it you see how soft he had become, his face puffy and his general bearing heavy and lifeless, which used to be so finely drawn and alert. For he believed in living well, frequenting expensive cafés and eating expensive dinners in expensive establishments, appreciative as he was of all the refine-ments that a modern Babylon could offer him.

To be plunged back into the comparatively primitive society, physically and intellectually, of Dublin would have horrified him. So when the war came he fled to Switzerland rather than return to his native land. That it had changed greatly for the better and had modernized he would not believe; in fact, to speak the truth, he was determined not to believe. And then there was this imaginary grievance against Ireland which could not be erased.

Also, more practically, he was nervous as to what might happen to him or his family if he returned. He told me that he had heard of some man who had gone into a Dublin bookshop, and asked if they had a copy of *Ulysses*. He was told that they had not. 'Well,' the man remarked threateningly, 'the writer of that had better not come back into this country.'

'A fanatic!' I protested.

'Yes, but it is such a person who does it.'

When his family, Nora, Lucia and his son Georgio, were on holiday in Galway, he told me he had a special aeroplane chartered in readiness to rescue them, if necessary. I must say this extraordinary precaution irritated me, even though it was in the period of the civil war, for I was sure at that time, when his fame was limited to a few intellectuals, he could have walked from one end of Dublin to the other without being accosted, or recognized even, and his family was in no greater danger than any other family.

No – immersed in Continental life he felt safe and happy, as an international genius, where the physical life pleased him at every turn. And after he died, Mrs Joyce maintained the same attitude.

Meeting her in Paris once I suggested, since she complained of loneliness, that she should go over to Ireland.

'What!' she cried, her voice hysterical. 'They burnt my husband's books.'

To burn or not to burn an author's works – is it important? So long as they don't burn him, or his family, or his house. . . . Could it not be beneficial?

But no, I thought it better to shut up. Evidently she was determined to maintain his imagined, and by this time historical, grievance against his native country – this pleasant-natured woman who was now so anxious to be loyal to him.

For years past, writers on Joyce have tended to ignore her because she was non-intellectual, and non-literary. Also, some of those who surrounded Joyce in his later years were more interested in their own

literary gymnastics than in general humanities. Reflected literary glory
was what they were after, and so they did not take her very seriously.

It is true in conventional terms that she was not well educated. One
remembers that story of how, after a particularly troublesome episode
in Trieste, she had decided to leave him. Sitting down at the table she
started to write a letter to her mother in Galway, beginning with a small
'i'. Joyce, who was looking over her shoulder, remarked to her with
some amusement: 'If you are going to leave me, then at least you might
start with a capital 'I'.' To which she replied with her usual good sense
'What difference does it make?' – an answer which conveys that spontaneous air of innocence which she never lost.

However, those who took Mrs Joyce for a fool made a great mistake.
For she was extremely shrewd; judged character in a flash, and was firm
in her judgments.

In addition she had, as someone remarked to me the first time that
they met her, that thing that you often hear about – Irish charm. Indeed,
one of her chief attributes was that she was perfectly natural in a society
where most were hopefully acting a part, and were given to ideas of
their own importance.

Some writers have compared her to Molly Bloom. And there is some
basis for it. According to a photograph taken in Galway while she was
on holiday there from Trieste, she was in the colloquial phrase 'a
smasher', with the same magnificently robust figure as her mother, and
was no doubt capable of raising tumultuous passions.

When I first met her in Paris her son, Georgio, was almost a young
man, and Lucia in her late teens. But she was still attractive, with a
latent sensualism which one felt it would not take much to stir. However, at that time a mother's responsibility for her family and her man
was her main interest, though I do remember her talking to me once
with enthusiasm about the handsome men she had put her eye on in
Trieste.

'Nora, my faithful darling, my sweet-eyed blackguard schoolgirl,'
wrote Joyce, and it conveys something of her natural waywardness.
Even in Paris, where things are apt to become over-sophisticated, she
never lost that characteristic.

I have no doubt that she was sensual and passionate in her youth,
when she took him, knowing and caring nothing whatsoever about
literature, just for the man she liked and had decided to go the the Continent with.

Probably after the suppressed, innuendo-riddled, sex atmosphere of Dublin the frank sex-life of an Italian seaport town stimulated her. And if there were excesses, well – they are common enough, except that the participants are not famous people afterwards, and they have not written detailed accounts of them, which were taken and sold to a ready market by a relation.

In several letters to her Joyce mentions her eyes, and they were her chief attraction: dream-filled, heavy-lidded, mysterious and alluring. Also the way her hair grew across her forehead was very attractive, but on the other hand her long upper lip and dwindling chin weakened her general appearance in later life. But her lovely, friendly manner always charmed one.

In fact my admiration and liking for her helped to cement my friendship with Joyce, for he would not be friends with anyone who was not friends with her. If they ignored her, he ignored them; and if he was the sun, she was the encircling moon, and, in this tower of Babel of the many tongues, it was delightful to find myself seated in a typical Irish home, where she – for she was the outspoken one – had never lost her turn for the vernacular: the breeze of the West in a stuffy Paris apartment.

In the early days she did not seem to take much interest in his writing, being too much occupied, as in Trieste, in making him toe the line, which was not easy.

Even in Paris, when I met them before the publication of *Ulysses*, she did not appear to be much impressed, and in the early days of its final publication she maintained her jaunty, amused detachment.

For instance, when he used to come into the room in the late afternoon wearing his special short white writing-coat, and flop exhausted into an armchair, she used to say to him: 'For goodness' sake, Jim, take that coat off you. It makes you a show.' But the only response she got was an all-meaning and amused smile.

I was present in the room when he presented her with the first copy of the first edition of *Ulysses*. She turned to me and offered to auction it then and there. For that was Mrs Joyce – gay and natural and provocative. Later, it is true, she succumbed to the remarkable success of his work, and remained deeply impressed. 'It is a wonderful story,' she said to me at the end – starting as it did in poverty and confusion, and ending in a blaze of fame.

The last time I saw her was when she came to dine with me at what used to be their favourite café, 'Chez Francis', a café on the right bank of the Seine facing the Pont d'Alma and the Tour Eiffel. But it was a tragic evening, with former happy memories crowding in on her bereavement, and finally, as I helped her to the waiting taxi, for she was then crippled with arthritis, I heard her utter disconsolately 'This too, too solid flesh . . . ' for she did not want to go on.

Literary commentators on Joyce have wanted to make her into a kind of Jezebel to suit their book; but it was not so when I knew her anyway.

Like most, she had had hot blood in her youth: what would a woman be without it?

A warm, human plumpness settled down in his brain. His brain yielded. Perfume of embraces all him assailed. With hungered flesh obscurely, he mutely craved to adore!

And again:

Joy, young life, her lips that she gave me pouting . . . .
Hot I tongued her. She kissed me. I was kissed.
All yielding she tossed my hair.
Kissed, she kissed me.
Me. And me now.

Downes's Cakeshop and Williams's Jam

Bernard Share

The fiftieth anniversary of Bloomsday was not, in itself, much to write home about. The Joyce industry had not yet remigrated from America back home, and Bord Fáilte were still more bemused with beaches and racehorses than with the mind-jogging trot of a funeral equipage headed for Glasnevin cemetery. In the *Irish Times* Benedict Kiely could write 'Superficially, Dublin has little changed . . .' and proceed to take the reader over the course without having to fill in too many obvious lacunae. Superficially, of course, he was right: in 1954 you could still turn your eyes to heaven without the imaginary dotted line between them and the nearest hunk of cumulus being intersected by anything more vaunted in its ambition than the dome of the Custom House; the citizens, similarly, assumed the horizontal and wondered at those in other places who preferred to spend their days going agitatedly up and down. Pubs were still pubs, not suburban parlours with the next-door neighbour's overblown radio eternally in evidence.

Compare and contrast Bloomsday 1969: much more organized by now, with plenty of elegantly printed *Ulysses* maps, a Joyce Museum, junketings various, and a solemnly convened James Joyce Symposium exhibiting the latest line in holy relics. The only thing missing was James Joyce's Dublin, which is now being schematically pulled down without anyone, not even, apparently, the disciples with both the funds and the fanaticism, raising a dollar to prevent it. The house in Eccles Street is now nothing more than a door that leads nowhere in a Dublin pub, and whilst it might be a bit much to expect any devotee, however flush, to buy up Sandymount Strand to prevent the Corporation covering it with the contents of the city's dustbins, there are numerous corners of this foreign field that could be, for the addicts, for ever Bloomsday, had they

a mind to exert themselves. But they don't. One contributor to the
Symposium, who confessed he was going to miss out on the conducted
tour of the shrines, even went as far as to hint that he, as a scholar,
would be happier when all physical vestiges of the Dublin of 16th June
1904 had been swept away. Exegesists like himself would then be left
with a *tabula rasa* upon which to build, using cut-outs from the canon
like the back panels of cereal boxes, their own Joycean Dublin. Brute
facts can sometimes be a damned nuisance.

Working happily inside this process of natural dereliction and un-
natural destruction is a nice, happy little Joycean irony. Miles and
miles of typewriter ribbon have passed under the hammer to propound,
prove and illustrate Joyce's love-hate relationship with his native
country in general and his native city in particular. Every Summer-
Schoolboy knows that having shaken the sphagnum of the 'inhospitable
bog' off his feet for good and all, he never tired of wanting, in theory at
least, to get stuck back into it; and that his 'wild goup's chase across the
Kathartic Ocean' never really took him further than a twopenny tram-
ride from the Pillar. He put into his early books, in the words of his
city's present Commissioner and Joyce scholar, Andrew Cass, 'a
motiveless malignancy against various Dubliners' as well as every other
tiny detail he could beg or remember of this physical shape and feel of
the place. A man called Lionel Chouchon has written a novel, *La Tête
Enflée*, which is described on the jacket as *un roman qui fait 'Pop'*.
Inside you find, besides a good deal of unconventional typography, an
assortment of actual objects, metro tickets, jam labels, hairpins, glued on
to the pages as three-dimensional extensions of the story. If Joyce had
thought of the idea first I am sure he would have insisted upon actual
tram tickets, betting slips, facsimiles of *The Sweets of Sin* and so on
being incorporated in *Ulysses*, though his publishers would no doubt
have kicked up at some of the items he might have wished to include in
the Circe and Penelope episodes, Whatever his dallyings with the heady
notions of Giambattista Vico and Giordano Bruno, there is never any
equivocation about the ground upon which his feet are firmly planted.
And the irony lies in the fact that his legions of commentators and
expositors, for all their questioning of almost every other aspect of every
other concept which he ever formed, have in this respect taken him at
his word.

When we come to consider Joyce's Dublin from this point of view
we discover that art has taken a stranglehold on life and that nothing

short of the most violent academic blasphemy is likely to dislodge it. It is vain for the tourist boys to hope to interest the visiting Joyceman in the current beauties of the capital, the concrete boxes, the O'Connell Street ice-cream parlours, the parking meters. They have no need to look at Dublin: They know it from *Dubliners* and *Ulysses*, and they know that nothing can possibly change it. This is not mere fantasy, based, like bad market research, on a knock upon one academic door. Never mind what is said in the hot airlessness of a Joyce Symposium (though speaker after speaker produced the uncomfortable feeling in the non-committal listener that the trams were indeed still clanking past outside the Gresham, and that the latest edition of the *Freeman's Journal* was just on the streets: this is simple crowd-psychology and to be expected). But when the same kind of thing emerges from the academic caroll we realize that Joyce's belated attempt, in *Finnegan*, to make amends to his much maligned country and city has either gone unnoticed – scarcely possible – or just not been believed. Consider these passages from W. M. Schutte's book *Joyce and Shakespeare*:

> One of the major causes of the enervation in Dublin is the lack of any integrating force in the lives of the citizens. All of the pressures drive man away from man.

And again:

> The forces in society which are assumed by the inhabitants to be capable of integrating Dublin life are seen in *Ulysses* to be every bit as maimed and impotent as they were in *Dubliners*. Of religion one hears much talk, but one finds no indication that it can help man to a balanced, creative life . . . another potential integrating force, the political, is equally ineffective.... In *Ulysses* the instability of Irish political life is kept constantly in the reader's mind.... At the heart of Dublin there is nothing but memory, cant, misery and self-pity.

Notice that the whole thing is in the present tense, and that though the comments are ostensibly about literature the implication carries over without any noticeable jerk into life: when John William Corrington says in a recent essay on the short story 'The Sisters': 'There is no need, I think, to attempt a definition of corruption or frustration in connection with *Dubliners*' what he really means is that there is no need to do the same thing in connection with Dublin. Of course it was corrupt and frustrating; of course it was suffering from 'spiritual paralysis', as Robert Scholes had it in a reading of *Counterparts*, because Joyce says so. I have seen no research – though of course I am nowhere near up to date in latest developments within the industry – which has tabulated the happy, cheerful things that happened in Edwardian Dublin to happy, cheerful people, nothing which really exposes Joyce's city for the sophistic vision that it is. Andrew Cass has clearly pointed out (page 169) that the reasons for Joyce's leaving Ireland had as much to do with Joyce as with Ireland, and that when he had purged his spleen in *Dubliners* and *Ulysses* he made a belated attempt to set the record straight in *Finnegan*, which is more or less clearly dedicated to Ireland, *con amore* rather than *con furore*. Critics and public alike, however, have preferred to disregard this late aberration; they continue to a man to take Joyce's earlier, bitter picture of his city as the factual and atmospheric truth, and, to judge from the implicit attitudes evinced at the Symposium, to assume that nothing has changed. Now that *Ulysses* in paperback is reaching a mass market more and more people will be confirmed in the impression that Dublin not only was, but is, a repository of 'cultic twalette' and every social and spiritual ill the flesh and the psyche are heir to. That the love was ultimately to prove stronger than the hate in Joyce's attitude to his city few will quarrel with; but all the resources of the Grand Funferall were not enough to wipe away the early bitter indictment. There is thus a special poignancy in his farewell in verse, 'Gas from a Burner', written in rage and desolation in 1912:

> I printed folklore from North and South
> By Gregory of the Golden Mouth:
> I printed poets, sad silly and solemn:
> I printed Patrick What-do-you-Colm:
> I printed the great John Millicent Synge
> Who soars above on an angel's wing
> In the playboy shift that he pinched as swag
> From Maunsel's manager's travelling-bag.
>
> Shite and onions! Do you think I'll print
> The name of the Wellington Monument,
> Sydney Parade and Sandymount tram,
> Downes's cakeshop and Williams's jam?

Sad and ironic, but for anyone with a taint of iconoclasm, great gas.

Doctors and Hospitals

Dr J. B. Lyons

Joyce boasted with pardonable exaggeration that if Dublin were destroyed the physical city could be rebuilt from his works. The topographical detail in *Ulysses* is certainly remarkable when it is realized that its author, living abroad, had no opportunity to check his facts personally. Now and then he asked Mrs Josephine Murray, his aunt, to verify some point or other but in the main he relied on a remarkable visual memory.

Many medical institutions are mentioned in *Ulysses*, those alluded to most frequently being the Mater, Holles Street and Mercer's Hospitals.

Leopold Bloom, whose meanderings are followed throughout a long, June day in 1904, lives in Eccles Street. Passing along Berkeley Street in the morning he muses: 'The *Mater Misericordiae*. Eccles Street. My house down there. Big place. Ward for incurables there. Very encouraging'. Later he hears a medical student discoursing on the affectations of the profession. 'The bedsides manner it is they use in the Mater hospice. Demme does not Doctor O'Gargle chuck the nuns there under the chin?'

Bloom has had first-hand knowledge of 'the house of misericord'. He has been to the Casualty Department with a bee sting. The student – 'Dixon yclept junior of saint Mary Merciable's' – who treated him has moved to Holles Street Hospital, then under the Mastership of Dr Andrew Horne.

Seventy beds keeps he there teeming mothers are wont that they lie for to thole and bring forth bairns hale so God's angel to Mary quoth. Watchers they there walk, white sisters in ward sleepless.

Smarts they still sickness soothing: in twelve moons thrice an hundred. Truest bedthanes they twain are, for Horne holding wariest ward.

Walking through Molesworth Street, Bloom notices a placard advertising the Mirus Bazaar. 'In aid of funds for Mercer's Hospital. The Messiah was first given for that. Yes Handel. What about going out there. Ballsbridge'. In the afternoon he encounters the Viceroy who, 'on his way to inaugurate the Mirus Bazaar in aid of funds for Mercer's Hospital, drove with his following towards Mount Street'. Many others view the Viceroy and his Countess: from the Ormond Hotel 'gold by bronze' the barmaids watch and admire; Simon Dedalus 'stood still in mid-street and brought his hat low'; Blazes Boylan 'offered to the three ladies the bold admiration of his eyes and the red flower between his lips.'

Late in the evening Bloom is again reminded of Mercer's when *'Mirus Bazaar fireworks go up from all sides with symbolic phallopyrotechnic designs'*. Meanwhile two minor characters, M'Coy and Lenehan, have passed along Sycamore Street beside the Empire Music Hall: 'At the Dolphin they halted to allow the ambulance car to gallop past them for Jervis Street'. Phillip Gilligan, one of Bloom's friends, died in Jervis Street Hospital.

M'Coy had a job on the *Freeman's Journal* before he got the job in the morgue, under Louis Byrne. 'Good idea a post-mortem for doctors. Find out what they imagine they know. He died of a Tuesday'.

There is an inexplicit reference to Sir Patrick Dun's Hospital; Dr Steeven's Hospital is not included but the founder's sister, Madame Grissel Steevens (who, according to an ill-informed legend, had a face like a pig's snout), is recalled in a discourse on monstrous births.

Our Lady's Hospice for the Dying, the Royal Hospital Kilmainham and 'Simpson's Hospital for reduced but respectable men permanently disabled by gout or want of sight' are briefly mentioned. And is not Joyce's description of neglected senility a more oppressive reality today than in 1904? 'Nadir of misery: the aged impotent disfranchised ratesupported moribund lunatic pauper'.

There is a reference to 'Dr Eustace's private asylum for demented gentlemen', and 'Dottyville' is Grangegorman Asylum, known today as St Brendan's Hospital. The Lock Hospital, which is no longer in existence, is not forgotten. In the Circe episode a whore speaks of 'Mary

Shorthall that was in the lock with the pox she got off Jimmy Pidgeon in the blue caps off him that couldn't swallow and was smothered with the convulsions in the mattress and we all subscribed for the funeral'.

Stanislaus Joyce was a clerk at the Apothecaries' Hall, an item duly fitted into the mosaic of *Ulysses*, a book in which, as in life, irrelevance is relevant: 'Where is your brother? Apothecaries' Hall. My whetstone'.

Stephen Dedalus, who plays Telemachus to Bloom's Odysseus, lives in the Martello Tower, Sandycove, with Buck Mulligan. 'And what is death?' Mulligan asks rhetorically. 'You saw only your mother die. I see them pop off every day in the Mater and Richmond and cut up into tripes in the dissecting room. It's a beastly thing and nothing else'.

During the course of the day Bloom meets an old flame. He asks about a mutual acquaintance, Mrs Purefoy, to be told: 'She's in the lying-in hospital in Holles Street. Dr Horne got her in. She's three days bad now'.

After their marriage the Blooms had lived in Holles Street. Unknown to Leopold his wife ogled the students from her window but she found them slow on the uptake. ' . . . not a notion what I meant aren't they thick never understand what you say even youd want to print it up on a big poster for them . . . where does their great intelligence come in Id like to know grey matter they have it all up in their tail if you ask me. . . . '

The College of Surgeons is referred to in *Dubliners*. Lenehan, a character in 'Two Gallants', is waiting for a friend. 'He went as far as the clock of the College of Surgeons. It was on the stroke of ten'. Baggot Street Hospital is featured in another story; the inquest on the body of an alcoholic, Mrs Smily Sinicio, was held there. 'Dr Halpin, assistant house-surgeon of the City of Dublin Hospital, stated that the deceased had two lower ribs fractured and had sustained severe contusions of the right shoulder. The right side of the head had been injured in the fall. The injuries were not sufficient to have caused death in a normal person. Death, in his opinion, had been probably due to shock and sudden failure of the heart's action'.

In the first draft of 'A Painful Case' the scene of the inquest on Mrs Sinicio was St Vincent's Hospital but with his customary attention to detail, Joyce wrote to Stannie for information: 'Would the city ambulance be called out to Sydney Parade for an accident? Would an accident at Sydney Parade be treated at Vincent's Hospital?' Stannie's suggestion that 'in all probability the body would have been sent in on the tram' may not reflect the inadequacy of the ambulance service but indicate a measure of expediency in days of horse-drawn ambulances. Meanwhile it probably occurred to Joyce that accident cases are taken to the *nearest* hospital and the Royal City of Dublin Hospital, Baggot Street, is a good deal nearer to Sydney Parade than is St Vincent's Hospital.

The background to 'Araby' is a bazaar held in aid of Jervis Street Hospital. This was the first of an annual series of bazaars and we have already seen that from noon to night in *Ulysses*, Bloom is reminded of another of these great bazaars. 'A long lost candle wandered up the sky from Mirus Bazaar in search of funds for Mercer's Hospital and broke, drooping, and shed a cluster of violet but one white stars. They floated, fell: they faded'.

The *Report of Mercer's Hospital* for 1903 contains an anticipatory reference to the event: 'Many of the friends of the Hospital are making strenuous efforts to raise a sum of money for the benefit of the Hospital by the 'Mirus' Bazaar to be held at Ball's Bridge. . . . Unfortunately, the *Report* for 1904 is missing but from that of the following year we learn that the success of the fete enabled the governors to provide a new operating theatre, an anaesthetic room, an X-ray department, and four bedrooms for the Sisters – 'all of which will be electrically lighted'. The bazaar was held in splendid weather (the total attendance was 54,565 and Mercer's received £4,399 3s. 4d.) but it commenced on 31st May and if on 16th June 'bronze by gold' heard 'the viceregal hoofs go by, ringing steel' the Earl of Dudley's purpose was not to open the Mirus Bazaar. Furthermore, had Blazes Boylan been about on the actual opening day, his leer would have disconcerted two ladies rather than three. Countess Dudley, who was pregnant, did not attend.

For most readers *Finnegan's Wake* is as impenetrable as a mediaeval palimpsest. Who knows what topographical riches lie hidden in its pages? There is a fairly obvious reference to the late Dr Bethel Solomons and the Rotunda Hospital: 'in my bethel of Solyman's I accouched their rotundaties'.

Madame Stevens and a number of hospitals are referred to in the following passage:

> . . . he, after having being trying all he knew with the lady's help of Madame Gristle for upwards of eighteen calendars to get out of Sir Patrick Dun's, through Sir Humphrey Jervis's and into the St Kevin's bed in the Adelaide's hosspittles (from these incurable

welleslays among those incarable wellasdays through Saint Iago by his cocklehat, good Lazar, deliver us!) without after having been able to jerrywangle it anysides.

And we have already seen that there is an allusion in *Finnegans Wake* to the Medical School in Cecelia Street where Joyce was so briefly enrolled as a student. He never 'walked the wards' of the Dublin hospitals but he would have known many of the faculty by the name and reputation. Many medical practitioners and scientists are mentioned in *Ulysses*, the latter group including Pasteur and Röntgen the chemist and physicist who made discoveries of epic importance. Some are historical, some fictional; a number were Dublin celebrities of Joyce's youth, and there is one quack, Henry Franks, a purveyor of pills for V.D.:

All kinds of places are good for ads. That clap doctor for the clap used to be stuck up in all the greenhouses. Never see it now. Strictly confidential. Dr Hy Franks. Didn't cost him a red. . . . Got fellows to stick them up or stuck them up himself for that matter on the q.t. running in to loosen a button. Fly by night. Just the place too. Post no bills. Post 110 pills. Some chap with a dose burning him.

The earliest historical medical figures included are Empedocles (504–443 B.C.) and Maimonides (1135–1204), the latter a famous Jewish physician, philosopher and Rabbi whom Bloom mimics. And Joyce utilizes the well-known saying, 'from Moses to Moses there was none like Moses', which refers to the Biblical Moses, Moses Mendelssohn and Moses Maimonides respectively.

Next we find mention of some of the Irish families in which the role of physician was hereditary:

It is now why therefore we shall wonder if as the best historians relate, among the Celts, who nothing that was not in its nature admirable admired, the art of medicine shall have been highly honoured. Not to speak of hostels, leper yards, sweating chambers, plaguegraves, their greatest doctors, the O'Sheils, the O'Hickeys, the O'Lees, have sedulously set down the divers methods by which the sick and the relapsed found again health whether the malady had been the trembling withering or the loose boyconnell flux.

The O'Sheils who lived at Ballyshiel (in the present Co. Offaly) were physicians to the Mc Mahons of Oriel and are credited with the *Book of the O'Sheils* c. 1657. The O'Hickeys were physicians to clans living in

what is now Co. Clare. Nicholas O'Hickey translated *Lilium Medicinae*
during the last quarter of the fifteenth century. The O'Lees lived in
Connacht. They, too, had a book, a translation of a Latin text.

Paracelsus – the most original medical thinker of the sixteenth
century according to Garrison – is included among a list of notabilities
in the Cyclops episode. J. S. Atherton (*The Books at the Wake*) thinks
it improbable that Joyce ever read Paracelsus but if Gogarty is to be
believed Lyster urged the medicals who used the National Library to
read him. 'Before pursuing Osler, who is quite a modern author and
divorced from European tradition, might I not suggest that you dip, for
a little, into Paracelsus, that Doctor of both Faculties, neither of which
he deigns to define? Surely your mind is not impervious to the charm of
those inadequately appreciated Middle Ages?' Is it likely that Joyce
could have resisted the librarian's challenge?

R. M. Adams has pointed out in *Surface and Symbol* that it was
Rualdus Columbus who first recognized the clitoris as an anatomical
entity, an item which Joyce uses with comic effect. 'All possess bachelor's
button discovered by Rualdus Columbus. Tumble her. Columble her'.
Columbus (1516–59), whose anatomical work was published post-
humously in 1559, was assistant to Andreas Vesalius, the founder of
modern anatomy, and succeeded him in the chair of anatomy at Padua.
He showed that the lens of the eye is not situated in the centre of the
globe and proved experimentally that blood flows from the lungs into
the pulmonary vein.

Nicholas Culpeper (1616–54), Lazaro Spallanzani (1729–99), Johann
Friedrich Blumenbach (1752–1840), Graham Lusk (1866–1932), C. G.
Leopold (1846–1911), Oscar Hertwig (1849–1922) and G. Vallenti
(1860–1917) are referred to as embryologists although only the last
three merit the title. Hertwig proved that the spermatozoon enters the
ovum, accomplishing fertilization by union of male and female pro-
nuclei.

Must we accept the view of Empedocles of Trinacria that the right
ovary (the post-menstrual period, assert others) is responsible for the
birth of males or are the too long neglected spermatozoa or nema-
sperms the differentiating factors or is it, as most embryologists opine,
such as Culpeper, Spalanzani, Blumenbach, Lusk, Hertwig, Leopold
and Vallenti, a mixture of both?

Charles Lucas (1713–77), who has been called 'the Wilkes of Ireland'.

is better remembered as a politician than as a doctor. In 1747 he started a weekly paper, the *Citizen's Journal*, but had to flee the country because of his opinions. He took a medical degree in Leyden and practised in London before returning to Ireland. For a time he was M.P. for Dublin and, as Joyce recalls, he founded the *Freeman's Journal:* 'Grattan and Flood wrote for this very paper, the editor cried in his face. Irish Volunteers. Where are you now? Established 1763. Dr Lucas'.

In the funeral cab Bloom sits listening to his companions but he is watchful by habit. Passing through College Street he notes: 'Plasto's. Sir Philip Crampton's memorial fountain bust. Who was he?' The question, like so many questions in life, is left unanswered. Joyce tells us nothing about the distinguished surgeon to the Meath Hospital who had been Surgeon General, President of the R.C.S.I. and a chief founder of the Dublin Zoo, but later in the afternoon Bloom, pondering on communal kitchens, recalls Crampton: 'After you with our incorporated drinking-cup. Like Sir Philip Crampton's fountain. Rub off the microbes with your handkerchief. Next chap rubs on a new batch with his'.

Two landmarks used to guide us in following Cashel Boyle O'Connor Fitzmaurice Tisdall Farrell's walk through the city are 'Mr Lewis Werner's cheerful window' (Louis J. Werner, F.R.C.S.I., Ophthalmic Surgeon to the Mater Hospital, lived at 31 Merrion Square) and 1 Merrion Square, the corner house formerly occupied by Sir William Wilde, whose distinction as a surgeon and antiquarian tends to be overshadowed by the notoriety of his famous son.

Sir Andrew Horne's prominence in the Oxen of the Sun episode has already been noted. He was Master of the National Maternity Hospital where, on 16th June, Mrs Purefoy was in labour. In selecting that surname for his fictional patient, Joyce had his tongue in his cheek: Richard Dancer Purefoy (1847–1919) of 62 Merrion Square was an ex-Master of the Rotunda Hospital. Incidentally, he established the hospital's first pathology laboratory by organizing the 'Lucina' Bazaar.

Other medical notabilities of the time who figure in *Ulysses* are Louis A. Byrne, the Dublin coroner, Sir Charles Cameron, the city M.O.H., Connolly Norman, R.M.S. Richmond District Asylum, Surgeon Macardle, Sir Thornley Stoker (whose brother wrote *Dracula*), George Sigerson and Austin Meldon. The last-named, who was Surgeon to Jervis Street Hospital and President of the Royal College of

Surgeons in Ireland in 1889–90, was famous for his dinner-parties at which exotic items such as kangaroo tail and shark's fin were served. His corpulence explains Joyce's reference to 'a wolf in the stomach' and also a riddle current in the Dublin of the 1890s: 'What is more wonderful than the passing of a camel through the eye of a needle?' 'Dr Austin Meldon getting into a fly'.

Stephen Dedalus's reference to his mother's last illness – 'Dr Bob Kenny is attending her' – derives, of course, from Mrs Joyce's terminal illness. She died from cancer and her doctor was Robert J. D. Kenny, F.R.C.S.I., of 30 Rutland Square, West, Visiting Surgeon to the North Dublin Union Hospital and to Cabra Auxiliary Hospital.

Metchnikoff ('And to such delight has Metchnikoff inoculated anthropoid apes') and A. Conan Doyle ('The Stark-Munro Letters by A. Conan Doyle, property of the City of Dublin Library, 13 days overdue' was on Bloom's bookshelf) are well-known celebrities but a number of the doctors in *Ulysses* are fictional. The latter include Dr Finucane who certified Paddy Dignam's death, 'snuffy Dr Murren', Dr Francis Brady, Dr Rinderpest (rinderpest = cattle plague), 'the best quoted cow catcher in all Muscovy', and the Rt. Hon. Sir Hercules Hannibal Habeas Corpus Anderson, F.R.C.P.I.

One cannot, however, designate as fictional any character in *Ulysses* without hazard. Leopold Bloom's reflections on the vogue of Dr Tibble's Vi-coca suggest a fiction or a quack and *Ulysses* had already been published before Joyce consulted Sydney Granville Tibbles (1884–1960), a London ophthalmologist. Another questionable fiction is young O'Hare for whom, as Bloom recalls, Nurse Callan had a soft spot.

> Her he asked if O'Hare Doctor tidings sent from far coast and she with grameful sigh him answered that O'Hare Doctor in heaven was . . . he was died in Mona island through bellycrab three years agone come Childermas.

The young doctor had died from cancer but in the spring of 1902 John J. O'Hare took a degree at the Royal University and was appointed to the Mater Hospital. In the following February *St Stephen's* included a news item: 'Dr Jack O'Hare the popular Bohemian footballer is at present in Holles Street Hospital'. And at the Mater 'smoking concert' at the Rotunda on Shrove Tuesday 1904 O'Hare, still very much alive, sang a ditty with an obstetrical theme – 'The kiddie's still there but the waters are gone. . . .'

Dr Collins, whom Molly Bloom recalls with vivid detail, poses a particularly interesting conundrum:

When I had that white thing coming from me and Floey made me go to that dry old stick Dr Collins for women's diseases on Pembroke Road your vagina he called it I suppose that's how he got all the gilt mirrors and carpets getting round those rich ones off Stephens Green running up to him for every little fiddle faddle her vagina and her cochin china . . .

It has been said that Joyce's model for Dr Collins was Dr Joseph Collins, an American physician and author whom he had met in Paris, but R. M. Adams points out that there was an actual Dr J. R. Collins, M.B., B.S.Dub., at 65 Pembroke Road. On looking into the matter further, we find that in 1904 the Rev. T. R. S. Collins, B.D., lived at that address. Dr Jno. Rupert Collins, who had not graduated from Dublin University until 1901 and cannot have been a dry old stick, had left Ireland and was then practising in Cheltenham.

It is pointless to analyse Joyce's motives too closely. The search for correspondences should not be pursued too rigorously. However ardent Joyce's desire for verisimilitude it must be remembered that he did have a novelist's licence to trim his facts to suit his purpose. *Ulysses* is a superb prose cathedral richly adorned with a multitude of decorations; presumably its author was moved by the same impulse that led mediaeval masons to chisel the faces of their patrons and enemies on the soaring walls, depicting them at a whim as saints or devils, the reality altered sometimes by mere caprice.

Crampton ('so inseulated as Crampton's peartree'), Tibble, Lucas, Sigerson ('Sisurd Sigerson Shygmomanometer Society for bledprusshers'), Horne ('Ho, he hath horn hide!') and possibly Gogarty ('Gougerotty') re-appear in *Finnegans Wake* and the names of several doctors and scientists are woven into the text of this book where one word may have many meanings, e.g., 'through all Lavinia's volted ampire' commemorating Volta and Ampère.

One of the most unequivocal allusions is to Sir Dominic Corrigan, a leading nineteenth century Dublin physician – 'Corrigan's pulse and varicoarse veins'; perhaps the best-known – 'when they were yung and easily freudened' – concerns Jung and Freud who also perform a tandem act in 'Jungfraud's Messongebook'. Carl Jung, whom Joyce consulted about Lucia and who wrote a critique of *Ulysses* which displeased its author, is also referred to in 'the law of the jungrel', 'the jest of junk the jungular', 'no junglegrown pineapple', and 'Junglemen in agleement'. Vogt, who operated on Joyce, is worked into Ann van Vogt, an amusing modification of Ireland's legendary Shan Van Vocht, and Virchow, pathologist, anthropologist and politician, author of the celebrated *Cellular Pathology*, is referred to in 'by virchow of those filthered Ovocnes.'

A British affectation in the pronunciation of certain surnames (e.g. Home pronounced Hume) amused Joyce, and Gustavus Hume, who gave his name to Dublin's Hume Street, affords scope for punning: 'hume sweet hume', 'and send him to Home Surgeon Hume'. Another Dublin worthy included is the Quaker physician, John Rutty, an austere man who extolled the virtue of mineral waters. 'The use of cold water, testificates Dr Rutty, may be warmly recommended for the subjugation of cungunitals loosed. Tolloll, schools!'

The reference to 'the skall of a gall' becomes clear when it is recalled that Gall was a prominent phrenologist, and that to Hairductor Achmed Borumbored is a tribute to the audacity of a Kilkenny man.

In 1771 an impressive, bearded Turkish physician, Dr Achmet Borumbodad arrived in Ireland and proposed to set up baths in Dublin. Obtaining support among the local medical fraternity and receiving grants from the House of Commons and the College of Physicians, he established 'Dr Achmet's Royal Baths' on the quays at Bachelor's Walk. They were well patronized and Borumbodad claimed that from 1775 to 1781 '10,000 destitute and miserable objects have been restored to the blessings of health'. His charges were modest and the expense of enlarging the baths led him into insolvency. Meanwhile, the Turk had fallen in love with a Miss Hartigan. He offered to shave off his great black beard and to become a Christian. This was not enough to win the lady and eventually he disclosed that he was no foreigner, but Patrick Joyce of Kilkenny.

Details of many other scientists who have been identified by Adaline Glasheen in Joyce's pages – 'thought he weighed a new ton when there falled his first lapapple' (Sir Isaac Newton), 'Charley, you're my darwing' (Darwin), 'ignerants show beneath suspicion like the bitter halves of esculpuloids' (Aesculapius) – can be found in her *A Census of Finnegans Wake.*

Stephen Hero and A Portrait of the Artist as a Young Man: the Intervention of Style in a Work of the Creative Imagination

Francis Harvey

The aloof Dosenesque hero of *A Portrait of the Artist as a Young Man* – Stephen Dedalus: that insufferable prig, spoiled Jesuit and solipsist extraordinary – may not differ in essentials from the figure that emerges from the pages of *Stephen Hero,* but a comparison of the two works, despite the fact that the surviving portion of the latter only corresponds to the last ninety pages of the *Portrait (Travellers' Library* ed., Jonathan Cape), can be illuminating, not only in its revelation of how Joyce's protagonist is given a depth and sophistication he lacks in *Stephen Hero* but also in showing how the intervention of *style* can modify, indeed vitiate, a work of the creative imagination. Ignoring the fact that *Stephen Hero* is fragmentary and that it is a first draft which was subsequently disowned by its author as a 'school-boy's production', we can, nevertheless, draw some interesting conclusions about the writer and his work from even the most cursory perusal of the two texts.

Joyce was intensely concerned with projecting a certain kind of Flaubertian literary *persona* – the artist as God? – in both these works, particularly in the *Portrait,* and while we may doubt very much whether the picture of him that emerges from *Stephen Hero* is an authentic self-portrait, we can assume with certainty that it is closer to the truth than the carefully romanticized one we dimly (a word which appears in the later work as frequently as in the early Yeats) perceive through the intricate veils of elegiac *fin-de-siècle* prose in the *Portrait. Stephen Hero* may be an artistically inferior work – we can't, after all, justly compare a fragment with a whole – but, surprisingly, one of the first things that struck me on a rereading was the fact that it did not seem *dated* – which, curiously enough, was the predominant impression left on me by a rereading of the *Portrait.* Its flaccid languorous paragraphs, clotted with sensuous adjectives, are full of Ninetyish nuances and cadences and, ironically enough, again and again echo the language of the Celtic Twilight which Joyce so despised: words from the early Yeats like *dim, grey, soft, dark, sad, low, gentle,* wilt and droop on page after page.

Stephen Hero makes a much more immediate impact on the reader; it is, of course, far less contrived stylistically and, one supposes, is a factual record of Joyce's life at the time; it is full of long passages of excellent dialogue which do not appear in the *Portrait;* it has a natural human warmth and spontaneity conspicuously absent from the studied self-conscious posturing – literary and personal – of the other book; and it reproduces the *texture* of life as one imagines it at the time in a hard clear light and not as if through a glass dimly – which is what occurs in the *Portrait* where everything is seen through a complex highly wrought curtain of obfuscating prose and each character seems a sort of wraith trapped in the interstices of Stephen's subjectivity. (The contrasting manner in which Emma Clery is treated in both books is relevant here and I will refer to it later.) If we are interested in finding out what the young Joyce may have been like; if we want to know more about his background, family and friends; if we want to read something that is much closer to genuine warts-and-all auto-biography, then it is to the truncated text of *Stephen Hero* that we should turn and not to the gilded self-portrait Joyce so subtly paints in the later work. Of course, we should not forget that the author was writing what was ostensibly a work of fiction and not an autobiography and like all writers he selected and falsified – which he was perfectly entitled to do.

The *Portrait,* as it progresses from the apparently simple but in fact highly organized baby-talk prose of the hero's childhood – the growth of the child's mind matched step by step with an increasing complexity of language – to the sophisticated Pateresque pages describing his youth and early manhood, stands or falls on *style.* And as far as I'm concerned it falls – and very heavily indeed. Style is a legitimate weapon in the armoury of any literary artist, but when it begins to obtrude itself between writer and reader; when it makes one more conscious of *how* a thing is written than of what is being said or is happening; in short, when it makes one stop and say 'Wasn't that marvellous but why did he use the word *touch* six times in six lines?' then surely there is something that smacks of virtuosity for the sake of virtuosity. (One thinks at once of the Old Pretender himself and of Well's savage, if unjust, parody of his work.)

The *Portrait* is a book vitiated by style. This is not quite so evident in the early pages but as we read on we discover a sort of stylistic patina darkening every paragraph, blurring every contour and subduing every colour – like a varnish that dulls an old canvas. Joyce was perhaps the greatest master of pastiche in the history of the English language – all his work, from *Chamber Music* to *Finnegans Wake*, bears ample witness to this – and the *Portrait*, if it is nothing else, is a masterpiece of pastiche, its rich cadenced prose recalling again and again the influence of, among others, Flaubert and Pater. They say that the style is the man; and in the whole corpus of Joyce's work it is only in *Stephen Hero* that we can clearly discern his individual signature: the rest is pastiche of a brilliance unmatched in English literature but pastiche nevertheless. Words are no longer instruments: they are the be-all and the end-all of everything.

Let us take a passage in the *Portrait* and compare it with one in *Stephen Hero*. This is from the *latter*.

When she had gone in he went along by the canal bank, still in the shadow of the leafless trees, humming to himself the chant of the Good Friday gospel. He thought of what he had said to Cranly that when people love they give and he said aloud 'I will never speak to her again'. As he came near the lower bridge a woman emerged from the shadows and said 'Good night, love'. Stephen stood still and looked at her. She was an undersized woman and even in that chilly season her clothes gave off an odour of ancient sweats. A black straw hat was set rakishly above her glazed face. She asked him to come for a little walk. Stephen did not speak to her but, still humming the chant of the passion, transferred his coins to her hand and continued on his way. He heard her benedictions at his back and he walked and he began to wonder which was better from the literary point of view: Renan's account of the death of Jesus or the account given by the evangelists.

The following is from the *Portrait*.

A girl stood before him in midstream, alone and still, gazing out to sea. She seemed like one whom magic had changed into the likeness of a strange and beautiful seabird. Her long slender bare legs were delicate as a crane's and pure save where an emerald trail of seaweed had fashioned itself as a sign upon the flesh. Her thighs, fuller and softhued as ivory, were bared almost to the hips, where the white fringes of her drawers were like feathering of soft white down. Her slateblue skirts were kilted boldly about her waist and dovetailed behind her. Her bosom was as a bird's, soft and slight, slight and soft as the breast of some darkplumaged dove. But her long fair hair was girlish: and girlish, and touched with the wonder of mortal beauty, her face.

The writing in the first passage is lucid, vigorous, unpretentious and remarkably free of soft-centred adjectives. There is little of that repetition of key words which mars so much of the *Portrait* and the only questionable phrase, *an odour of ancient sweats,* immediately evokes the inflated prose of that book. This, in fact, might well be a piece of excellent contemporary prose: there is nothing dated about it.

The second passage is hard to stomach. First of all, notice the deliberate repetitions: *bare: bare: bared: white: white: softhued: soft: dovetailed: dove:* the appalling *soft and slight: slight and soft.* The whole passage is cluttered with adjectives – *strange and beautiful* must have been a cliché even in Joyce's day – there is an almost ostentatious concern with euphony and rhythm and, apart from *bosom,* which at once dates the piece, the tone and cadence of this stylistic confection is cloyingly *fin-de-siècle.* The inversion in the last sentence is unforgivable.

The passage immediately following this is, if anything, worse.

She was alone and still, gazing out to sea: and when she felt his presence and the worship of his eyes her eyes turned to him in quiet sufferance of his gaze, without shame or wantonness. Long, long she suffered his gaze and then quietly withdrew her eyes from his and bent them towards the stream, gently stirring the water with her foot hither and thither. The first faint noise of gently moving water broke the silence, low and faint and whispering, faint as the bells of sleep; hither and thither, hither and thither; and a faint flame trembled on her cheek.

This is so bad that it reads like a parody – self-parody. It is invertebrate, static, narcissistic, so verbally introverted that it seems to be admiring itself. It is dead: embalmed in its own virtuosity. Notice how *gaze* is repeated three times; *faint* four times; *gently* twice; *eyes* three times; *water* twice; the phrase *hither and thither* three times; and then there is the appalling *Long, long*. It is the prose of a man so intoxicated by words, their sounds and their colours, the patterns they make on the page, that he sees each of them as an end in itself: every paragraph a carefully plotted *tour-de-force* of arid verbal ingenuity; Flaubert's search for *le mot juste* degenerating into empty preciosity.

I have already commented on the way in which each character in the *Portrait* seems like a wraith doomed to wander through the mists of Stephen's subjectivity while, on the other hand, the characters in *Stephen Hero* have solidity and substance and seem endowed with purposeful lives of their own. Perhaps the outstanding example of this is the radically different treatment of Emma Clery – the girl Stephen wanted to sleep with – in the two books. In the *Portrait* she hardly exists at all except as a sort of foil for the hero's sexuality, a shadowy figure, so attentuated indeed that it seems only fitting she should be referred to by her initials. Emma as we see her in *Stephen Hero* is a girl with a mind of her own but in the *Portrait* she is deliberately reduced to the indistinctness of an adumbration: a moth-like creature existing only in the light of Stephen's overpowering ego. The passages in *Stephen Hero* describing the hero's encounters with Emma are among the best in the book – natural, direct, unliterary – but in the *Portrait* she is wrapped up in so many layers of verbal cellophane that she becomes a kind of life-size doll who'd be no good in bed anyway – a masturbatory image. And in many ways this seems to sum up the difference between the two books – the difference between a living person (warts and all) and a perfect waxen effigy.

The *Portrait* is a great *dead* masterpiece – as expertly embalmed in its own prose as that other classic of literary mummification, *Marius the Epicurean*, a glittering verbal confection concocted by a virtuoso in words – and it is nothing else.

The Unraised Hat

Monk Gibbon

About Joyce, and my endeavours to be doubly fair to him because I have been perhaps unfair and captious?... There is a tremendously strong impulse in me to beg him not to shock me! One can stand much, but that kind of shock which is the result of vulgarity and commonness, one is frightened of receiving. It's as though one's mind goes on quivering afterwards. . . . It's just exactly the reverse of the exquisite rapture one feels for instance with that passage which ends a chapter where Proust describes the flowering apple trees in the spring rain.

The speaker is that much-emancipated young woman, Katherine Mansfield, in a letter to a friend in the year 1922. A little afterwards I was in Paris and *Ulysses* was still the favourite topic of conversation in the small restaurant in the Rue Git le Coeur which I frequented nightly.

It was a favourite with Americans and, though I had never read a syllable of the book, I joined ardently in these debates. Tom Bodkin had told me that his whole mental life had been overcast for three months by reading it. That was enough to go on.

I encountered Joyce himself in Sylvia Beach's bookshop and, later, in the American library, where a nervous movement of the lower jaw as he handled the great dictionaries in which he sought for words was a noticeable aspect of the sharp-featured, spectacled face.

Later, Richard Ellman, in his excellent if massive biography, and Stanislaus Joyce in *My Brother's Keeper* brought me considerably nearer the man.

The Joyce cult must be nearing its grand climacteric. Of his seriousness as a writer and of the originality and prodigality of his talent, in certain aspects, there can be no doubt. All the same I do not feel inclined to raise my hat outside the Martello Tower at Sandycove, as once as a young man I used to, passing the house in Marine Terrace in Jersey where Victor Hugo had lived as an exile.

We are forced to admit something like genius in the finale of *Finnegans Wake*, a passage that with its overtones and undertones wins my even more immediate homage than the famous washerwoman episode. But the verdict of the American judge who passed *Ulysses* for general consumption on the grounds that it was an emetic and not an aphrodisiac, though much quoted by the happy publisher in the U.S.A., has always seemed to me a pitiful attempt upon the part of the aspiring legal mind to be 'with it' in the literary world by exalting vomiting at the expense of another much discussed and more agreeable human activity.

As for Joyce's own occasional claims to strike useless fetters from the human soul, they do not ring very true. There was only one thing to which he was steadfastly and consistently loyal, and that was his own genius. Professor Anders quotes Ezra Pound's penetrating verdict to John Quin: 'Joyce – pleasing; after the first shell of the cantankerous Irishman, I got the impression that the real man is the author of *Chamber Music*, the sensitive'.

The real man possibly; but certainly not the real writer, whose métier it became to share with us every scabrous recollection and aberration of youth's angry consciousness. Katherine Mansfield was wasting her time when she begged that he might not shock her. Undoubtedly there existed a huge gulf between Joyce the sentimental author of little lyrics which Edward Dowden would have been proud to father, and Joyce the author of Molly Bloom's soliloquy.

It is not the first antithesis to be found in the field of literary biography.

I discover other anomalies as between the man and the artist. Joyce's much publicized love of Dublin is one of them. Of course the writer loved Dublin. It was his theme. And the man, consciously or perhaps subconsciously, loathed and detested it, and no wonder.

How could he love a city where he had endured much hardship and humiliation until it had provided him with a masterpiece; and then – very naturally – placed it immediately upon a sort of pedestal, since he owed it the only sort of gratitude which the hundred-per-cent writer knows.

Joyce became the arch-enemy of all forms of genuine human aspiration, reserving a little tenderness for Bloom, provided it never runs too much counter to our contempt for mankind. The effect of *Ulysses* on a mind like E. M. Forster's was cataclysmic enough. One wonders what someone like Carlyle would have had to say to it.

It helped the trend of denigrating human personality and revealing the depths; and, so far from frightening our western civilization away from those depths, there has appeared a school of writers who, it would almost seem, would like us to think these depths typical.

Moses came down from Sinai and found the Israelites worshipping a gold calf. The impulse to worship is strong and as soon as men lose faith in the gods or in God they tend to look for a substitute, as in the deification of the Caesars, or the apotheosis of Hitler, Stalin or Mao. Literary godhead tends to last longer than political godhead and it should always be remembered that the calf *was* gold and that a great many earrings and bracelets had gone into its composition. But the sacrifices offered to it can even so be in excess of its deserts.

I do not think that it would have surprised Joyce if he had been told that professors would one day dance round his work and slash themselves with knives or with their latest thesis. But a critical Moses may yet come down from the mountain and protest about the matter. Joyce will not be discredited for any literary alloy in his writings but rather for certain fundamental philosophic defects in both purpose and performance. He was a good defender of himself and could put the thing pungently. Take his claim for *Ulysses*, 'If it isn't fit to read, life isn't fit to live'. This is effective only to an unthinking mind, for the argument fails when we retort that life often isn't fit to live – for the soldier crouching in a flooded trench waiting for the next sixteen inch shell to burst on the parapet, for the dipsomaniac in the final throes of *delirium tremens*, for the sex maniac stalking his next victim. Joyce's assumption that we would reply with a pious affirmation 'Of course life is fit to live' and that he could then add his triumphant 'And *Ulysses* to read' is countered the moment we challenge the questionable premise.

Ulysses came into a world whose optimism – if 1913 could be called an epoch of optimism, which is very doubtful – had been completely overthrown by one of the most disastrous wars in history. The world was ready for a poor view of life and for a very poor view of humanity. That Joyce's work tends to reveal all the most trivial as well as the baser activities of the human mind is not a crime. It might even be a service. But the revelation is made as though it were the whole truth. Nothing seems to have existed for Joyce except his own literary intention and anything that could feed its fuel. His work has the qualities of a powerful microscope directed on to the sediment of last week's milk bottle. The range of Proust's interests is limited, concentrating upon a particular social milieu in France in a particular epoch. But it is worldwide compared to Joyce's preoccupation with certain aspects of shabby-genteel Dublin.

S. L. Goldberg, speaking of a fairly early moment in Joyce's literary career, says:

> Soon he was assuring himself by checking that all the details in the stories were accurate *(Dubliners)*; and he ended by persuading himself and trying to persuade others that the 'style of scrupulous meanness' and the 'special odour of corruption' he had achieved would have a morally liberating effect on his country. *Dubliners* would let in fresh air; 'it is not my fault', he wrote to a recalcitrant publisher, 'that the odour of the ash-pits and old weeds and offal hangs round my stories. I seriously believe that you will retard the course of civilization in Ireland by preventing the Irish people from having one good look at themselves in my nicely polished looking-glass'.

Goldberg says elsewhere: '*Ulysses* leaves out too much to make it the final encyclopaedic epic it obviously aims to be'. Joyce's world, utterly man-centred, practically ignores any aspect of Nature except man. His talent was prodigal and it would be very strange if one were not impressed by it. But, as well, he excites in some of us a fundamental antipathy, like that of a man who cannot stop telling us about the dog-dirt on his boots.

There was more to the Irish people than that. Just as there was something irrational in Joyce's trivial personal superstitions so there is something in his work, disproportionate, distorted, almost a disease. Preoccupied exclusively with certain obsessions on which he can exercise his verbal activity and despite his brilliant intelligence, he has no ultimate comment to pass upon life. Though a master of subtle evocation as in those closing pages of *Finnegans Wake,* placed beside the humanity, the universality and the sanity of Tchekov he becomes almost *fin-de-siècle.*

The Catholic Element in *Work in Progress*

Thomas McGreevy[1]

The technique of Mr Joyce's *Work in Progress* has probably been explained sufficiently already to give readers interested in serious literature a line of approach to it. Technique is, of course, important always and there are still technical aspects of the work the implications of which will continue to interest the critic. It seems to me, for instance, to be noteworthy as marking not a reaction from realism but the carrying on of realism to the point where it breaks of its own volition into fantasy, into the verbal materials of which realism, unknown to the realists, partly consisted. This fantasy is obviously richer than the fantasy of, say, Mr Walter de la Mare, which turns away from reality and takes refuge in a childishness which at its best is no more than charming. Perhaps the best justification for the technique of *Work in Progress*, however, was that implied in the phrase of the late President of the English Royal Academy of Art at the 1928 Academy Banquet in London. (See the *Observer*, 6th May, 1928.) 'There are', he said, 'examples in our language so perfect in their beauty and fitness that one feels they cannot have been formed out of a language already fixed but that a language had been created in order that they may emerge'. I do not know whether Sir Frank Dicksee had *Work in Progress* in mind when he was speaking. I scarcely think it likely. But evidently he might have. For Mr Joyce has created a language that is necessary precisely to give beauty and fitness to his new work.

It is well to remember, however, that the beauty and fitness are the important things, and technical considerations may be put aside for a moment in order to consider *Work in Progress* from the point of view of

---

1 From *Our Exagmination Round His Factification for Incamination of Work in Progress* (i.e., Finnegans Wake), Faber and Faber Ltd., 1929

A Bash in the Tunnel

other beauties and fitnesses than verbal ones. Obviously, the book being still unfinished, one may not yet say that it is marked by beauty and fitness as a whole. But every chapter and passage that has appeared is so admirably realized and so related to every other chapter and passage that one has no doubts that when the end does come the author of *Ulysses* will have justified himself again as a prose writer who combines a well-nigh flawless sense of the significance of words with a power to construct on a scale scarcely equalled in English literature since the Renaissance, not even by the author of *Paradise Lost*. The splendour of order, to use St Thomas's phrase, has not been the dominating characteristic of modern English prose and it is partly because the quality was demonstrated on a vast scale in *Ulysses* that that book marked a literary revolution. And signs are not absent that, in spite of the difficulty of having to invent a new language as he writes, Mr Joyce, in his latest work, has lost nothing of his amazing power in this direction.

That the conception of the story as a whole is influenced by the Purgatorio and still more by the philosophy of Vico is well known. Mr Joyce is a traditionalist, a classicist. That is why he is regarded as a revolutionary not only by the academic critics but by those of the fervidly scientific advanced school whose attitude towards the biology of words is not what, if they were consistent, they ought to wish it to be. The deep-rooted Catholicism of *Ulysses* was what most upset pastiche Catholicism of many fashionable critics in England. The enthusiastic converts who discover the surface beauties of Catholicism at the older universities – 'temporary' Catholics one might call them – tend always to be shocked by the more profound 'regular' Catholicism of Ireland. And one remembers the difficulties of even the true born English Catholic Bishop Ullathorne in trying to keep the over enthusiastic converts Newman and Manning in order. To an intelligent Irishman, and to Mr Joyce least of all, Catholicism is never a matter of standing on one leg. It is not a pose, it is fundamental. Consequently, it has to face everything.

But the temporary Romanizers were as shocked by the unsavoury element in *Ulysses* as a sentimental Saracen of the Middle Ages might have been by the way in which Dante put popes in hell. (Compare, incidentally, the introduction of the phantoms of the Catholic and Church of Ireland primates into the Night-town scene in *Ulysses*.) Again Irish Catholics are not shocked by finding amongst the detail in the superb monogram page (Christi autem generatio) of the Book of Kells two rats tearing the Host from each other with their teeth. They face the fact, as the monk who painted the page faced it, that devilry exists. The *Introibo ad altare diaboli* with its response to the devil which hath made glad my young days intoned by Father Malachi O'Flynn and the Reverend Mr Love in *Ulysses* should be taken in exactly the same spirit as the rats in the work of the monk. But an English Catholic critic, writing of *Ulysses*, wanted it all to be like the passage relating to the chanting of the Creed:

> The proud potent titles clanged over Stephen's memory the triumph of their brazen bells: et unam sanctam catholicam et apostolicam ecclesiam; the slow growth and change of rite and dogma like his own rare thoughts, a chemistry of stars. Symbol of the Apostles in the Mass for Pope Marcellus, the voices blended, singing alone aloud in affirmation: and behind their chant the vigilant angel of the church militant disarmed and menaced her heresiarchs. A horde of heresies fleeing with mitres awry: Photius and the brood of mockers and Arius, warring his life long upon the consubstantiality of the Son with the Father and Valentine spurning Christ's terrene body and the subtle heresiarch Sabellius who held that the Father was Himself His own Son . . . idle mockery. The void awaits surely all them that weave the wind: a menace, a disarming and a worsting from those embattled angels of the Church, Michael's host who defend her ever in the hour of conflict with their lances and shields.

He went on glibly to say: 'It is a case of *corruptio optimi pessima* and a great Jesuit-trained talent has gone over malignantly and mockingly to the powers of evil'. He presumably rejects and would eliminate the rats from the Book of Kells, the gargoyles from the thirteenth-century cathedrals of all Europe.

Actually, it is worth while to note, malignance and mockery are precisely the things that are absent in *Ulysses*. In this inferno from which Stephen is ever trying spiritually to escape – for he, unlike the Jewish Bloom, knows the distinction between the law of nature and the law of grace and is in revolt against the former however unable he be to realize the latter – even the most obscene characters are viewed with a Dantesque detachment that must inevitably shock the inquisitorially minded. These do not notice that as Stephen leaves after having put out the light on the scene that revolted him by smashing the chandelier the

Voice of All the Blessed is heard calling. 'Alleluia, for the Lord God Omnipotent reigneth!' The inquisitorially minded, I hasten to add, however, exist in Ireland as well as in England. We in Ireland have been, though only to a relatively slight extent, affected, first during the Penal times when our priests had to be educated abroad, by French Jansenism and the orientally fanatical Catholicism of Spain, and later during the nineteenth century by our political association with the censorious nonconformity of England. We are even now founding an Inquisition in Dublin, though one may believe that it is not likely to be a very successful obstacle to the self-expression of a people who, with fewer pretensions have a sense of a larger tradition than that of the half-educated suburbans who initiated the idea of a new censorship. These latter understand no more than the enthusiastic converts who lay down the law to nobler men than themselves in England that Catholicism in literature has never been merely ladylike and that when a really great Catholic writer sets out to create an inferno it will be an inferno. For *Ulysses* is an inferno. As Homer sent his Ulysses wandering through an inferno of Greek mythology and Virgil his Aeneas through one of Roman mythology, so Dante himself voyaged through the inferno of the mediaeval Christian imagination and so Mr Joyce sent his hero through the inferno of modern subjectivity. The values are not altered but, because Mr Joyce is a great realist, it is the most real of all – one notes for instance that the Voice of All the Damned is the Voice of All the Blessed reversed, a realistic and understandable effect (cf. Dante's mysterious and not altogether intelligible 'Pape Satan, pape Satan aleppe . . . ') – and it is as terrible and pitiful as any.

The purgatorial aspect of *Work in Progress* is most obvious, of course, in the purgatorial transitional language in which it is written. This language is adequate to the theme. Purgatory is not fixed and static like the four last things, death, judgment, heaven and hell. The people there are not as rooted in evil – or, for Dante or for Mr Joyce, even in personality – as the people in the inferno. And therefore, for literary purposes, not in definitive language either. In *Work in Progress* the characters speak a language made up of scraps of half the languages known to mankind. Passing through a state of flux or transition they catch at every verbal, every syllabic, association. It is not natural that in such circumstances, without irreverence – on the contrary indeed – *Qui tecum vivit et regnet* should become for one of them Quick tekaum whiffat and drainit and that In the name of the Father and of the Son and of the Holy Ghost should become In the name of the former and of the latter and of their holocaust. The former is surely the Eternal, the latter the world and the holocaust the world consumed by fire as preordained from eternity.

Then there is a politically purgatorial side to the work dominated by the figure, intermediate from every point of view, of the Anglo-Irishman, Earwigger, Persse O'Reilley. And there is, perhaps, the personal purgatory of the author. I imagine – though it is an interpretation of my own – that the writer himself is suggested in that transitional stage of self-realization when he was still James Joyce the musician who, to find himself finally as an artist, had to become James Joyce the writer. All through his work it is evident that Mr Joyce never loses sight of the fact that the principality of hell and the state of purgatory are in life and by the law of nature not less within us than the kingdom of heaven. The questions of the law of grace triumphant and of a modern Paradiso will probably be more appropriately raised in some years' time.

Vico is the imaginative philosopher, the Dante, of the Counter Reformation, little known though there is a road bearing the Neapolitan name in Norwegian Dalkey, a suburb of Dublin. The conception at the back of *Work in Progress* is influenced by the Vico theory of the four stages of human society's evolution. But the working out of the parallel between the Vico conception and the reconstruction of it in regarding Dublin's life history in *Work in Progress* must wait till the complete work has appeared. The thunder clap, in Vico's system the most dramatic manifestation to primitive man of a supreme, incalculable being, is there in Part I, however, and students of Vico will be able as the work moves to completion to recognize the second, third and fourth of the Neapolitan's main ideas, marriage according to the auspices, the burial of the dead, and divine providence, in the other parts of it. They may be taken as comically foreshadowed in the childish sing-song repeated in one of the chapters that have already appeared, 'Harry me, marry me, bury me, bind me'.

Coming thus to less vast considerations, there are details of the work which, in their beauty and fitness, are unsurpassed even by the finest things in *Ulysses*. As characters, the mysterious viking father of Dublin – Dublin was founded by the 'Danes' – and his hustru (woman of the house), the wayward Anna Livia, the River Liffey, Dublin's mother, stand out above all, in some ways more than any of the whole gallery of amazing figures in the earlier work; but the Pecksniffian Earwicker, protean and purgatorial, though less epic is not less vivid. Then there is that broth-of-a-boy Seigmund-Shaun, sometimes figuring as a cherub, sometimes imagining himself a priest, a much more muscular type of Christian than Stephen Dedalus, entirely uninfluenced by Greek or Judaistic thought, the burliest Norse-Irish convert who ever escaladed the walls of Maynooth. As for verbal beauties and fitnesses, there are passages and phrases all through that have the delicate magic and dramatic force that one takes so much for granted from Mr Joyce, simply because he is Mr Joyce. There is the first paragraph of all with the voice of Brigid answering from the turf fire, mishe! mishe! (I am, I am) to tauf tauf (baptize!) thuartpeatrick (peat, Patrick). There is the final passage from the Anna Livia chapter when the two women are discovered as tree and stone; there is the paragraph at the beginning of Part III beginning 'Methought as I was dropping asleep in somepart in nonland of where's please' and the other 'When lo! (whish o whish) mesaw, mestreamed through deafths of durkness I heard a voice'. There is the meditation on the death of Mrs Sanders to compare with an earlier Dublin meditation (Swift's on the death of Hester) and the delicious little story of the Ondt and the Gracehoper[1] (the champions of space and time respectively) told by Shaun immediately afterwards. The portrait of the Ondt is worth reproducing.

> He was a weltfall fellow, raumybult and abelboobied, by near saw altitudinous wee a schelling in kopfers. He was sair sair sullemn and chairmanlooking when he was not making spaces in his psyche, but laus! when he wore making spaces on his ikey he ware mouche moore secred and wisechairmanlooking.

This little interpolation is a satire, but it is satire that is, like all good satire, intensely serious and it is subjected to the discipline of literary form. There is much talk of time in it – see for instance the passage describing the saturnalian funeral of the old earwig (here transformed into Besterfarther zeuts) piously arranged by the Gracehoper to an accompaniment of planetary music:

> The whool of the whaal in the wheel of the whorl of the Boubou from Bourneum has thus come to town.

Much, perhaps all, art consists in seeing the funeral of one's past

---

[1] Republished in *Three Fragments from 'Work in Progress'*, Black Sun Press, Paris

from the emotionally static point of artistic creation – emotion re-collected in tranquillity, time recollected in space. The London master of spaces should read Mr Joyce's fable. He might learn from it that Gracehopers, for all their seeming time-ness, are much more in space than the Ondts, who decide that they will 'not come to party at that lopps'. The author of *Time and the Western Man* is a writer of remark-able potentialities but he has so much contempt for time that he never takes enough time to finish anything properly. If he would read the story of the Ondt and the Gracehoper, not impatiently, he might learn from it how to write satire not like a barbarian, ineffectively, but like an artist, effectively.

Diseases of the Ox

J. F. Byrne[1]

In the *Portrait of the Artist* Joyce writes of 'Stephen pointing to the title page of Cranly's book on which was written "Diseases of the Ox" '. This apparently trivial incident affords much material for rumination. Here is the story.

In July 1899, something occurred to a cow owned by my farming friends in the County Wicklow; in the National Library I sought for, and with the help of the librarian, Mr Lyster, finally located, a book in which I hoped to find some information that might be useful should a similar emergency occur. When the librarian handed me the book at the counter, he indicated a section or chapter in it with the title 'Diseases of the Ox,' and although I was serious in mood, I immediately smiled. 'Diseases of the Ox,' I read aloud, and remarked to Lyster, who also had a broad smile on his visage: 'Sounds funny, somehow, that title'. Yes, it does,' he agreed, 'but maybe it covers what you are looking for'.

I took the book with me and sat down at a table near the balcony door, and I had just begun to peruse it when Joyce came in and sat down beside me. At that period Joyce was cramming himself with the Norwegian language, and he had brought with him to our table a pile of books on Ibsen including some of his plays, a Norwegian dictionary and a Norwegian grammar. For a moment he was silent, but then he leaned over to look at the large book I had open before me. 'Good Lord, Byrne,' he ejaculated, 'what are you reading?' I didn't say anything but I turned the pages to the title of the chapter where printed in large type was 'DISEASES OF THE OX'. The instantaneous effect on James Joyce was the detonating expulsion of a howl that reverberated through

---

[1] Author of *Silent Years* from which this extract is taken. He was 'Cranly' in the novels.

the reading room; and no Assyrian ever came down more swiftly on a fold than did Lyster on Joyce, who was in a convulsion of laughter. 'Mr Joyce,' the librarian ordered, 'please leave the reading room'. By way of calling attention to an ameliorating circumstance, I pointed to the title, but Lyster snapped: 'Yes, Mr Byrne, I know, but Mr Joyce should learn to control himself, and I must ask him to leave the reading room, and to stay out of it until he does'. Compliantly Joyce struggled to his feet, and I got up to go with him. 'I don't mean you, Mr Byrne. Of course, you can stay.' 'That's all right, thank you, Mr Lyster, but I'm afraid I'll have to help my friend out of the room. He would never be able to navigate as far as the turnstile'.

Outside the library Joyce slowly regained his composure, but neither of us felt inclined to make an immediate return to the vicinity of that book. Instead we went for a walk through the Green and, needless to say, we talked; and the one big question that interested us was why that title was so funny. Why, for instance, was it that if that title had been 'Diseases of Cattle', or 'Bovine Diseases', we would not have thought it a bit funny? But 'Diseases of the Ox' yes; for some obscure reason it was funny.

The consideration of this question suggests two other questions which, being more closely related than might appear at first sight, we may take up here in connection with the mammoth *Ulysses*. In that book Joyce employs three elemental four-letter words. According to Hanley's *Word Index to James Joyce's Ulysses* these words, with variations, are employed by Joyce in that book a total of thirty times; and the two questions that arise are 'What effect did the employment of these words have on the book considered as a work of art?' and 'What effect did the appearance of these three words in the book have on its sales?'

I have already told how I took up with Joyce the matter of that yarn he had written in the *Portrait* about the 'conversation' between Stephen and Father Butt in the Physics Theatre, and as a corollary to our talk on this point, we had gone on to mull over his use of the three four-letter words. The upshot was that I found Joyce not at all positive about the artistic value of the words; but inflexibly positive about their sales or popularity value. And with this judgment of Joyce's I could largely agree.

Two points in this general connection I want to stress. The first of these is that Joyce rarely, indeed scarcely ever, uttered orally any of these words; and it is all the more strange, therefore, that he had a leaning to write them, and it is also a little strange that he was so addicted to putting a plethora of expletives and fulminations into the mouths of some of his characters. In this regard, he made another mistake of over-embellishment, but the reason he did this was simply that he believed it was becoming for strong men, or strong characters, to talk that way.

To illustrate my point, let us look at and note the language in a letter he wrote to his brother, and which is reproduced in part in Mr Gorman's book. In it Joyce fulminates:

> For the love of the Lord Christ change my curse-o'-God state of affairs. Give me for Christ's sake a pen and an ink bottle . . . and then, by the crucified Jaysus, if I don't . . . , send me to hell. . . . Whoever the hell you are . . . I'm darned to hell if. . . . For your sake I refrained from taking a little black fellow from Bristol by the nape of the neck and hurling him into the street. . . . But my heroic nature urged me to do this because he was smaller than I.

Let me stress the fact that Joyce was no coward; but muscularly he was weak and he knew it. It would have taxed his strength to take a one-year-old baby 'by the nape of the neck'. In writing this letter Joyce was consciously posing as the eldest and strongest of the brothers – mentally, physically and muscularly. And he wrote as he fancied a man of his 'heroic nature' should thunderously express himself.

And now coming to the second of my two points, it is that I believe one of Joyce's principal purposes in insisting on the use of elemental words in his works was in protest against popular insincerity, cant and hypocrisy; and against a puritanical prudery which is essentially prurient.

Harking back to the 'conversation' between Stephen and Father Butt, I reminded Joyce that toward the end of his *Portrait* he made Stephen say: 'That tundish has been in my mind for a long time. I looked it up and find it English and good old blunt English too'. I asked Joyce where did he look up the word tundish and he told me in the dictionary. Then I asked him: 'Did you ever look up the word in Shakespeare, you know he uses it once in that piffly *Measure for Measure?*' 'Probably I did, but I couldn't say for certain'.

'Well, the point I am getting at is this: In that play the Duke says to Lucio: 'Why should he die sir?' And Lucio replies: 'Why? For filling a bottle with a tundish'. Now we can well imagine the guffaw that went up from the surrounding audience when it heard these words issue with ribald flippancy from the mouth of a character whom Shakespeare was depicting as the lowdown skunk, Lucio'.

'I see what you're driving at,' interrupted Joyce. 'Your point is that if Lucio had used all three of the elemental words in this seven-word sentence, as he could have done, he would have expressed himself with less indecency. This never occurred to me before, but if that is your point I fully agree'.

'Yes,' I said, 'that is my point'.

There is another aspect to this matter to which I will advert briefly. James Joyce valued many words for their sounds and for their own sake as much as he did for their connotation. Indeed the meaning of a word or group of words often was less important to Joyce than the word itself, or the grouping. Milton could say, and did, when he was imprecating on – of all things – Urania: 'The meaning, not the name, I call'. Joyce could scarcely ever have so spoken. He would have insisted on his Urania – and a rose to him by any other name would have been just another weed.

To retrace my steps once more after this digression, that incident in the National Library of Joyce's outburst of mirth at the title 'Diseases of the Ox' occurred during the period when he was studying Ibsen and preparing his essay on that playwright – an essay which found prompt acceptance, on its very first offering, in the *Fortnightly Review*. While Joyce was writing it, a period of about two months, he sat as usual beside me in the Library, and at his insistence I read it and reread it as it progressed, and when it was finished I could have recited it verbatim. Whether it was a good thing for Joyce that his essay was accepted by the *Fortnightly*, and that it was accepted so promptly, is a point I won't discuss here.

It must, however, in this connection be emphasized that it would be impossible for a young collegiate of the present day to realize the importance attached in Joyce's time by some persons, in certain circles, to the *Fortnightly Review*. Joyce was well aware, however, that this was not my attitude; and he knew that my opinion of him, or of the essay he wrote, would not be modified in the slightest degree by the *Fortnightly* acceptance. To some extent *Blackwood's* mantle, or to speak more aptly, *Blackwood's* 'muddy vesture of decay', had fallen on the *Fortnightly*. Joyce knew that I was a reader of Poe's works and that I admired the great American; and he knew that whereas Poe's opinion of

Blackwood's stood at freezing point on Poe's thermometer, my opinion of the literary importance of that magazine, or, indeed, of any other magazine with similar pretensions, stood down near absolute zero.

More than a year before the *Fortnightly* acceptance, I had been reading Poe's *Review of Elizabeth Barrett Browning's Poems*, and I had expressed to Joyce my unstinted admiration for it and for the selected excerpts illustrating what Poe called 'her wild and magnificent genius'. I cull here a few lines chosen by him from her Drama of Exile:

> With his calm massive face turned full on thine,
> And his mane listening.
>
> As if the new reality of death
> Were dashed against his eyes, – and roared so fierce
> (Such thick carnivorous passion in his throat
> Tearing a passage through the wrath and fear) –
> And roared so wild, and smote from all the hills
> Such fast keen echoes crumbling down the vales
> To distant silence, – that the forest beats,
> One after one, did mutter a response
> In savage and in sorrowful complaint
> Which trailed along the gorges.

And then Poe goes on to write anent *Blackwood's* literary critic:

> But, perhaps, we are guilty of a very gross absurdity ourselves, in commenting at all upon the whimsicalities of a reviewer who can deliberately select for special animadversion the second of the four verses we here copy:
>
> > 'Eyes,' he said, 'now throbbing through me! are ye
> > eyes that did undoe me?
> > Shining eyes like antique jewels set in Parian
> > statue-stone!
> > Underneath that calm white forehead are ye ever
> > burning torrid
> > O'er the desolate sand desert of my heart and
> > life undone?'
>
> ... when we take into consideration the moral designed, the weirdness of effect intended, and the historical adaptation of the fact alluded to in the line previously mentioned (a fact of which it is possible that

H

the critic is ignorant), we cannot refrain from expressing our conviction – and we here express it in the teeth of the whole horde of the Ambrosianians – that from the entire range of poetical literature there shall not, in a century, be produced a more sonorous – a more vigorous verse – a juster – a nobler – a more ideal – a more magnificent image – than this very image, in this very verse, which the most noted magazine of Europe has so especially and so contemptuously condemned.

In his recent biography of his grandfather, Lord Alfred Tennyson, Charles Tennyson tells us that Alfred was driven into nine years of public silence by the cruelty of a sneering review in the *Quarterly Review*. It sounds almost incredible that anyone should have been so deeply affected by such a cause; but the fact is only too well established that many persons were, and Tennyson was more than ordinarily sensitive. He was, fortunately for himself, not so sensitive or so delicate as Keats, whom the damnable reviewers almost literally stoned to death.

Down through the years, from '. . . Scotch Reviewers' through Keats' killers, and from *Blackwood's* through the *Quarterly,* and through the *Fortnightly,* gross ignorance pontificated incessantly from the pulpit of some 'magazine' or 'review'.

After his article on Ibsen had been published, Joyce's relationship with his few associates became impaired by either their jealousy or their sycophancy; and so it happened that Joyce was forced during the next couple of years to rely more than ever on me for companionship.

Immediately after the publication of the Ibsen article, Joyce began occasionally, and when in the mood, to seek expression in writing short poems. In the production of these he was not prolific; and even as he sat beside me in the library he would write and rewrite and retouch, it might almost seem interminably, a bit of verse containing perhaps a dozen or a score of lines. When he had at last polished his gem to a satisfying degree of curvature and smoothness, he would write out the finished poem with slow and stylish penmanship and hand the copy to me. Many a time he said to me as he did this: 'Keep all these, J.F. – some day they'll be worth a pound a piece to you'. Joyce always said this jokingly; but I never took his remark as a joke for I was even then quite sure that, no matter what my own personal opinion of his bits of verse might be, these bits of polished verse in Joyce's equally polished handwriting would some day be collector's pieces.

The finished poems were invariably done on slips of good quality white paper provided free and in abundance to the readers of the National Library. The slips were approximately 7⅝ inches in length by 3⅜ inches in width. Joyce gave me copies of all the poems he wrote prior to October 1902; and I kept all of them, as well as I could, for more than twenty years. Then, finding that many had been either lost or, more likely, pilfered, and realizing that they would probably be safer in a collection, I yielded to the importunities of John Quinn and sold him the few originals I had left. With these I also sold to Mr Quinn a signed copy of Joyce's The Holy Office, which he gave to me on one of his visits to my place at 100 Phibsboro Road. The price I got for these several items averaged about six dollars. That certainly wasn't much; but still it was more than even Joyce had jokingly told me they would some day be worth.

One day late in March 1902 Joyce said to me: 'I have another poem for you'.

'Good,' I said, 'give it to me'.

'I have it in the rough here, but I'll write it out for you'.

'You know I told you I had an appointment at four o'clock in connection with the handball tournament, and it is nearly that now. Give me the rough, and I'll copy it myself in one-quarter the time it would take you to write it'.

He did; and I did. And that copy of Joyce's poem written by me with a pencil on two library slips so many years ago is still in my possession. On the second slip where the word 'sorrow' occurs in the poem, Joyce drew a mark over that word, and he wrote in the margin 'Accent divided equally'.

Here is a reproduction of the poem, *verbatim et literati,* as I copied it from Joyce's rough:

I

O, it is cold and still – alas! –
The soft white bosom of my love,
Wherein no mood of guile or fear
But only gentleness did move.
She heard as standing on the shore,
A bell above the water's toll,
She heard the call of 'come away'
Which is the calling of the soul.

II

They covered her with linen white
And set white candles at her head
And loosened out her glorious hair
And laid her on a snow-white bed.
I saw her passing like a cloud,
Discreet and silent and apart.
O, little joy and great sorrow
Is all the music of the heart.

III

The fiddle has a mournful sound
That's playing in the street below.
I would I lay with her I love –
And who is there to say me no?
We lie upon the bed of love
And lie together in the ground:
To live, to love and to forget
Is all the wisdom lovers have.

Joyce was fond of music, and at that time I was even fonder of it than he was. During the far-flung visits of the Rouseby and Carl Rosa Opera Companies, we went to as many operas as we could afford. In our very youthful days we enjoyed such popular favourites as *Trovatore; Maritana; The Bohemian Girl; Lily of Killarney*, and such like; but as we grew older, it was Wagner who attracted us – especially by such of his music dramas as *Tristan and Isolde* and *Lohengrin*.

In the dramatic field we looked forward to the occasional visits of, for instance, Osmond Tearle, whose repertory was chiefly, but not exclusively, Shakespearean. Tearle's locale was always the Gaiety Theatre; and in that theatre, whether we were attending opera, play or pantomime, Joyce had the peculiar whim to sit at the extreme right of the top gallery (the gods). From this vantage point you looked down almost vertically on the players. I did not like the spot at all, but Joyce was so childishly eager to sit there that, of course, I agreed to sit with him.

Once in a while during the period of which I have been writing, Joyce developed an urge to set something to music. Usually it was one of his own pieces of verse, but at one time in 1902 he laboured lovingly over composing an accompaniment for James Clarence Mangan's beautiful poem 'Dark Rosaleen'. Towards the south end of the Aula

Maxima in University College, and on its west side, there was a door leading to a small room in which was a pianoforte. Joyce and I went there on many a night so that I could hear him sing the airs he had in mind and then play them for him. And sometimes on these nights, in order not to attract attention, we stayed in that room in pitch darkness – Joyce singing almost sotto voce and I playing the piano pianissimo. Whether Joyce's accompaniment to Mangan's 'Dark Rosaleen' has ever been published I do not know. But I do know that after all these years I remember perfectly the air for it which he sang to me, and which I played for him, in the dark.

The handball tournament I organized in 1902 was so successful and popular, especially in bringing the medical and art students together, that I was importuned by many, including professors, to organize another tournament in the following spring of 1903. With this request I complied willingly, and proceeded to do the job, on the tacit understanding that the handball alley at University College would again be available for the event. But when I had organized the tourney, and it was ready to start, some prigs and bounders among the boarders at University College objected to the use of what they claimed was their ball alley; and, to my astonishment, the objections of these dogs in a manger among the boarders was sustained by the college authorities, and the use of the handball alley for the tournament was denied. This unexpected and thoroughly unsportsmanlike development was one which I could not leave unchallenged. I had to meet it.

I am dealing with this incident briefly; it is told in detail in *A Page of Irish History*. I will only say that I went to the head of the Dublin Metropolitan Police, Sir John Ross of Bladensburg, and asked him for permission to hold the tournament in the splendid ball alley attached to the Mountjoy police station. Sir John was most agreeable and immediately granted my request, stipulating only that there should be no play during certain hours when the night-duty bobbies were sleeping. This proviso was entirely acceptable; indeed, it proved a fortunate circumstance in that it prolonged the tournament – which turned out to be just as popular with the bobbies and prison warders as it was with the students.

During the progress of the tournament we engaged in athletic competition including some weight-lifting stunts. One of these stunts was the repeated lifting from the ground with one hand of two 56-pound dumbbells to arm's length above the head. In this event I easily out-lifted all competitors; a result which vastly surprised me because the bobbies in Mountjoy were the C Division, the athletic pick of the metropolitan police. Joyce arrived back in Dublin from Paris at this time, and the superiority of 'Cranly's arm' *(Ulysses)* in the weight-raising event was no surprise to him.

During Joyce's absence in Paris something had occurred which hurt me deeply, I cannot go into detail about this, but I felt so badly about it that I wanted to speak with him. In long rambles about Dublin during the week after Easter, I talked the matter over with him exhaustively, but it seemed to me that his explanation explained nothing, and I would not agree to a continuation of our friendship. With this understanding, we parted finally on Friday night. On the following Sunday morning, the postman delivered to me this letter from James A. Joyce:

Dear Byrne,

Would you care to meet me tomorrow (Sunday) in Prince's St. at one o'clock? Perhaps you will not get this tomorrow morning as the post is upset.

J A J
7 S Peter's Terrace, Cabra
Saturday Night

In writing this letter to me Joyce proved that, in a way, he knew me better than I knew myself. We had said goodbye to each other – definitely; and yet only twenty-four hours later he wrote to ask me to meet him. And, of course, I did meet him – in Prince's Street at one o'clock.

That Sunday afternoon, evening and night, we walked through all the southern suburbs of Dublin. And as we walked we talked; and gradually James Joyce won, in substantial part, his battle for a continued friendship.

Towards the end of *A Portrait of the Artist*, Joyce writes about this long walk and talk. As usual, however, he mixes this event with events of other times and places. In one passage, he writes: 'Their minds, lately estranged, seemed suddenly to have been drawn closer, one to the other'. I would distinguish here that it was not our minds that were estranged. Indeed, Joyce's mind was at one with mine in apprehending the cause of my grievance. He knew and admitted that he was at fault; he tried to explain, and he told me he was sorry. His explanation I did not accept – at that time; but he did succeed in convincing me of the earnestness of his sorrow. Looking back on this incident in the light of maturity, I think now that I was wrong – I should have realized more clearly his difficulty in formulating an explanation, and if I had realized this I would have been able more adequately to interpret the one he gave me.

Notwithstanding our reconciliation, there was a modification in our relationship. This condition persisted for more than twelve months, but became gradually ameliorated, and by the time Nora Barnacle came into his life, James Joyce and I were again at one.

Harking back to Joyce's account of our walk and talk in *A Portrait of the Artist* there are some passages in which Joyce tells of my trying to get him to yield to the wish of his ailing mother. Of Cranly he says:

His hat had come down on his forehead. He shoved it back: and in the shadow of the trees Stephen saw his pale face, framed by the dark, and his large dark eyes. Yes. His face was handsome: and his body was strong and hard. He had spoken of a mother's love.

And in another passage he quotes Cranly:

Whatever else is unsure in this stinking dunghill of a world a mother's love is not.

The point at issue between Joyce and his mother was her wish that he would make his Easter duty, and his refusal to do so. In his narration of our discussion of this point, Joyce reports on Cranly:

'It is a curious thing, do you know' – Cranly said dispassionately – 'how your mind is supersaturated with the religion in which you say you disbelieve'.

And in Stephen Hero he quotes Cranly as remarking:

'You say you're emancipated but, in my opinion, you haven't got beyond the first Book of Genesis yet'.

Joyce would have been more accurate had he reported me as saying 'chapter' instead of 'Book' of Genesis. In commenting thus I am not making the merely captious point that Genesis is not divided into books – my point is that, as Joyce quoted me, my remark implies my opinion that in order to become 'emancipated' you have to read 'beyond' the Book of Genesis. That wasn't what I had in mind at all. For I was satisfied that a perusal of the Book of Genesis was in itself sufficient to lead one to 'emancipation'.

Joyce's attitude towards his mother affected me keenly, as had his attitude a short time back to his dying sister Isabel. I thought he was callous, and did not hesitate to tell him so; and when he sought to defend himself on religious grounds, while at the same time proclaiming his freedom from religion, and his emancipation, I was doubly angered. Look at one bit of the conversation between Cranly and Stephen, as told in *A Portrait*, which for academic purposes I accept as he reported it.

– Let me ask you a question. Do you love your mother? –
Stephen shook his head slowly.
– I don't know what your words mean – he said simply.
– Have you never loved anyone? – Cranly asked.
– Do you mean women? –
– I am not speaking of that – Cranly said in a colder tone.
– I ask you if you ever felt love towards anyone or anything. –
Stephen walked on beside his friend, staring gloomily at the footpath.

Let me make it clear that this incident of Joyce and his mother was not the cause of the near rupture in our relationship. But I did feel deeply his refusal to comply with what he knew was practically her dying wish; and my feeling, I repeat, was further deepened by the explanation he gave for his refusal. To quote once more from *A Portrait*.

– Cranly, I had an unpleasant quarrel this evening. –
– With your people? – Cranly asked.
– With my mother. –
– About religion? –
– Yes – Stephen answered.
After a pause Cranly asked:
– What age is your mother? –
– Not old – Stephen said. – She wishes me to make my Easter duty. –
– And will you? –
– I will not – Stephen said.
– Why not? – Cranly said.
– I will not serve – answered Stephen.
– That remark was made before – Cranly said calmly.
– It is made behind now – said Stephen hotly.
Cranly pressed Stephen's arm, saying:
– Go easy, my dear man. You're an excitable bloody man, do you know. –

He laughed nervously as he spoke and, looking up into Stephen's face with moved and friendly eyes, said:
– Do you know that you are an excitable man? –
– I daresay I am – said Stephen, laughing also. –

As partly bearing on, and undoubtedly stemming from, Joyce's attitude towards his mother, it is noteworthy that in his youth and early manhood his attitude towards older people, generally, was distant, unresponsive, unwelcoming, guarded and cold – to the point of frigidity. I do not recall one older person in whose company he was at ease.

With my cousin Cicely he could sit for a while without being in obvious discomfort but this was because Cicely would wait for him to say something, or else nothing would be said. But with my cousin Mary he didn't get along at all. Mary was a little bit of a gusher; she wouldn't let many gaps occur in a conversation, and she would always be trying to cap a story told by anyone else; or cap even a simple statement of fact, with something better, or funnier, or more strangely factual. Mary was an oddity; she was as unselfish a person as ever lived, and although she was capable and brainy she never learned even the elementary facts of life.

One evening when Joyce was in number 7 Eccles Street, a lady friend of my two cousins came in to pay them a visit; and during the conversation, which was confined almost entirely to Mary and the visiting lady, there was a bit of dialogue which was truly stereoscopic in the light it threw on Mary – her deep ignorance of life, and her desire to go one better. The visitor was lugubriously telling us about the troubles in a family she knew: the husband had just died leaving his widow with three children, and, what was much worse, there was a posthumous child that would not be born for a full six months.

And to this what did Mary say? Did she express her sympathetic commiseration? She did not. She said:
'Why that's nothing. My father was dead years before I was born.'

Mary did not like Joyce, partly because, as she said of him once, 'When he holds out his hand for you to shake, you feel nothing but five little, raw, cold sausages'. And Joyce did not like Mary. And that is why in his *Ulysses*, Mrs Fleming is the lady who cooks and darns socks for Poldy and Molly Bloom in number 7 Eccles Street.

J

The Artist on the Giant's Grave

Benedict Kiely

North Richmond Street, being blind, was a quiet street except at the hour when the Christian Brothers' School set the boys free. An uninhabited house of two storeys stood at the blind end, detached from its neighbours in a square ground. The other houses of the street, conscious of decent lives within them, gazed at one another with brown imperturbable faces.

It was also the street along which a refined Quaker lady had walked to pay a visit to a Christian Brother who had once been a novelist, a poet and a playwright, and who had halved what seems to have been a gentle platonic fluttering with the Quaker lady, and who, in a fit of flight from the world, had destroyed what remained of his manuscripts and taken to unalloyed religion. When he was told that the Quaker lady, who was also blamelessly wedded, was in the parlour to pay him a call he gave the matter prayerful thought, sent her a message that he could not see her, and went on being unalloyed.

The crisis of conscience of Gerald Griffin, the author of *The Collegians,* found no place in *Dubliners,* perhaps because Griffin was not a Dubliner nor ever could be, being a Limerick man. But it is at least interesting that that moment in his life should have taken place in the same street in which the quest for love and Araby began, and ended in a boy's disillusion. Those brown imperturbable faces, behind them the consciousness of decent lives, looked out on that darkness of agony in which man knows himself 'as a creature driven and derided by vanity'.

Brown but perturbed, even outraged faces, here and elsewhere, looked out on the man who had written 'Araby' and more besides. When I settled in Dublin in 1940 that sawed-off street, going nowhere and leading nowhere, seemed, for two reasons, a natural place of pilgrimage, the easier to get to because my first tent in that city was pegged down a few minutes walk away across the banks of the Royal Canal in Bally-bough.

Curiously enough, too, the first person I'd heard, up to that moment, making a favourable, an impassioned, statement on James Joyce had been an Irish Christian Brother. This had happened during a class in trigonometry in a secondary school in a town in Ulster some time during the 1930s, and the brother was given to digression into matters closer to his heart than sines and cosines, although long afterwards the digression did not seem as far or as fanciful as it then did. He was a cultured man with literary tastes and he defended Joyce to a class of half-comprehending boys, not just because Joyce was a great writer but because he was a great Irish writer, a national possession, something to be proud of, and because it was evident from the attitude of certain parties in Britain and the U.S.A. towards *Ulysses* that yet another attempt was being made to do the Irish down. That the book had been published and praised in France simply went to show that the most civilized people in Europe were with us as they had been with us in the past, sails cracking in Bantry Bay, if only luck and the weather had also been with us. He could not approve, he told us, of literary criticism by customs and excise.

For an Irish Christian Brother that was an unusual approach to James Joyce but then that teacher was an unusual man and we were lucky to have him. He made us realize that there was a world where books mattered and also that all writers were not, as the curriculum assumed, dead. The curriculum, needless to say, made no mention of Joyce, and found room only for a few early poems of Yeats, who might have been embalmed for centuries for anything the notes to our texts had to say. The history of English literature that we used said that Irishmen had often made a fresh and lively contribution but that, as a rule, they were uneducated, uncultured men. The Irishmen the historian, an English schoolteacher, was mentioning in that comment were Burke, Goldsmith and Berkeley who clearly might have achieved something if they had had the benefit of an education. That sort of textbook did badly need correction.

For our benefit, too, and to relieve his own soul of an indignation, our teacher of trigonometry came down like thunder on a hostile review that a learned, versatile and turbulent professor had written of a book of poetry by F. R. Higgins, and we came to know that learned professors could also be obtuse, and we were treated to a colourful making of comparisons between the poems of Higgins and *The Love Songs of Connacht*. So that those of his pupils who cared about such things and who went that way got to Dublin with their eyes wide open. The reading of *Dubliners* was a preparation for walking the streets of the golden city where so many of the great had been.

Joyce was, then, the writer who proved to whatever was chauvinistic in one that an Irish writer could shake the world: it was also pretty obvious that he was neither uneducated nor uncultured although Virginia Woolf, God help her, had her own ideas about that. Then he was in the 'style of scrupulous meanness' of *Dubliners*, the guide to the city. The famous declaratory passage was an interesting parallel to the passage in which William Carleton, an Ulster man like myself, had explained why he had taken it upon himself to write *The Traits and Stories of the Irish Peasantry*. The Joycean declaration had to be learned by heart in much the same way as, at an earlier age, Pearse's speech at the grave of O'Donovan Rossa had been learned by heart:

> I do not think that any writer has yet presented Dublin to the world. It has been a capital of Europe for thousands of years, it is supposed to be the second city of the British empire and it is nearly three times as big as Venice. Moreover, on account of many circumstances . . . the expression seems to me to bear some meaning and I doubt whether the same can be said for such words as 'Londoner' and 'Parisian' . . . .

There was, in that, all the arrogance of a young man zealous to make a case for his own city and his own book. But nothing appeals to young men like an arrogant young man; and all the sideswipes that the young Joyce had made at repression and obscurantism seemed well justified in the 1940s when the repressions of a silly literary censorship were at their worst. When he wrote of Dublin as the centre of the country's moral paralysis he was attacking not the city which he loved and celebrated but a narrow group of narrow minds that one could easily identify as being still with us. A Dublin daily newspaper, renowned for success through dullness, did the young men of that time a favour by failing to carry even a news report of the death of Joyce, and thus helping to identify and delineate the enemy.

As a student of U.C.D., too, one could so easily and arrogantly identify with the arrogant Joyce. Newman's head was there in the church in St Stephen's Green to remind one of Newman's hopeless struggle against the obscurantism, or plain bloody ignorance, of Cardinal Cullen whose broad bucolic back could be studied, by way of contrast, in the pro-cathedral.

Brinsley MacNamara had, when I was but new to Dublin, persuaded me that the backs of statues were so much more revealing than their fronts. He demonstrated his thesis by a study of the back of the statue of old Dargan, the financier, outside the National Art Gallery. 'Never show your teeth,' old Dargan had said, 'unless you mean to bite.' That message could be as good as read on the back of his statue.

Newman's calm head reminded one a little about the development of Christian doctrine; something about the fact that Thomas Huxley had said – in relation to the knife-edge on which Newman had balanced his thoughts – that, with a few changes, the *Grammar of Assent* could be transformed into a handbook for unbelievers; but mostly it reminded one that Joyce (or Stephen) had given praise to Newman's prose, cloistral and silver-veined. Joyce was, in that, so much wiser than George Moore who in *Hail and Farewell* devoted so many tedious pages to attacking Newman's prose: the attack of an irascible pedant or, worse still, a bigot, and an attack that was so painfully part of Moore's anti-Catholic kick, which one could not take seriously because it seemed that he had never been close enough to the thing to feel anyway deeply about it. Joyce had felt deeply and spoken fairly and made his problems yours, and made your problems his own.

In one of the rooms, too, in St Stephen's Green, Stephen Dedalus had talked to the English Jesuit who owned a language of which a Dubliner was to take violent possession. The curving marble banister on the stairway of the National Library was, as it had been to Stephen, smooth-sliding Mincius crowned with vocal reeds. Kind air in the evening still defined the coigns of the buildings. The planks of the Bull Bridge still resounded to the thumps of the boots of young Christian Brothers going down to the sea, and out on the wide strand, Howth floating in the background, any pool could have been the pool in which the barelegged girl waded and revealed to Stephen all beauty, all desire, all life and its agony:

> Her slate-blue skirts were kilted boldly about her waist and dove-tailed behind her. Her bosom was as a bird's, soft and slight,

slight and soft as the breast of some dark-plumaged dove. But her long fair hair was girlish; and girlish, and touched with the wonder of mortal beauty, her face.

For all this a Jesuit interlude was a good preparation. Down in the woods of Laois, in the Irish midlands, where I spent a while in a Jesuit novitiate, then situated in what had once been the country house of the Earl of Portarlington – Edward the Seventh had slept there and, by way of contrast, the last countess to live there had become a Roman Catholic – I found out that it really mattered to some people whether James Joyce had been an O.B. or an O.C. But brotherly charity could be preserved and the controversy resolved by realizing that he had been both: that is, an old boy of both Belvedere and Clongowes. As they had had on Voltaire and Renan the Jesuits had their claim on him, and he had his claim on them, and used it to the extent of, in *A Portrait*, a most morbid presentation of *The Spiritual Exercises of Saint Ignatius*. Joyce's books were not to be found on the shelves of the novitiates' *ad usum* library but some of the titles there to be found would have appealed to him.

There were the works of Dom Columba Marmion, O.S.B., Abbot of Maredsous in Belgium; of Mother Mary St Paul and Mother Mary Loyola whose name became, on the tongue of a Galway novice who must have been thinking of *Finnegans Wake*, Mother Mary Lie Over; the works and pomps of Father Faber, an effeminate English priest of the Oratory who wrote a hymn 'Faith of Our Fathers' that was to be used on public occasions by the Gaelic Athletic Association, sons of Polyphemus the Citizen, as a pious addition to the Irish national anthem; the works of Fr Peter Gallwey, S.J., of the English province, who wrote *The Watches of the Passion* and who was as popular but not as fashionable as that Father Vaughan who came from London to Dublin to preach and was, ironically, immortalized only by James Joyce; the Spiritual Treatises of the Ven. Fr Rodriguez, S.J.; the writings of Père Plus and the Abbé Fouard and Archbishop Goodier, of Scaramelli, Pourrat's *Christian Spirituality*; and, oddly enough and for a little mundane relaxation, Bell's *Reciter* and Bartlett's *Familiar Quotations*, and a book called *Is Life Worth Living?* by an American cleric called Fulton Sheen, a name not then so well known and clearly matter for a master punster; and a pamphlet called *Old Times in the Barony* by the Rev. Fr Conmee, S.J., who had once set off from

Belvedere to make a journey to Donnycarney.

But naturally, or supernaturally, no Joyce. Hadn't the American Catholic critic, Blanche Mary Kelly, said that *A Portrait* was the classic portrayal of the soul saying 'no' to God: Stephen was a sore case of spoiled priest or lost vocation. Losing God he had found the sea-surrounded symbol of the girl on Dollymount Strand, the chalice secretly carried through enemies, the soul of the old artificer.

In other Jesuit houses, I was told, there was a part of the library, jocosely called Hell, in which special books were kept to be read only for special purposes and not to be treated lightly. Although by the time I was wandering the streets of Dublin and the roads of Ireland with Kevin Sullivan when he was writing his *Joyce Among the Jesuits*, Hell had, long before Pope John, been abolished. The Jesuits were always in the forefront of such cooling-off policies and the man who, when he was a novice, had been discussing with most authority the Obeeism or Oceeism of Joyce had become a very audible voice, speaking for rational liberal values in Irish cultural life. Was that Jesuitry or Joyceanism or both combined? For the Irish writer after him Joyce did not dictate an attitude towards the Catholic Church in Ireland, but he certainly helped to form it, just as the Jesuits, even by his revolt and contradictions, had helped to form him. The Jesuit Kinch had his summer residence in Mecklenburg Street and the cave of Circe was only a hop and a jump downhill from the sodality chapel.

Students who have listened to me in the United States have told me afterwards that they noticed in me a tendency to make reference more often to Yeats than to Joyce. Until they told me I was not aware of this but, on examination of conscience, the reason seemed simple enough. The accident of having, when a boy, relatives at Ben Bulben's foot and on the shores of Lough Melvin means still that the very name of Yeats automatically brings up memories of horse-races on the sands at Mullaghmore, of trout fishing on the Bunduff River, when one 'had the livelong summer day to spend'. The name of Joyce calls up memories of conflict with all the dark demons the young man wrestled with as he walked between Fairview Corner and St Stephen's Green.

In the Yeats country you can experience a sense of floating unreality that makes it possible to ask: which came first, the poetry or the country? So skilfully has the poet used rock and reed, cairn and thornbush, quayside and old houses. But here in this city there is no question as to which came first: ancient established city or the artifice to map it as the model of all cities and in so doing to forge the uncreated conscience of his race.

Mr James Duffy lived in Chapelizod because he wished to live as far as possible from the city of which he was a citizen and because he found all the other suburbs of Dublin mean, modern and pretentious.

H.C.E. was located there not to separate himself from the citizens but to draw all men together, making all things one, the past and the present, the beginning and the end.

A tall obelisk is erected (the only word) as a memorial to a longnosed duke and becomes the Willingdone organ of all men. A magazine is built to hold bullets and becomes a place of revelation for all women. An iron urinal becomes a mystic part of the homeward night journey of the father and the son. In the later history of the city it is to be removed by corporation decree because it has become a centre for homosexual offences. The Joycean irony was prophetic.

From Howth and environs, where Grania of the Ships shamed the lord of the castle, to the humps of Castleknock beyond Iseult's chapel, the earth quakes as the giant turns in his sleep, awakened by Dedalus, and remembers everything. But, even though asleep, he was there before the young man walked on his grave.

What the Irish Papers said

The obituary memoirs below appeared in the Irish papers of January 1941.

With Joyce dead in Zürich, and an end made to a forty years' friendship, one's thoughts inevitably revert to the first meeting. It was my first lecture at University College. The class was in English literature, and the lecturer began with Aristotle's Poetics, as seemed to me very right in the circumstances. Towards the end of the lecture the professor put in some remarks about Stephen Phillips, who had just written *Paolo and Francesca*. He asked had anyone read it, and then immediately: 'Have you read it, Mr Joyce?' A voice behind me said 'Yes'; I looked around, and saw my first poet.

I grew very familiar with that figure in the next three years, and in my eyes it did not change much in the next forty. Tall, slim and elegant; an erect and loose carriage, an up-tilted, long, narrow head, with a chin that jutted out arrogantly; firm, tight shut mouth, blue eyes that for all their myopic look could glare suddenly or stare with indignant wonder; a high forehead that bulged under stiff-standing hair. Some of these items changed later. The elegant adumbration of a beard tentatively came and went, and the eyes that since then saw and suffered so much were obscured by powerful lenses; but the graceful figure and carriage remained the same, and the cane that replaced the famous ash-plant of his later Dublin days still swung casually, disguising but aiding the dimmed vision.

That is how he looked in Paris, where he lived in the years between the two wars, in different apartments from the Faubourg to the Invalides. The talk within might be as much in Italian as in French, but there were pictures by Jack Yeats looking down from the walls – pictures, I need hardly say, of Anna Liffey – and above them a great wood-carving of the Arms of Dublin, that once looked out on the

Liffey herself. And gradually the spirit of Dublin would prevail. He would sing old Tudor songs and Dublin street ballads in an admirable tenor voice, trained years before in Dublin by Signor Palmieri when he won distinction at the Feis Ceoil in 1904. I once asked Joyce when was he coming back to Dublin. 'Why should I?' he said. 'Have I ever left it?' And, of course, he never really had. He contained Dublin. His knowledge of the town by inheritance, by observation, by memory was prodigious, and he was at pains to keep his picture of it up to date. When he challenged me to mention some new feature of Dublin to justify his return I could only instance the new smell of petrol. If Dublin were destroyed, his words could rebuild the houses; if its population were wiped out, his books could repeople it. Joyce was many things, but he was certainly the last forty volumes of *Thom's Directory*[1] thinking aloud.

In those early days, as since, Joyce was a figure apart. It would be easy to exaggerate his apparent arrogance and reserve. If he seemed arrogant and aloof it was in defence. Silently or with some abrupt, devastating phrase he stood in fierce defence of his own integrity – his liberty to think differently. He was far and away the most mature of our student group. We were all conscious of it; cheerfully and disrespectfully aware that he was in correspondence with Ibsen, Arthur Symons and William Archer, and that his verse was beginning to appear in the *Saturday Review* and his prose in the *Fortnightly*. He was just past eighteen then, reading Danish as well as French and Italian, and his early papers in University College were curiously highly wrought and recondite performances. The casual allusion to the Nolan in the first sentence of the 'Day of the Rabblement' is an instance of the out-of-the-way reading that kept us all guessing. His literary idols of that time – never, I think, to be overthrown – were Dante and Ibsen, and I cannot help thinking that he saw himself in relation to the Ireland of his day as the disdainful Florentine or as Ibsen among the Norse Nationalists.

His later life belongs to world literature, where his influence has been as widespread, as profound and as disruptive as that of Picasso in painting. He was as great a master of English prose as Yeats was of English verse – that is to say, he was one of the two greatest figures in contemporary English literature. In his last work he chose to abandon the writing of English and to formulate his own idiom. He shattered

---

[1] The Dublin street directory

the categories of time and space, and sought, by the incantation of sound and otherwise, enormously to extend the sensitiveness of our apprehension. The success or failure of this experiment may not be considered here, but it is relevant to the two points which I am content to isolate. The first is the constant preoccupation with Dublin to which I have sufficiently referred, the other is more significant. Joyce lived much of his life in desperate and tragic suffering. We have had in Ireland many generous artists who have not hesitated to mix in public affairs. Joyce was not one of them. To preserve his independence for the sake of his art was with him a passion. It led him to more than one painful parting and through much suffering. The fierce intensity of his will made his life a struggle against circumstance. He followed his inflexible purpose in poverty, in exile, in physical suffering, in good and ill, and even in the manner of his literary expression, with a sort of heroism not easy to understand and certainly not common. The integrity and independence of the artist may be vilified by a catchword. It was the essence of Joyce. One might like at this moment to dwell on his loyalty, his courtesy, his gaiety amongst friends, the gallant companionship of his wife. In the end one comes back to this indomitable integrity of his, 'holding to ancient nobleness that high unconsortable one'.

C. P. CURRAN

Irish Times, 14th January 1941

The first time I met Joyce he was living in the Rue de Grenelle. I went down armed with a box of Olhausen's black puddings. I did this on Paddy Tuohy's advice – I mean on the advice of my friend, the late Patrick Tuohy, R.H.A., at that time living in Paris, having completed the now famous portrait of Joyce's father and one of Joyce himself. Tuohy wired me just in time. James's birthday was approaching. He loved Olhausen's black puddings. They recalled his student days in Dublin. So I came armed with them, and Tuohy and I enjoyed them, too, that night in the Rue de Grenelle.

The strongest man is he who stands most alone. Ibsen's dictum was especially true of Joyce in letters. He stood aloof from other writers, having set them a new fashion in prose. In that consciousness he worked slowly, laboriously, with his failing sight, like a spider at the intricacies of his web. External contacts occurred, but unless they were relevant to the world of Dublin he had created he took no interest in them.

In his linen coat, his legs tucked under him on the divan, leaning back to ease the pain in his eyes, or listening to your news of the new Dublin, he looked a little bored and exotic. And the blond face, the neat moustache and the air of personal aloofness were a little chilling, conveying mostly that your news was no news at all to him. Which was probably true. His flat was full of Irish newspapers – even provincial ones – and I remember his quoting quips made by witnesses in my own court in Kilmainham.

One night, dining in a restaurant – I think it was the Trianon, opposite the Montparnasse Station – he took Tuohy and myself on (as the phrase is) in an effort of photographic memory. After twenty years' absence he challenged us, who had just left Dublin, to name the shops from Amiens Street Station to the Pillar. First one side and then down the other. Mostly he was three or four shops in front of us. When Tuohy and I left a gap, he filled it. When we named a new proprietor, he named, and remembered the passing of, the old. I remember his flat in the Rue de Grenelle, and, later, the one up off the Étoile. I remember them for him, for Mrs Joyce's beautiful Galway voice, her hospitality and constant good humour; remember them for the good Irish whiskey they provided, for the Dublin street ballads sung by the host himself, and for the never-changing sense of a Dublin transported abroad.

I was the Irish delegate to the international Congress of P.E.N. in Paris in 1937. Immediately I arrived Joyce rang me. He subsequently attended one of the meetings, receiving an ovation, and delivered a speech on the pirated editions of *Ulysses* in America. At the banquet held at the close of the Congress he personally organized an Irish table, presided at it and, again receiving an ovation from a very distinguished literary gathering, made a short speech in reply to the toast 'Ireland'. Afterwards in the foyer in the hotel a whole world of writers surrounded him.

Joyce was worth half a dozen Irish legations in any country he had chosen to live in. All European writers knew of him, and he took care to let them know that he was Irish. In making Dublin famous he made Ireland famous in European letters.

KENNETH REDDIN

Irish Times, 14th January 1941

SISTERS OF JAMES JOYCE MOURN FOR TWO BROTHERS

Three sisters of James Joyce, the distinguished Irish writer, who died yesterday, talked of a double sorrow as they sat together last night in a top flat in Mountjoy Square, Dublin.

They had heard not only of the death of their brother, James, but also of another brother, Charles, who died at Hastings, Sussex, on Saturday.

The other sisters were the Misses Florence and Eva Joyce. Another sister, Mrs Mai Monoghan, lives in Galway, and yet another is a nun in the Mercy Order, Sister Mary Gertrude, in New Zealand.

To their burden of sorrow is added their uncertainty about the fate of a third brother, Stanislaus, who was living in Trieste until the outbreak of war and of whom they have heard no news since.

James Joyce used to write regularly to his sisters in Dublin. 'He always expressed his love of Dublin and of the Dublin people, and often said that he would love to live here again,' said Miss Eva Joyce.

'WAS OUR IDOL'

'He suffered much from rheumatic fever though, and the climate would not suit him.

'However some people may criticize what he wrote, he was our eldest brother and our idol, and to us, at least, his writings had the stamp of genius.

'He had the kindest disposition, hated show and publicity, and spent all his spare time with his family, enjoying trips with them in the French countryside.'

Mrs Schaurek, with whom James Joyce lived while he was working on *Ulysses* and later while he was engaged on his unfinished *Work in Progress*, told me:

'He seemed tireless; wrote everything in his distinctive, though spidery, hand. For leisure, he would turn to the piano and sing in a clear tenor voice Irish melodies of the sentimental kind.

'They say he was anti-Catholic, but he never missed a service during all the Holy Weeks he spent with me in Trieste.'

Irish Press, 14th January 1941

James Joyce, the famous Irish-born writer, died in hospital in Zürich at 2.15 a.m. today. He was 58.

Though he was pronounced out of danger earlier yesterday his condition became worse last night. Blood transfusions were given at once. On Saturday he had undergone an emergency abdominal operation.

MUCH DISCUSSED

James Joyce was one of the most discussed figures in contemporary literature.

Born on 2nd February 1882, he was educated at Clongowes Wood and later at Belvedere and took his B.A. degree at the Royal University.

Even as a university student he became known as a writer and he was regarded as one of the most brilliant students of his generation.

His chief publications before he went to live on the Continent were his collection of short stories *Dubliners* and his semi-autobiographical work *A Portrait of the Artist as a Young Man*.

NOTABLE BOOKS

Opinions about his later work vary, but there is a general agreement that those two books were notable contributions to English literature and that they showed great imagination, a fine use of words, an extraordinary sensitiveness to the social, political and religious life of the Dublin of that day. When he left Ireland not long before the 1914-18 war, he went first to Trieste, as a teacher, and later lived in Rome and Zürich before settling in Paris. His chief works of the Continental period were *Ulysses* and *Work in Progress*, the latter published in fragment.

By that time he had changed his whole idea of writing. It might even be said that he had changed his whole idea of language. Those latter publications were written in a language that the ordinary reader would recognize only here and there as English.

He had become hostile to the Catholic Church, in which he had been brought up. But in all his writings it seems as if he were never easy about his attitude to the Church, as if his quarrel with it preyed on his mind continually.

Visitors to him in Paris of late years have spoken of him as always being very much interested in news of Dublin and very fond of talking about his native city. They have described him as usually being dressed in white, and finding it necessary, owing to failing sight, to write with a great red pencil on huge sheets of paper.

His last book, *Work in Progress*, was published about a year ago, though he had begun work on it as far back as 1923.

He married Nora, daughter of Thomas Barnacle, of Galway, in 1904. They had one son and one daughter.

Irish Independent, 13th January 1941

Notes on Contributors

JOHN MONTAGUE was born in New York in 1929 and raised in Tyrone, Northern Ireland. A poet and lecturer, he was educated at University College, Dublin, and lectured at Berkeley University, U.S.A. His books include *Poisoned Lands, A Chosen Light* and *Death of a Chieftain* (short stories).

BRIAN NOLAN was born in Dublin in 1911 and died in 1966. A novelist and journalist, he used the pseudonyms 'Flan O'Brien' for his novels and 'Myles na Gopaleen' for a satirical column in the *Irish Times*. He was educated at University College, Dublin, and later spent some time in Germany on research work. He was an acquaintance of James Joyce. His books include *At Swim-Two-Birds, An Beal Bocht* (in Irish), *The Third Policeman, The Hard Life* and *The Dalkey Archive*. Some of his books have been adapted for the stage and produced in the Abbey and Gate Theatres, Dublin.

SAMUEL BECKETT, author and playwright, was born in Dublin in 1906 and educated at Portora Royal School and Trinity College, Dublin (M.A.). From 1928 to 1930 he was English Lecturer at École Normale Supérieure, Paris, and from 1930 to 1937 French Lecturer at Trinity College, Dublin. Since 1932 he has lived mostly in France – in Paris since 1937. He was awarded the Nobel Prize for Literature in 1969. His books include: Verse: *Whoroscope* (1930), *Echo's Bones* (1935); short stories: *More Pricks than Kicks* (1934); plays: *Waiting for Godot* (1952), *End Game* (1957); novels: *Murphy* (1938), *Watt* (1944) and *Molloy* (1951).

W. B. STANFORD was born in 1910 and educated at Trinity College, Dublin (M.A., D.Litt., M.R.I.A., Fellow of T.C.D.). He became Regius Professor of Greek at Trinity College, Dublin, and has been a senator in the Senate of the Republic of Ireland since 1958. He was the Irish Representative to the Council of Europe in 1951 and to the Parliamentary Conference of the European Movement in Vienna in 1956. His books include: *Greek Metaphor, Ambiguity, Aeschylus in his Style* and *The Ulysses Theme* (1954). He is the Editor of *Hermathena* (T.C.D.).

EDNA O'BRIEN was born in Scariff, Co. Clare. Her books include *The Country Girls*, *The Lonely Girl*, *Girls in Their Married Bliss*, *August Is A Wicked Month*, *Casualties of Peace* and *The Love Object* (a collection of short stories).

PATRICK KAVANAGH, poet and novelist, was born in Monaghan in 1906 and died in Dublin in 1967. His books include *The Great Hunger* (poems), *Collected Poems* (1964) and a novel *Tarry Flynn*. He produced and wrote almost exclusively a newspaper in Dublin called *Kavanagh's Weekly*.

JOSEPH M. HONE was born in Dublin in 1882 and died in 1959. His books include two biographies, *W. B. Yeats 1865-1939* and *Life of George Moore*.

AIDAN HIGGINS was born in Kildare in 1927 and now lives in Germany. His books include *Felo De Se* (1961) (short stories) and a novel *Langrishe Go Down* (1966).

NIALL MONTGOMERY was born in Dublin in 1915, and is an architect. When asked if he could be described as a Joycean scholar he answered: 'Good lord no! Can't stand Joyce. I am a Proustian myself'.

ULICK O'CONNOR, writer, playwright, poet, lecturer and journalist, was born in Dublin in 1929 and educated at University College, Dublin, Loyola University, New Orleans, U.S.A., and Kings Inns, Dublin (called to the Irish Bar). His books include two biographies, *Oliver St John Gogarty* and *Brendan Behan* (1970).

JOHN STANISLAUS JOYCE, a brother of James Joyce, was born 17th December, 1884. His book *My Brother's Keeper* was published in 1958. Died Trieste 1955 aged 70.

JOHN JORDAN, poet and lecturer, was born in Dublin in 1930 and educated at University College, Dublin, and Oxford University. He is at present a lecturer in English at University College, Dublin, and he was Editor of *Poetry Ireland* 1962-65.

EOIN O'MAHONY was born in Cork in 1904 and died in 1970. He was educated at Clongowes Wood, University College, Cork, and University College, Dublin. He held the awards of K.M. (Knight of Malta), Chevalier of the Royal Stuart Society and the Cross of the Order of Merit of the German Federal Republic. A lecturer and geneaologist, he was called to the Irish Bar in 1930 and the English Bar in 1933.

PATRICK BOYLE, novelist and short story writer, was born in Ballymoney, Co. Antrim, and is a Fellow of the Irish Academy of Letters. His books include the novel *Like Any Other Man* and collected short stories *At Night All Cats Are Grey* and *All Looks Yellow To The Jaundiced Eye*.

DENIS JOHNSTON, writer, broadcaster, professor and playwright, was born in Dublin in 1901 and was educated at St Andrews College, Dublin, and Christ Church, Cambridge (M.A., LL.M. 1926). He was a director of the Gate Theatre 1931-36 before moving to the B.B.C. He was a war correspondent from 1940 to 1946. His plays include *The Old Lady Says No!*, *The Moon in the Yellow River*, *A Bride for the Unicorns* and *Strange Occurrence on Ireland's Eye*. He has also written two volumes of autobiography, *Nine Rivers from Jordan* (1953) and *The Brazen Horn* (1969), and the biographies *In Search of Swift* (1959) and *J. M. Synge* (1965).

ANDREW CASS, author of *Childe Horrid's Pilgrimace*, was the pen name of John Garvin, secretary of the Deparment of Local Government in Ireland from 1948 to 1966. Under his pen name Mr Garvin has written and lectured widely on Anglo-Irish literature, particularly James Joyce. Since his retirement he has been chairman of An Chomhairle Leabhrlanna (the National Library Council), Vice Chairman of the Higher Education Authority and Dublin City Commissioner, replacing the members of the Dublin City Council who were removed from office by the Minister for Local Government in April 1969.

ARTHUR POWER, playwright, art critic and painter, met Joyce while art critic for the *New York Herald* in the 1920s in Paris. His plays include *The Marriage Packet* and he wrote short stories in *Dublin Magazine*, etc.

BERNARD SHARE, writer, journalist and lecturer, was educated at Trinity College, Dublin. His books include *Inish* and *Merciful Hour* (1970).

J. B. LYONS, M.D., F.R.C.P.I., surgeon, novelist and essayist, was born in Dublin in 1923. His books include *The Citizen Surgeon*, a biography of Sir Victor Horsley (1857-1916). His novels (published under the pseudonym Michael Fitzwilliam) include *A Question of Surgery*, *South Downs General Hospital* and *When Doctors Differ*.

FRANCIS HARVEY was born at Enniskillen, Co. Fermanagh, but is at present living in Co. Donegal. Poet, playwright, short-story writer, critic, labourer, clerk, warehouse porter and assistant bank manager, but presently unemployed. He is married with five children; an enemy of technological society and bourgeois values, and a radical.

MONK GIBBON, Ph.D., F.R.S.L., poet and writer, was born in Dublin in 1896 and educated at St Columba's, Dublin, and Keble, Oxford. His books include three volumes of autobiography, *The Seals* (1935), *Mount Ida* (1948) and *Inglorious Soldier* (1968), the novel *The Climate Of Love* (1961) and poetry *The Tremulous String* (1926), *The Branch Of Hawthorn* (1927) and *Collected Poems* (1968).

THOMAS MACGREEVY was born in Co. Kerry in 1893, was educated at Trinity College, Dublin (B.A.), and lectured in France. He became a D.Litt. (N.U.I.) in 1957. He worked on the *Connoisseur* and other magazines and published several monographs of literary and artistic criticism. He is better known as a poet outside Ireland than inside. He was Director of the National Gallery of Ireland from 1950 to 1963, and was awarded the Chevalier (1948) and the Officer (1962) of the Legion of Honour (France).

JOHN FRANCIS BYRNE, author and cryptoanalyst, was born in Dublin in 1879 and died in the U.S.A. in the 1960s. J. F. Byrne was 'Cranly' in James Joyce's *Ulysses* and lived at No. 7 Eccles Street, the home of 'Bloom' in *Ulysses*. (The door of No. 7 Eccles Street is now in the Bailey Tavern, Duke Street, Dublin.) His books include *Silent Years* (U.S.A. 1953).

BENEDICT KIELY was born in Northern Ireland in 1919. A novelist, short story writer and lecturer, he was educated at University College, Dublin, and lectured at Hollins College, Virginia, U.S.A., the University of Oregon and Emory University, Atlanta, U.S.A. He is at present lecturing at University College, Dublin. His books include *In A Harbour Green*, *The Captain's Whiskers* and *Cards Of The Gambler*. He has also published a number of collections of short stories.

CONSTANTINE P. CURRAN, writer and barrister, was born in Dublin in the late 19th century of a Nationalist family and was a contemporary of James Joyce at the National University, Dublin. He entered the legal profession and became Registrar of the High Court of Ireland. His books include *James Joyce Remembered* (1968).

KENNETH REDDIN. A district court justice of Ireland and author of *Another Shore*.

INDEX

page

Abbey Theatre - - - - 148
Achilles - - - - - 23
Adam - - - - - - 33
Adams, R. M. - - - - 198
Adrian IV - - - - - 110
Adventures of Ulysses 37, 38, 40, 42
'A.E.' - 74, 79, 86, 94, 99, 144, 145
Alexander - - - - - 23
America - 73, 75, 95, 103, 246
Amiens - - - - 14, 154
Anna Livia - 29, 31, 217, 218, 243
Anna Livia Plurabelle - 66, 177
Apollo - - - - - - 36
Archer, William - - - 133, 244
Aristotle - - - - 64, 144
Ascham - - - - - 37
Assisi - - - - - - 152
Atherton, J. S. - - - - 198
Athlone - - - - 150, 152
Atlantic Ocean - - - - 46
Australia - - - - 150, 153

Baggot Street - - 137, 195, 196
Bailey, The - - - 16, 17
Bantry Bay - - - - - 236
Barnacle, Nora - - - - 231
Barnacle, Thomas - - - 249
Bayle - - - - - - 22
Belfast - - - - - 148, 175
Belgium - - - 151, 154, 239
Bell, George 83, 84, 89, 91, 92, 98
Belvedere - 66, 102, 105, 110, 120
   121, 124, 139, 147, 148, 150, 153,
                  154, 239, 240, 248
Blackrock - 104, 105, 106, 108, 110
Blenheim - - - - - 84
Bloom, Leopold - 75, 143, 144, 165,
      173, 193, 196, 197, 199, 200
Bloom, Molly 145, 186, 201, 210, 233
Bodkin, Tom - - - - 209
Bohemian Girl, The - - - 228
Book of Kells - - 175, 214, 215

page

Books at the Wake, The - - 198
Borumbodad, Achmet, Dr - 202
Bossuet - - - - - 24
Brandes, Georg - - - - 144
Bray - - - - - - 105
Bridges, Robert - - - - 37
Bruno, Giordano - - 22, 31
Byrne, Alfie - - - - 55
Byrne, Davy - - - 68, 144
Byron - - - - 50, 112, 171

Caesar - - - - - 23, 211
Calderon - - - - 36, 41
Caligula - - - - - 23
Cambridge - - - - - 56
Canada - - - - - 163
Carl Rosa Opera Co. - - 228
Carleton, William - - - 237
Carthage - - - - - 46
Casement, Sir Roger - - - 139
Castleknock - - - - 241
Catullus - - - - - 77
Cézanne - - - - - 47
Chamber Music - - - - 205
Chesterton - - - - - 49
Chiari - - - - - 95
Chopin - - - - - 119
Chouchon, Lionel - - - 190
Churchill, Winston - - - 149
Clare Street - - - - 75
Clery, Emma - - - - 207
Clongowes 19, 56, 66, 101, 102, 105,
      113, 130, 139, 147, 148, 150, 151,
               152, 153, 154, 239, 248
Cockcrows - - - - - 95
Collegians, The - - - - 235
Colum, Padraic - 73, 74, 78, 79, 82,
               94, 117, 135, 144
Columbus, Rualdus - - - 198
Connolly, Cyril - - - - 56
Cork 104, 106, 108, 109, 115, 148
Cornell University - - - 82

255

page

Corrington, J. W. - - - 191
Coward, Noel - - - - 56
Crampton, Sir Phillip - 199, 201

Dalkey - - - - - 107
Dante 24, 29, 32, 34, 35, 41, 50,
63, 82, 104, 216
Dargan, W. - - - - - 238
'Dark Rosaleen' - - 142, 228, 229
David Copperfield - - - 116
de Kock, Paul - - - 159, 160
De Monarchia - - - - 33
de Valera, Eamon - 20, 62, 177
Dedalus, Stephen 15, 19, 24, 61, 68,
72, 73, 74, 76, 85, 88, 106, 107
123, 127, 145, 169, 170, 171, 195,
203, 218, 223, 238
Dickens - - 30, 67, 116, 129
Dicksee, Sir Frank - - - 213
Dinan - - - - - - 84
Disraeli - - - - - 149
Divine Comedy, The - - - 33
Don Quixote - - - - 65
Dowden, Edward - 84, 144, 210
Dublin 16, 31, 45, 55, 58, 59, 61,
75, 78, 79, 83, 86, 89, 91, 93, 95,
96, 97, 101, 102, 104, 106, 107,
109, 111, 115, 116, 117, 118, 119,
123, 124, 128, 130, 135, 137, 138,
140, 143, 144, 145, 146, 148, 153,
160, 165, 169, 171, 173, 175, 176,
182, 185, 189, 190, 191, 192, 193,
197, 202, 210, 212, 216, 217, 218,
230, 235, 237, 238, 241, 243, 244,
245, 246, 247, 248

Eccles Street - 44, 189, 193, 233
Edinburgh Review - - - 171
Edward VII - 53, 54, 145, 239
Eliot, T. S. - - - - 50, 66
Ellman, Richard - 76, 135, 209
Elwood - - - - - 84
Ely Place - - - 75, 96, 97
Euripides - - - - - 36
Exiles - - - - - 44

Falmouth - - - - - 91
Fénelon - - - 36, 39, 40
Fenian - - - - - - 66
Finnegans Wake 19, 20, 51, 56, 58,

page

61, 62, 63, 65, 66, 67, 69, 70, 72,
137, 141, 164, 166, 174, 175, 176,
177, 191, 192, 196, 197, 201, 205,
210, 212, 239
Flanders - - - - - 55
Flaubert - - - - 205, 207
Florence - - - - - 33
Forster, E. M. - - - - 211
France - - 15, 85, 128, 137, 141
Freeman's Journal - - - 118
Freyer, Dermot - - - - 95
Freyer, Peter - - - - 94

Gaiety Theatre - - - - 228
Galway 47, 125, 148, 186, 247, 249
George V - - - - - 54
Germany - - - - - 149
Gilbert, W. S. - - - - 151
Gladstone - - - - - 149
Glasgow - - - - 115, 116
Goethe - - - - 50, 144
Gogarty, Oliver St John 56, 73, 74,
75, 76, 77, 78, 79, 80, 81, 82, 83,
84, 85, 86, 87, 88, 89, 91, 93, 94,
95, 96, 97, 98, 99, 100, 102, 142,
148, 163, 164, 167, 198, 201
Goldberg, S. L. - - - - 212
Gorman, Herbert 136, 170, 172, 223
Gould, Nat - - - - 30
Grafton Street - - 137, 144
Grammar of Assent - - - 238
Grattan - - - - - 199
Great Expectations - - - 30
Greene, Graham - 140, 146
Gregory, Lady - 56, 85, 148
Griffin, Gerald - - - 235
Griffith, Arthur - - 54, 76
Grozio, Ugo - - - - 21
Guinness - - - - 30, 94
Gulliver's Travels - - - 65

Hadow, W. H. - - - - 83
Hail and Farewell - - - 238
Hajer - - - - - 95
Hamlet - - - - 15, 169
Hanley - - - - - 222
Harcourt Street - - - 18
Hardy, Thomas - - - 126
Harvard - - 51, 64, 72
Hastings - - - - 247

page

Hercules - - - - - 29
Hermes - - - - 27, 36
Higgins, F. R. - - - 236, 237
Hitler - - - - - - 211
Hobbes - - - - - 22
Hollywood - - - - - 65
Homer 26, 35, 36, 37, 39, 40, 41, 50,
77, 165, 216
Hoult, Norah - - - - 74
Hours of Idleness - - - 171
Hume Street - - - 137, 202
Huxley, Aldous - - - - 62
Huxley, Thomas - - - 238

Ibsen - - 44, 133, 226, 244, 245
Iliad - - - - - 35, 39
Innsbruck - - - - - 150
Irish Independent - - - 249
Irish Names of Places - - 18
Irish National Theatre - - 90
Irish Press - - - - 247
Irish Times - - 59, 176, 189, 246
Is Life Worth Living? - - 239
'It's a Long Way to Tipperary' 47

Jersey - - - - - 210
Jonson - - - - - 144
Joyce Among the Jesuits - - 240
Juno and the Paycock - - 50

Kavanagh, Patrick - - 144, 146
Kazantzakis - - - - 35
Keats - - - 39, 146, 226
Kelly, Blanche Mary - - 240
Kettle - - - - 55, 79
Kildare Street - - - - 137
Kilmainham - - - - 246
Kipling - - - - - 53
Knox, Ronald - - - - 56

Latini, Brunetto - - - 144
Lee, F. W. - - - - - 82
Lee, Sidney - - - - 144
Leto - - - - - - 36
Levin, Dr - 65, 66, 67, 69, 70, 72
Lily of Killarney - - - 228
Limerick - - - 79, 170, 235
Liszt - - - - - - 119
Locke - - - - - - 22
Lohengrin - - - - - 228

page

London 54, 59, 85, 145, 161, 183,
184, 213
Louvain - - - - - 154
Louys, Pierre - - - - 87
Love Songs of Connacht, The - 237
Love the Greatest Enchantment 36
Lucan - - - - - - 25
Lucifer - - - - - 15
Lydgate - - - - - 36
Lyster, T. W. - - - 221, 222

Macaulay, Lord - - - - 139
McCormack, John - - - 46
McGreevy, Thomas - - - 71
Machiavelli - - - - - 22
Mackenzie, Compton - - 89
Macran - - - - 82, 83
Magennis, W. - - - - 44
Mahaffy, John Pentland - 83, 98
Malta - - - - - - 154
Mangan, James Clarence - - 228
Manning, Cardinal - - - 214
Mansfield, Katherine - 209, 210
Mao - - - - - - 211
Maredsous - - - - - 239
Margate - - - - - 91
Maritana - - - - - 228
Marius the Epicurean - - - 207
Marlay Abbey - - - - 56
Marscilles - - - - - 54
Martello Tower - 52, 73, 74, 76, 91,
93, 94, 141, 165, 195, 210
Martyn, Edward - - 144, 148
Maynooth - - 62, 147, 149, 218
Measure for Measure - - - 223
Mendelssohn - - - 119, 197
Meredith, George - - 79, 144
Meredith, Sir James - 53, 118
Milton - - - 50, 136, 144, 224
Molesworth, Mary - - - 155
Monte Carlo - - - - 63
Moore, George - 19, 59, 73, 74, 144,
238
Morris, William - - - - 89
Moscow - - - - - 65
Mountjoy Square - 110, 124, 247
Mulligan, Buck - 50, 73, 74, 75, 76,
85, 141, 142, 143, 195
Mulligan, Malachi - - - 130

Index

page

Napier, Sir Charles - - - 56
Nassau Street - - - - 137
National Art Gallery - - - 238
National Library 41, 169, 198, 221,
224, 227, 238
Nero - - - - - - 23
New York - - - - 95, 163
New Zealand - - - - 247
Newdigate - - - - 84, 86
Newman, John H. 148, 153, 214,
238
Nice - - - - - - 57
Norway - - - - - 133

O'Brien, Kate - - - - 56
O'Casey, Sean - - - - 50
O'Connell, Daniel - - 147, 148
O'Connell Street - - 138, 191
O'Donovan Rossa - - - 237
Odyssey - - - - 35, 39
O'Neill, Senor - - - 84
O'Sullivan, Sean - - 75, 91
Ovid - - - - - 36, 39
Oxford 46, 82, 83, 84, 86, 87, 88, 89,
91, 94, 151

Page of Irish History - - - 229
Paolo and Francesca - - - 243
Paradise Lost - - - 136, 214
Paris 19, 43, 47, 58, 75, 82, 94,
114, 150, 170, 182, 184, 186, 187,
230, 243, 245, 246, 248
Parnell, James 105, 138, 139, 140,
149
Pascoli - - - - - 35, 41
Pater - - - - - - 205
Pearse, Patrick - - - 152, 237
Peel, Sir Robert - - - - 148
Père Plus - - - - - 239
Phillips, Stephen - - - 243
Phoenix Park - - 18, 31, 110
Picasso - - 64, 69, 70, 244
Pius VII - - - - - 147
Plato - - - - - - 144
Poe - - - - - 224, 225
Pola - - - - - - 171
Poliziano - - - - - 33
Polyphemus - - - - 23
Pope - - - - - 37, 40
Pope Giovanni XXII - - 33

page

Pope John - - - - - 240
Pope Marcellus - - - - 215
Portrait of the Artist 24, 51, 65, 89,
106, 107, 110, 112, 114, 115, 123,
124, 127, 130, 139, 140, 151, 153,
169, 171, 181, 203, 204, 205, 206,
207, 221, 224, 225, 226, 233, 242
Poseidon - - - - - 36
Pound, Ezra - - 44, 54, 210
Prague - - - - - - 152
Pritchett, V. S. - - - - 57
Proust - - - - - 209, 212
Purgatorio - - - - - 214

Queens Colleges - - - 148
Quinn, John - - - - 227

Red Cross - - - - - 47
Redmond, J. E. - - - - 147
Renan - - - - - 144, 239
Richmond Prison - - - 128
Rimbaud - - - - - 94
Roehampton - - - 150, 151
Rome - - - - - 86, 248
Romulus - - - - - 27
Ross, Sir John - - - - 229
Rouseby Opera Co. - - - 228
Rousseau - - - - 59, 62
Rue de Grenelle - - 245, 246
Russia - - - - 104, 147
Rutty, John - - - - 202

Saturday Review - - - 244
Scholes, Robert - - - - 192
Schubert - - - - - 119
Schumann - - - - - 119
Scipio - - - - - - 23
Scott, Michael - - - - 93
Scott, Walter - - - - 129
Shakespeare 29, 37, 39, 144, 169,
223, 224
Shaw - - - 59, 141, 166, 167
Sheen, Fulton - - - - 239
Shelbourne Hotel - - - 56
Shelley - - 50, 56, 77, 78, 144
Sigerson, George - - - 144
Sinn Fein - - - - - 54
Somme - - - - - 55
Sophocles - - - - - 36
Sorceries of Sin - - - - 36

page

page

Spinoza - - - - - 22
Stalin - - - - - 62, 211
Starkey, James - - 90, 91, 144
Stephen Hero 102, 106, 170, 203, 204, 205, 207, 231
Stephens, James - 79, 128, 144
Stephen's Green 119, 137, 149, 153, 201, 222, 238, 240
Stevenson, Robert Louis - - 53
Stone, C. - - - - - 89
Stonyhurst - - - - 150, 151
Sullivan, Kevin - - - - 240
Surface and Symbol - - - 198
Sweets of Sin - - - 159, 190
Swift 56, 60, 119, 141, 143, 166, 218
Swinburne, Algernon - - 74
Symons, Arthur - - - - 244
Synge - - - - - 79, 148

Tchekov - - - - - 212
Tearle, Osmond - - - 228
Télémaque - - - - 36, 39
Tennyson, Alfred Lord - 37, 226
Tennyson, Charles - - - 226
Tiberius - - - - - 23
Time and the Western Man - 219
Toynbee, Philip - - - - 75
Traits and Stories of the Irish Peasantry, The - - 237
Tranchiennes - - - - 154
Trench, Dermot - - - 84
Trieste 54, 95, 102, 103, 106, 117, 119, 130, 171, 184, 186, 187, 247
Trinity College 52, 78, 81, 88, 145, 148
Tristan and Isolde - - - 228
Trovatore - - - - - 228
Troy - - - - - 35, 38
Tuohy, Patrick - - - 245, 246
Tyrrell - - - - - 98

Ulster - - - - - 236, 237
Ulysses 18, 36, 38, 39, 49, 50, 51, 55, 58, 59, 61, 65, 66, 67, 69, 73, 75, 76, 86, 87, 94, 103, 108, 126, 130, 136, 140, 141, 142, 143, 145, 146, 163, 164, 169, 171, 172, 173, 176, 185, 187, 189, 190, 191, 192, 193, 195, 196, 197, 200, 201, 209, 211, 214, 215, 216, 217, 222, 230, 233, 236, 246, 247, 248
University College 135, 140, 150, 201, 229, 237, 243, 244

Venice - - - - - 237
Vienna - - - - - 95
Virgil - - - - 36, 77, 216
Voltaire - - - - - 239

Wagner - - - - - 228
Wangel, Hilde - - - - 133
Westland Row - - - - 17
Wilde, Oscar - - - 144, 183
Woolf, Virginia - - - - 237
Worcester - - - 83, 85, 88
Word Index to James Joyce's Ulysses - - - - - 222
Wordsworth - - - 77, 140
Work in Progress 21, 22, 25, 32, 47, 213, 216, 217, 248
Wyndham Lewis, D. B. - - 145

Yale - - - - - - 52
Yeats, Jack - - - - - 243
Yeats, W. B. 47, 54, 56, 63, 90, 91, 94, 99, 100, 139, 142, 145, 148, 236, 240, 244

Zürich - 35, 100, 171, 243, 247, 248

DATE DUE
